Modeling Pension Systems

Modeling Pension Systems

András Simonovits
Hungarian Academy of Scientists
Budapest
Hungary

First published 2003 by
PALGRAVE MACMILLAN
Houndmills, Basingstoke, Hampshire RG21 6XS and
175 Fifth Avenue, New York, N.Y. 10010
Companies and representatives throughout the world

PALGRAVE MACMILLAN is the global academic imprint of the Palgrave Macmillan division of St. Martin's Press, LLC and of Palgrave Macmillan Ltd. Macmillan® is a registered trademark in the United States, United Kingdom and other countries. Palgrave is a registered trademark in the European Union and other countries.

ISBN 1–4039–1524–5

This book is printed on paper suitable for recycling and made from fully managed and sustained forest sources.

A catalogue record for this book is available from the British Library.

Library of Congress Cataloging-in-Publication Data
Simonovits, András.
    Modeling pension systems / András Simonovits.
    p. cm.
    Includes bibliographical references and index.
    ISBN 1–4039–1524–5 (cloth)
        1. Pensions--Mathematical models. 2. Pensions--Hungary--
Mathematical models. I. Title.

HD7091.S426 2003
331.25'2'0151--dc21
                                                          2003055264

10   9   8   7   6   5   4   3   2   1
12   11   10   09   08   07   06   05   04   03

Printed and bound in Great Britain by
Antony Rowe Ltd, Chippenham and Eastbourne

Preface

Since the publication of Feldstein (1974), issues associated with unfunded public pension systems have been the focus of public discussion about retirement security worldwide. The publication of World Bank (1994) gave new impetus to this debate. Most of the discussion has been conducted at a qualitative level; questions and answers have been presented without quantitative analysis. World Bank analysts, for example, celebrate today the introduction of multipillar (or multitier) pension systems in Central Europe (in Hungary, Poland, etc.) without considering the divergence between the emerging structures and those planned; the unfunded public pillar has remained dominant and has evolved as purely earnings-related rather than modest and flat. Many publications omit discussion of the mathematics and economic theory that underlie recommendations and conclusions on pension systems.

One potential explanation for the omission of quantitative treatment may be the need to increase familiarity with underlying models in the policy community. It is with these consideration in mind that I have written this short book on pension models. Rather than omitting mathematical formulas and economic theories, I stress them.

I would like first to point out several of the book's features.

• Although I try here to clarify the *theory* behind discussion of pension issues, it is not my intention to neglect *practice*. Consequently, each chapter contains discussion and tables that present the characteristics of existing life insurance and pension systems.

• Although the book is short, I have attempted to provide a *comparative* treatment. I discuss and contrast different pension systems found in a range of countries, such as Chile, Germany, Hungary, the Netherlands, the United Kingdom, and the United States. Partly for historical reasons, each country has its own, distinct pension system, often with quite surprising features. However, I concentrate on types of system rather than those of particular countries.

• The *Hungarian pension system* plays a prominent role in this study. As a Hungarian, I have been scrutinizing our system for a decade. The Hungarian experience has some features in common with other countries and some that are distinctive in several respects. I hope readers will find this perspective useful.

• Although the book contains some original material, my main aim is to *summarize* the present state of research. To my knowledge, there are very few such surveys (for example, Verbon, 1988; World Bank, 1994; Gillion et. al, 2002; Feldstein–Liebman, 2001 and Simonovits, 2003).

• While I sample a range of types of pension policy, I am not neutral between them. I prefer a predominantly unfunded (or, equivalently, pay-as-you-go) and earnings-related pension system to the predominantly funded systems currently receiving broad attention.

• In writing a *book*, I have tried to relate its chapters to one another; it contains many cross-references. On the other hand, striving for a *modular* book, where the chapters can be read independently, I have repeated some definitions in several chapters.

• Although I have not designed the book as a textbook, I have included *problems* for the reader to solve as the treatment evolves. Consideration of these problems should facilitate command of the material. The *solutions* are, as usual, given at the end of the book. Again, I hope readers will find this feature helpful.

• At first I called the book an *introduction*, but its relatively high level of sophistication made me drop that word. In some cases, where my treatment is brief, I provide only references for readers who wish to pursue the topic in greater depth.

I have been studying these issues since 1992, and a survey related to this book appeared in the Social Security Bulletin "Perspectives".

I owe a special debt to Mária Augusztinovics, who initially sparked my interest in pension economics and has ever since been a source of inspiration. In addition, I owe special thanks to several persons. Peter Diamond has sent me his half-finished book (2002) and commented on a paper that Chapter 12 and Appendix A draw on. Péter Eső has shared with me his deep knowledge of the optimal mechanism design (as reflected in Chapter 12 and especially Appendix A). Robert I. Gál introduced me to the making of Hungarian generational accounts (see Chapter 18). György Molnár contributed to the analysis of Overlapping Cohorts, briefly analyzed in Chapter 13. János Réti has been answering my questions since 1992 and it was he who initiated the study of indexation (Chapter 14). John Francis, Michael Lovell and Michael Orszag have read and commented on an earlier version of the whole text. Last but not least, Michael James helped me improve the text. Gábor Hesz has made the final LaTeX version of the book.

I have learned much from Ilona Antal, Péter Bod, János Kornai, Béla Martos and János Stahl (Hungary); Johann Brunner, Peter Diamond, Martin Feldstein, Laurence Kotlikoff, Katharina Müller and Pierre Pestieau (abroad). Mária Augusztinovics, Katalin Lorschy, Michael Lovell, Béla Martos, Katharina Müller, Anna Patkós, Attila Rátfai, János Réti, Gergely Ujhelyi, Attila Tasnádi, Tamás Varga and János Vincze and several anonymous referees have made useful comments on earlier versions. I am indebted to all of them, but, of course, none bears responsibility for any of my oversights.

While working on the book, I have enjoyed the material and spiritual support of my workplace, the Institute of Economics, Hungarian Academy of Sciences (Budapest). I have a special obligation to the Central European University and the Budapest University of Technology and Economics, where I had the opportunity to try out the typescripts of this book at courses. My research was supported by the Hungarian National Research Fund OTKA 029135 and a Fulbright Scholarship at the Boston University.

Budapest, January, 2003.

Contents

List of figures

List of tables

Introduction

This study is devoted to a formal analysis of *pension systems*. For simplicity, it concentrates on old-age pensions, which ensure financial support during a period when most people lose much of their earning capacity. It excludes consideration of the important issue of disability and survivors' pensions, which require separate treatment.

As explained in the preface, this book surveys pension *models*. Its structure is simple. Part I deals with the *microeconomics* of pension systems; Part II covers *macroeconomic relations*; and Part III is devoted to the consideration of *special problems*. We assume that the reader has at least some familiarity with the basic concepts of pension systems.

Part I (Microeconomics) begins with the simplest *life-cycle* model, which captures the way the relative lengths of various stages of life affect the rate of saving from labor income necessary to finance childhood and old age.

The introduction of *stochastic complications* associated with random lifespan gives rise to many problems: unintended bequests, adverse selection, etc.

While mandatory private *funded systems* solve the problems of adverse selection and myopic behavior, they create others: for example, oscillating interest rates yield volatile benefits, and huge operational costs may undermine efficiency.

Most pensioners in developed countries today receive the bulk of their benefits from mandatory public *unfunded systems*. The variants of these systems differ mainly in their degree of redistribution. Flat-rate benefit systems, especially means-tested ones, may achieve significant redistribution toward the poor with minimal taxation, while earnings-related systems may achieve the same efficiency as mandatory private systems, without prior capital accumulation.

1

Recently a new trend has begun to emerge towards *mixed pension systems.* While diversification is reliable in insurance, possible inconsistency among the pillars of a mixed pension system may undermine its operation.

Taxation and inflation are not core concerns of this study but they nevertheless play very important roles in pension systems.

Part II, Macroeconomics, starts with a short introduction to *demography.* This allows us to formulate the simplest birth and death equations for an entire population. Such models—with the addition of suitable employment and eligibility data—yield, for example, the sizes of working and retired generations.

The analysis of the *macroeconomics of pension systems* underscores the close relationships among system characteristics: for example, the contribution (payroll-tax) rate and the ratio of average benefit to average net earnings. The description of the dominant role of demand for labor puts into perspective the demographic danger and the impact of raising the normal retirement age.

Issues surrounding the *transition from a mature unfunded system to a funded one* have attracted much attention. Careful thinking demonstrates the feasibility of the transition but also reveals the limits of the overall gains that can be expected.

Finally, no treatment of pension models is complete which fails to indicate the impact of pension systems on *income distribution.* In addition to the distribution of mandatory pension benefits, other benefits, such as free health services, must be taken into account.

Part III, on special topics, begins with *optimal consumption paths.* Special utility functions explain age-invariant growth rates and the initial value of an individual's consumption path.

A simple optimization model of *flexible retirement* with asymmetric information allows us to prove that so-called actuarial fairness—calculations using average life expectancy for everyone—favors people with longer (privately) expected lifespans over those with shorter ones.

The *Overlapping Cohorts* model is a framework for dynamic general equilibrium models, in which the interest rate is endogenous rather than exogenous. However, exclusive reliance on *rational expectations* may yield distorted and counterintuitive results. The analysis of other models—for example, *naive* expectations—may draw theory closer to practice.

The *indexation of benefits* is yet another interesting issue. Most governments rely on price indexation rather than wage indexation, which creates a wedge between earnings-related pensions granted in different years while aggregate pension expenditure follow the dynamics of aggregate wages.

The chapter on *prefunding the unfunded system* develops an analytical model of three scenarios of the transition from an unfunded system to a funded one, and presents empirical findings.

The *dynamic model of the German system* is an example of a rich collection of various reform scenarios. Its most noteworthy feature is its emphasis on distributive issues.

The chosen *political model* captures the interaction between age and income in voting for a pension system. Old people and lower-paid young people may vote for higher than reasonable contribution rates.

Generational accounting calculates the ratio of lifetime net contributions of the newborn to that of future cohorts, on the assumption that the entire extra burden is placed on the shoulders of future generations. Such a study of the Hungarian pension system confirms previous conjectures that the 'rationalization' of the public pillar contributes much more than the introduction of the private pillar to easing the long-run tensions in the system.

The last chapter *concludes*.

Appendix A continues the topic of flexible retirement and discusses the *design of optimal pension rules*. Appendix B, *Overlapping Generations* spells out the details of overlapping cohorts for two generations. *Solutions to Problems* help the reader check his own work.

Part I

Micro level

For didactic reasons, we begin the analysis of the pension system at the *micro* level, that is, from the point of view of the individual. Of course, certain data come from the macro level. We shall discuss the life-cycle theory (prework, work and postwork stages), the longevity risks, and the different types of pension systems (funded, unfunded, and mixed).

Chapter 1

Life cycle

In economics, 'life cycle' refers to an approach in which consumption and saving decisions depend on the age of the decision-maker.

Introduction

For purposes of employment, an individual's life can be divided into three *stages*: (i) childhood, (ii) working age, and (iii) old age. Only in the second stage does the individual work for a salary.

Of course, both the absolute and the relative lengths of the three stages have been changing over time. Two hundred years ago, children under ten years of age worked in British coal mines, and even now child labor is significant in the Third World. At the same time, *normal retirement age*—that is, the legal retirement age—was high. For instance, German pension law, introduced by Bismarck in 1889, applied only to workers over 70 years of age, who at the time represented only a minimal fraction of the population. By contrast, today it is common for West European students to continue their studies until the age of 28—at society's expense. At the same time, the age at retirement (not to be confused with the normal retirement age) has been falling worldwide.

Together with the lengths of the life-cycle stages, economic conditions have changed. Before the modern era, the bulk of people lived in big families in small villages, where the different stages were not clearly distinguished and the individual enjoyed only limited independence within the family. With industrialization and the emergence of nuclear families, social support for children and especially for the old has increased in importance.

In this chapter the life-cycle theory will be studied in a relatively simple model (Modigliani–Brumberg, 1954 and Ando–Modigliani, 1963, for a textbook treatment, see, Mankiw, 1997).

Life-cycle models

The simplest *life-cycle model* can be described as follows. Suppose that time is *discrete* and—to defer the use of *double* age-year indices until Chapter 7—assume that the individual is born at the beginning of year 0, enters the labor force at the beginning of year L, retires at the end of year R, and dies at the end of year D, $0 < L < R < D$. We shall introduce *years of service*: $T = R - L + 1$. (Note that we ignore the problems connected with the fine structure of events within the year.) The individual's earnings at age i are denoted by w_i, and his consumption at age j is denoted by c_j. For the sake of simplicity, here we ignore taxation and the social security contributions of both employers and employees. For convenience, 'earnings' means total earnings, that is, *total wage costs*. Furthermore, in order to avoid the complications associated with the production of a good when an individual is young coupled with its consumption when he is old, 'consumption' means consumption of non-durable goods.

Neoclassical economics prefers the individual to the family or the household. For the time being, we shall also assume a new-born baby takes up loans at birth to finance his childhood. In the first part of his active stage, he repays the loans, and in the second part he accumulates capital that he draws on in retirement. An alternative approach, used for example by Lee (1980), is to ignore childhood but replace individual consumption with family consumption. Kotlikoff–Summers (1981) call into question the zero-bequest assumption of the life-cycle theory. For convenience, we accept both simplifications (no family, no inheritance) in what follows.

Assume that there is no inflation and no interest margin between lending and borrowing. To simplify the formulas, I will work with *factors* rather than *rates*. So the interest factor is equal to 1 plus the interest rate, although I will denote the factor as others denote the rate: r. For simplicity, we assume that the factors of growth and of interest are age- and time-invariant. (Since these factors change over time, we should have written products of changing interest factors rather than powers of the same interest factor.)

For flows distributed in time, the so-called *present value* is the temporal aggregator. Let $\{c_j\}_{j=0}^{D}$ be the *consumption path*, r the interest factor used at discounting, then the present value of the consumption path discounted to the date of birth is

$$\text{PV} = \sum_{j=0}^{D} c_j r^{-j}.$$

Under our assumptions, the $D+1$ separate annual balance conditions $(a_k = r a_{k-1} + w_k - c_k)$ can be unified in one intertemporal budget constraint; the present value of the earning path is equal to that of the consumption path:

$$\sum_{i=L}^{R} w_i r^{-i} = \sum_{j=0}^{D} c_j r^{-j}. \tag{1.1}$$

Before continuing, consider the following classic example.

Example 1.1. No interest: $r = 1$, no growth: $w_L = \cdots = w_R$ and $c_0 = \cdots = c_D$. The ratio of consumption to total earnings is equal to the ratio of years of service to the length of life:

$$c_0 = w_L \frac{T}{D+1}. \tag{1.2'}$$

$\square$

This 'trivial' result is in fact very important since it reveals a most unwelcome truth: the longer people live and the earlier they retire, the lower their consumption is in relation to total wages. The ratio of consumption to total wages shows how much a worker can retain for his consumption from his total earnings.

We assume that the individual's annual earnings and consumption increase according to age-invariant growth factors Ω and γ, respectively. The earning and consumption paths in terms of initial values and growth factors are

$$w_i = w_L \Omega^{i-L}, \qquad i = L+1, \ldots, R, \tag{1.3}$$

$$c_j = c_0 \gamma^j, \qquad j = 1, \ldots, D. \tag{1.4}$$

Since the sum of the geometric series with $n+1$ terms will frequently be used, we shall introduce the following notation:

$$I_n(x) = \sum_{i=0}^{n} x^i = \frac{x^{n+1} - 1}{x - 1}. \tag{1.5}$$

Substituting (1.3)–(1.4) into (1.1), yields the quantified version of consumption smoothing:

Theorem 1.1. *(Retention rate.) Under our assumptions of exponential growth, the following relation holds between the parameters of consumption and earnings paths:*

$$c_0 = w_L \frac{I_{T-1}(\Omega/r)}{r^L I_D(\gamma/r)}. \tag{1.2}$$

Remark. In neoclassical economics, the consumer maximizes his *lifetime utility function* subject to his lifetime budget constraint. In our case, utility refers to the 'value' of a consumption path comprising $D+1$ years. It can be shown that in the derived optimization model the growth factor of consumption is age-invariant: it depends on the so-called discount factor, the interest factor, and the intertemporal elasticity of substitution (Chapter 12 and Varian, 1992, Chapter 19).

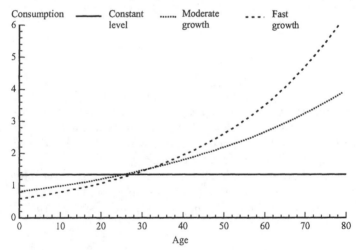

Figure 1.1. Consumption paths

The complex formula (1.2) can be illustrated in special cases. (a)–(b) Consumption grows in parallel with individual or average earnings: $\gamma = \Omega$ or $\gamma = g < \Omega$, respectively. (c) Constant consumption: $\gamma = 1$. In the numerical example, we shall work with annual data $L = 20$, $R = 59$, $D = 79$ (years).

Note the strong sensitivity of the initial and the closing values of consumption to the interest factor and the growth factors of earnings and consumption. In Figure 1.1, three consumption paths are considered with growth rates 0, 2 (the growth rate of average earnings) and 3% (the growth rate of individual earnings), while the interest rate is 4%. It can be seen that higher growth rate of consumption requires lower initial consumption.

This simple life-cycle model painted a stark picture of the relationship between the earnings path and the consumption path. Any pension model must capture this relationship.

At the end of this chapter, it would be useful to be able to present data on actual earnings and consumption paths. In the absence of such data, we have to be satisfied with *profiles*, depicting the age dependency of earnings and consumption in a given year rather than a typical path in time. Figures 1.2 and 1.3 have been constructed from István Baranyai's data from Hungary, 1998. The horizontal axes refer to age, while the vertical axes represent, respectively, wage and consumption with respect to the average. Note that consumption data have been averaged for certain age groups and broken down into cash and in-kind components. Of course, using certain assumptions, profiles can be converted into paths (see the proof of Theorem 8.4 below).

Table 1.1 displays international data on per capita social spending by age groups.

Table 1.1. Relative per capita social spending, by age group, 1980

| Country | Age group | | |
	0–14	15–64	65 and older
Great Britain	100	53.3	213
US	100	66.9	381
West-Germany	100	59.5	316

Source: World Bank (1994, p. 34) Table 1.1.

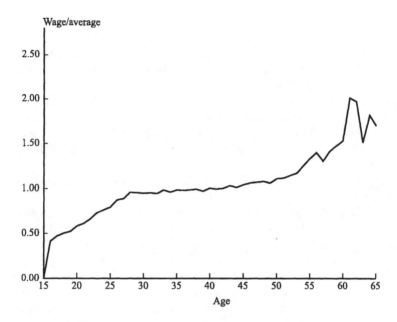

Figure 1.2. Age and real wage: Hungary 1998

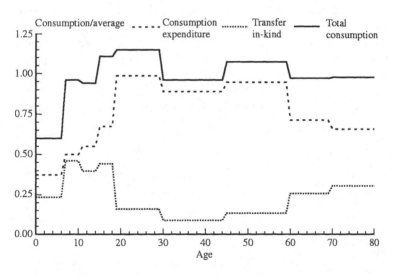

Figure 1.3. Age and consumption: Hungary 1998

In this book (apart from Chapter 17 and Appendix B), I consider the case of two cohorts only by way of illustration. It is widely believed that such models are good approximations to multicohort models; but this is not the case. The approximation is so rough that quantitative results can be quite distorted. Here, for example, is a striking, trivial, but common example. Suppose that the growth factor of wages (Ω) is a product of a seniority growth factor (ω) and an average growth factor g. It is well-known that, if we work with annual data, the growth rate of a product is approximately equal to the sum of the growth rates. (In formula: $\Omega - 1 \approx (\omega - 1) + (g - 1)$ rather than the exact $\Omega = \omega g$.) But, if we work with quarters of centuries, the approximation becomes grossly misleading. (For $\omega = 2$ and $g = 2$, $\Omega = 4$, but the usual approximation yields the absurd relation $4 - 1 \approx (2 - 1) + (2 - 1)$, that is, $3 \approx 2$.) Qualitative distortions, of course, are inevitable and even more serious.

Problem 1.1. We speak of a *credit constraint* if the consumer cannot receive any loans during his lifetime. Show that for the case of $R = 1$, $D = 2$, $w_0 = 1/4$, $w_1 = 3/4$ and $r = 1$, total smoothing of consumption is impossible.

Chapter 2

Life insurance with life annuity

We saw in Chapter 1 that a basic feature of human life is that the consumption path is much smoother than the earning path; people consume even when they do not earn. Another, equally important, characteristic is the so-called *longevity risk*: that is, the date of the death of any person is known in advance neither to him nor to others. Indeed, there are people who die just before retiring, and there are others who live for a hundred years. In the former case, lifetime consumption may be much lower than lifetime earnings; in the latter case, lifetime consumption may be much higher than lifetime earnings. Furthermore, this uncertainty makes self- or family financing much more difficult than it would be in a deterministic world (Fischer, 1973 and Walliser, 2000, 2001). Here we shall examine the ideal system of life insurance with life annuity and then turn to real-life complications.

Basic model

For the time being, let us assume that, at birth, the individual can buy a life insurance and life annuity at a reasonable price. *Life insurance* generally consists of monthly contributions over a long period; in return, it insures the insured person's survivors against his death. But the insured can also obtain a lump-sum benefit at the end of the

insurance period. *Life annuity* is traditionally purchased at the end
of the working period, and the purchaser obtains a monthly benefit
for the rest of his life. In this chapter, the two processes are combined
and we exclude lump-sum contributions and benefits.

We shall introduce the following notions from probability theory.
Let q_i be the probability of a person dying at age i (more precisely,
just before reaching his $(i+1)$-th birthday): $q_i \geq 0$ and $\sum_{i=0}^{D} q_i = 1$.
We shall also need *survival probability to age i*: $l_i = \sum_{j=i}^{D} q_j$. Finally,
we introduce the *remaining life expectancy at age i* as a weighted
average of the remaining years from age i:

$$E_i = \frac{\sum_{j=i}^{D} q_j(j - i + 1)}{l_i}. \tag{2.1}$$

In this context, it is important to keep in mind not only that older
people live longer than before but also much fewer infants die.

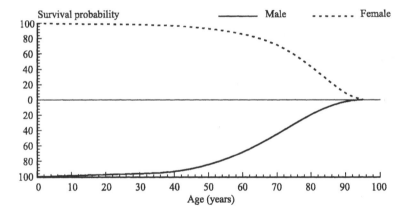

Figure 2.1. Survival probability: Hungary 1997

Figure 2.1 presents the gender- and age-specific Hungarian survival
data of 1997 (Central Statistical Office, 1998). The horizontal axis
represents age; the vertical axis shows the survival probability of a
person of each age. It is customary to place the curves for males and
females on opposite sides to form a pair of *symmetric survival curves*.
We emphasize that, all over the developed world, male mortality is
much higher than female. However, the widening of this gap in the
1990s is confined to the bulk of post-socialist countries.

To sum up vertically rather than horizontally, transforms (2.1) into

$$E_i = \frac{\sum_{j=i}^{D} l_j}{l_i}. \tag{2.2}$$

For the time being, we shall assume that, at birth, life insurance with life annuity can be bought without paying for the risk. (The assumption of zero fee for risk will soon be dropped.) Then (1.1) generalizes to

$$\sum_{i=L}^{R} l_i w_i r^{-i} = \sum_{j=0}^{D} l_j c_j r^{-j}. \tag{2.3}$$

In a general model, Yaari (1965) studied the *optimal* life-cycle consumption path under death risk. Here we confine our attention to constant consumption.

As well as cases where life insurance and life annuity are present, we shall consider the case where both are absent. In this case, an individual must be prepared for the 'worst' case: living until the final age. In calculating the corresponding consumption, the adjective *minimal* refers to the case where the subject receives no parental pension bequest, either because both parents reach the maximum age or because the government confiscates the bequest.

We shall prove

Theorem 2.1. *(Consumption under risk.) (a) If combined life insurance and life annuity without additional costs is available, then constant consumption is equal to*

$$c_0^I = \frac{\sum_{i=L}^{R} l_i w_i r^{-i}}{\sum_{j=0}^{D} l_j r^{-j}}. \tag{2.4}$$

(b) If no combined life insurance and life annuity is available, then the minimal constant consumption is equal to

$$c_0^N = \frac{\sum_{i=L}^{R} w_i r^{-i}}{\sum_{j=0}^{D} r^{-j}}. \tag{2.5}$$

(c) If insurance does not cover childhood, earnings are age-invariant ($\Omega = 1$), and the interest rate is zero ($r = 1$), then minimal consumption without insurance is lower than or equal to that with insurance:

$$c_0^N \leq c_0^I. \tag{2.6}$$

Remark. Some assumptions in (c) are required, but not necessarily those chosen (compare with Problem 2.1b below).

Proof. (a)–(b) follow from (2.3) and (1.1), respectively.

(c) Substituting (2.4)–(2.5) in (2.6) and rearranging the inequality yields

$$\frac{\sum_{i=L}^{R} l_i}{R - L + 1} \geq \frac{\sum_{j=L}^{D} l_j}{D - L + 1}.$$

Since l_i is non-increasing, the average for the first period cannot be lower than that for the whole period.   □

With the help of (2.2), Theorem 2.1 can be illustrated with

Example 2.1. If child's consumption is neglected and there is no interest: $r = 1$ and no growth: $\Omega = 1$, $\gamma = 1$, then

$$c_0^I = w_L \left(1 - \frac{l_{R+1} E_{R+1}}{l_L E_L} \right). \tag{2.4'}$$

The no-insurance case is given by (1.2'). Using the 1997 male life table for Hungary, we have $L = 20$ and $R = 61$ years, $l_L = 0.982$, $l_{R+1} = 0.646$, $E_L = 47.47$ years and $E_{R+1} = 13.84$ years. Then (2.4') yields $c_0^I / w_L = 1 - 0.6578 \cdot 0.2916 = 0.808$. For comparison, in the no-insurance case with $D = 99$ years, $c_0^N / w_L = 0.42$.   □

Problem 2.1. (a) Prove the following variant of Theorem 2.1c. If there is no childhood and nobody dies before retirement, then (2.6) holds.

(b) Demonstrate that the opposite inequality holds in the unrealistic case, where $R = 1$, $D = 2$, $w_1 = 2w_0$, $l_0 = 1$, $l_1 = l_2 = 1/2$, $r = 2$.

This simple model of life insurance and life annuity sheds light on the basic role of longevity risk in the financing of lifetime consumption.

Complications

It is important to point out that in most countries private markets for life annuities are rudimentary, probably because, where life annuities are not mandatory, the individuals who buy them tend on average to be wealthier and to have longer life expectancies (Friedmann–Warshawski, 1990 and Alier–Vittas, 2001). Arrow (1963) called attention to this so-called *adverse selection* in his classic article on health insurance (compare also Akerlof, 1970). Following Mitchell et al. (1999b) we can identify the following complications that arise in the real world (see also Mitchell, 2002).

In evaluating private life annuities, we should note that in the US the price offers of various insurance companies are highly dispersed; the average of the best offers is about 20% greater than that of the worst, although this difference also depends on gender and age.

It should be emphasized that different life tables give different annuities. It might be plausible to work with a life table of the general population, but Table 2.1 demonstrates that the life table of annuitants (people buying annuities) differs significantly from that of the general population. Each cohort of annuitants has a much lower mortality rate than the general population. For example, considering

Table 2.1. General population and annuitant mortality rates: US, 1995

Age (year)	1930 birth cohort general population	1995 individual annuitant	1930 birth cohort general population	1995 individual annuitant
	Men		Women	
65	22.2	11.5	13.4	7.3
70	31.5	18.8	19.8	11.5
75	46.7	30.9	29.1	19.4
80	73.7	50.4	44.3	33.4
85	113.8	79.8	69.6	57.6
90	169.0	120.6	116.7	101.3
95	238.4	172.6	189.5	158.4

Source: Mitchell et al. (1999b, p. 1308), Table 2, shortened and per 1000 persons.

the male members of the cohort born in 1930, the mortality rates of the general population and the annuitants were 22.2 and 11.5 per thousand in 1995, respectively. (The numbers referring to the older population are presumably estimates, since among the 1930 cohort nobody was older than 65 in 1995.)

Table 2.2 displays the differences in the annuity premiums resulting from the differences between the life tables of the general population and of annuitants. The basis of comparison is the so-called *money's worth of annuity*: the expected present discounted value of annuity payments per hundred premium dollars in 1995, using the treasury yield curve for discounting.

Table 2.2. Annuity values-per-premium hundred dollar, after-tax: US, 1995

Age (year)	General	Annuitant	General	Annuitant
	Population			
	Men		Women	
55	85.2	93.4	88.0	93.7
65	81.4	92.7	85.4	92.7
75	78.3	91.3	84.6	91.9

Source: Mitchell et al. (1999b, p. 1308), Table 3, shortened.

Note the strong dependence of the money's worth of annuities on gender and age for the general population and the lack of it for the annuitant population. These numbers confirm the well-known fact that the money's worth is much higher for the annuitants than for the general public. For example, a 55-year-old member of the public receives $85.2 from a hundred dollars, while a 75-year-old receives only $78.3. For male annuitants, this number is around $93. It is also noteworthy that between 1980 and 1995 the payout value per premium rose by roughly 13 percentage points.

Some economists claim that the *increasing annuitization* of old-age benefits makes people save progressively less (Gokhale et al., 1996). They suggest that, if it were possible to diminish the 'security' provided by Social Security, then the savings rate would increase (see Theorem 2.1). In contrast, the commentators of Gokhale et al. (1996) stress that denying people access to insurance reduces their welfare. Nevertheless, this misunderstanding—that annuitization is socially harmful—has a rational core: insurance and efficiency partially contradict each other, and a delicate trade-off exists between them (for example, Varian, 1992 and Drèze, 2000).

Voluntary or mandatory insurance

We have almost arrived at the *pension system*. Of course, pension insurance differs from combined life insurance and life annuity in several respects. For our purpose, the most important difference is that, while life insurance and life annuity are matters of individual choice, genuine pension insurance is mandatory and subject to significant regulation. Even economists who prefer a minimal state role would rarely if ever allow individuals to make no provision for their old age and then, despite this flouting of social solidarity, receive a public pension (see Chapter 17 and Lindbeck–Weibull (1988); for a critique of this argument, see Diamond, 2002b, p. 40). This consensus on the necessity of a mandatory pension system explains why it is easy to purchase life insurance without a life annuity, whereas mandatory pension systems generally stipulate that, at retirement, payouts on life insurance take the form of annuities rather than lump-sum payments. Therefore, in our approach, a *voluntary pension* is a long-term investment rather than a proper pension, since no life annuity is attached to it.

From now on we shall speak almost exclusively about mandatory pension systems. Dropping the costs of the first stage, child-raising, we set $c_i = 0$, $i = 0, \ldots, L - 1$.

Chapter 3

Fully funded systems

We start our discussion of pension systems with the so-called *fully funded* (for short, the *funded) system* or capital reserve system, which most closely approximates combined life insurance and life annuity. We shall discuss the complications arising in such a system—operating costs, volatility, annuitization—and present a case-study on Chile.

Basic model

A mandatory funded pension system pays a life annuity to every member (or his survivors) who has accumulated capital in an individual account from which the annuity is paid. In mandatory systems, it is customary to set the *pension contributions* as a time-invariant percentage of earnings, τ_w, which applies within certain bounds. (In this study, the subindex of a parameter often refers to the variable on which the parameter is based.) In return, a pensioner of age j receives *pension benefit* b_j, $j = R+1, \ldots, D$. To avoid complications, we assume that, when a worker retires, he stops working and claims benefits immediately. For the sake of completeness, we shall reformulate the intertemporal budget constraint (2.3) as the equality of the expected present values of lifetime contributions and benefits:

$$\tau_w \sum_{i=L}^{R} l_i w_i r^{-i} = \sum_{j=R+1}^{D} l_j b_j r^{-j}. \tag{3.1}$$

In essence, there are three types of funded systems: (a) provident funds, managed by the government; (b) occupational pension systems, managed by private firms; and (c) personal saving plans (or individual accounts), which are run by private pension funds. There is an emerging consensus that, of the three types, individual accounts, with their greater transparency and portability, are the most efficient (World Bank, 1994), even though their costs are higher and employers prefer occupational schemes (Blake, 2000, F54–58).

We shall confine our attention to *individual accounts*, showing the accumulation of contributions as pension wealth or capital. Some observers are convinced that these favored instruments promise fabulous yields. According to the most optimistic calculations (Feldstein, 1996), decent benefits, with funds paying 5–9% annual real returns, can be procured with contribution rates as low as 2–3%. We now reproduce some of the corresponding calculations.

We concentrate on the simplest form, namely, an annuity with a constant real value, a contribution span of 40 years, and a payment span of 20 years. It is customary to express the value of an annuity in terms of *final net (of pension contribution) earning* (u_R):

$$b_{R+1} = \hat{\beta}_u u_R, \text{ where } u_R = w_R(1 - \tau_w), \qquad (3.2)$$

and $\hat{\beta}_u$ is called the *individual net entry replacement rate*.

As an illustration, we assume that the individual net replacement rate is equal to 40% and determine the contribution rates for various real interest rates and real wage growth rates. Using the expressions from Chapter 1, we obtain Table 3.1.

Table 3.1. Contribution rate as a function of wage growth and interest rate, %

Real interest rate $100(r - 1)$	Growth rate of real wages $100(\Omega - 1)$	
	0	2
0	16.7	22.3
2	9.8	14.1
5	4.0	6.3

Problem 3.1. World Bank (1994, p. 205) computed its Table 6.1 using gross rather than net replacement:

$$b_{R+1} = \hat{\beta}_w w_R. \qquad (3.2^*)$$

As it is net replacement that is generally of interest (especially with varying contribution rates), the World Bank's result is misleading. Recalculate Table 3.1 with gross replacement.

Note the sensitivity of the result to the interest rate and wage dynamics (and also to the ratio of the length of active periods to that of passive periods, not reported here). World Bank experts also stressed that, for increasing real wages, the pension at death is a much lower share of the then prevailing average earnings (27%) than at retirement (40%). Finally, these calculations do not consider survivor and disability benefits, recurrent themes of the pension literature.

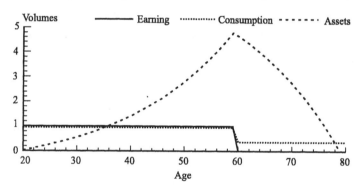

Figure 3.1. Life-cycle: optimistic view

We shall illustrate our findings in two figures. In the 'optimistic' case (Figure 3.1), the interest rate is equal to 5%, the growth rate of earnings is only 0%, and the corresponding contribution rate is a rather modest 4%. Observe also how small the accumulated capital remains even at the peak, amounting to only 5 times the final year's earnings (w_R). (Asset dynamics is described by $a_k = r a_{k-1} + w_k - c_k$.) In the 'pessimistic' case (Figure 3.2), the interest rate is equal to only 0%, the growth rate of earnings is a healthy 2%, and the corresponding contribution rate is a rather high 22.3%. Note the impressive accumulated capital, amounting to 13.4 times the final year's earnings at the peak.

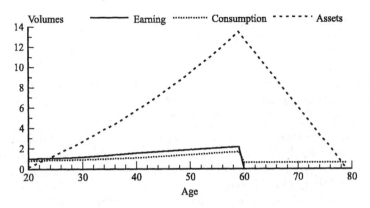

Figure 3.2. Life-cycle: pessimistic view

In what follows I treat problems arising with insurance, volatility, and fees.

Insurance vs. annuity

Perhaps the most common misunderstanding of the funded system relates to the *heritability* of the remaining pension capital. It is true (at least in Hungary) that, if the contributor to a private fund dies during the accumulation period, his designated survivors (not necessarily the widow or his children) inherit the accumulated savings. In the event that the contributor dies at the end of the accumulation period, when his children are grown up and the pension wealth is significant, his designated survivors stand to reap a substantial one-off benefit. In the case where the contributor dies at the beginning of the accumulation period, when his children are still young and the pension wealth is modest, they inherit almost nothing. Furthermore, the magnitude of the inheritance is independent of the number of survivors: the more children remain, the less support flows to each of them and other survivors. Would it not be wiser to have in place a life insurance scheme similar to that of unfunded systems (see Chapter 4 below)? A similar line of reasoning applies to the drawing-down stage; the wider the circle of survivors, the lower will be the benefit that each receives.

Many people may find it attractive to allow for a variable real value of the life annuity and for *accelerated or phased withdrawal*. The idea is the following. Assume an individual retiree at age $j - 1$ with an asset worth a_{j-1}. We divide his (or her) capital into E_{j-1} equal parts and allow the retiree to withdraw one part: a_{j-1}/E_{j-1}. (Recall that E_j is life expectancy at age j.) Assuming that the individual lives until age D', the dynamic is as follows:

$$c_j = \frac{a_{j-1}}{E_{j-1}}, \qquad a_j = r a_{j-1} - c_j, \qquad j = R + 1, \ldots, D'.$$

The remaining wealth is distributed among the survivors, whether within or outside the family.

Continuing the illustration in Example 2.1, we have

Example 3.1. If there is no interest: $r = 1$, then at accelerated withdrawal the ratio of consecutive consumptions is equal to

$$\frac{c_{j+1}}{c_j} = \frac{E_{j-1} - 1}{E_j}, \qquad j = R + 1, \ldots, D' - 1.$$

Because of decreasing survival probabilities, $E_{j-1} - 1 < E_j$, that is, consumption is a decreasing function of age. Using the data of Example 2.1, c_{j+1}/c_j drops from 0.967 at age $j = 62$ to very low positive values. □

Student loans and mortgages

The *student loan* is an interesting counterpart of the old-age pension (compare Augusztinovics, 1997b; Barr, 2001, Chapter 12): A student takes up a loan for a period of L years, the value of which is equal to b_j, $j = 0, \ldots, L - 1$. The repayment starts at age L and ends at age $L + S$, the repayment is equal to x_i, $i = L, \ldots, L + S$. There are two variants. (a) In case of a traditional bank loan, the repayment time $S + 1$ is given and the value of the annual repayment is constant (here in real terms, in reality in nominal terms): $x_i = x_L$. (b) In the case of an income-contingent student loan, the value of the annual repayment is proportional to concurrent earnings: $x_i = \xi w_i$, and the repayment time is endogenous.

Annual Hungarian data: $b_j = 210,000$ HUFs, $\xi = 0.06$, $w_0 = 1,200,000$ HUFs, $\Omega = 1.02$, where $w_i = w_0 \Omega^i$, $\$1 = 250$ HUFs in the

Summer, 2002. The real interest rates in the planned and the actual law are roughly $r = 1.06$ and $r = 1.00$, respectively.

Problem 3.2. Describe the relevant relations of the two types of student loan, when $S^a = 10$ years.

Mortgage is a more common and important counterpart of pensions. It is a special type of loan; repayment may extend over a long period of time and is secured by the property acquired with the borrowed funds.

Volatility

Business volatility influences both the capital and the life annuity of pension wealth. This risk can be diminished if (i) the individual portfolio is made increasingly risk-free as the owner approaches retirement, or (ii) the purchase of annuity is distributed in time (Alier–Vittas, 2001).

To give an idea of past trends, we cite several tables in condensed forms. Table 3.2 shows the history of US interest dynamics over the last 125 years.

Table 3.2. Real returns of financial assets in the US: 1871–1995, %

	S&P Stocks	15–year US bonds	Commercial papers	Combination 60–30–10*
Geometric average	6.87	2.81	3.11	5.66
Standard deviation	18.71	8.83	5.39	12.42
Correlations	30.06	8.62	68.79	

Source: Alier–Vittas (2001, pp. 399–401) Tables 11.1–11.4.

Remark. The last column shows the figures for the combination of stocks, bonds, and commercial paper in the proportions listed. The last row contains the correlations between stocks and bonds, stocks and paper, and bonds and paper, respectively.

We add that the (geometrical) average of annual growth rates of real earnings was about 1.5% with a standard deviation 3.75% (Alier–Vittas, 2001; p. 402, Table 11.5).

On this basis, the authors consider capital accumulation and annuities under various strategies (Tables 3.3 and 3.4, respectively). It

Table 3.3. Capital accumulation/final earnings
for alternative portfolios, %

Portfolios	100–0–0	0–100–0	60–30–10	30–60–10	baseline
Average	9.43	3.53	6.55	4.85	7.52
Standard deviation	3.02	1.33	1.55	1.44	0.88
Maximum	15.55	6.88	10.80	8.16	8.98
Minimum	3.83	1.80	3.43	2.76	6.14

Source: Alier–Vittas (2001, p. 404) Table 11.6.

Table 3.4. Gross individual replacement rates
for alternative portfolios, %

Portfolios	100–0–0	0–100–0	60–30–10	30–60–10	baseline
Average	60.5	22.6	42.0	31.1	48.2
Standard deviation	19.3	8.6	9.9	9.2	5.7
Maximum	99.7	43.7	69.3	52.3	57.6
Minimum	24.6	11.6	22.0	17.7	39.4

Source: Alier–Vittas (2001, p. 404) Table 11.7.

Remark. For the definition of replacement rate, see (3.2*) above.

is assumed that workers contributed 10% of their wages (increasing
annually by 2.5% on average plus by 1% for seniority) for 40 years
and lived in retirement for 20 years. As indicators of the performance of the systems, the authors show both the accumulated capital and the pension in terms of final earnings. We cite only their
simulation with a real discount rate of return of 2.5% for annuity
of constant real value. The authors consider four different portfolio strategies; two undiversified portfolios, 1) equities only: 100–0–0,
2) bonds only: 0–100–0; two balanced portfolios, 3) US-type: 60–30–
10 and 4) Chile-type: 30–60–10, and contrast them with the *baseline
case*, where the return on the pension fund investment is constant
over time. "... [F]or the sake of additional simplicity, we do not take
account of the operating fees and commissions charged by insurance
companies and pension fund managers" but ... "we do not underes-
timate the impact of high fees on pensions." (Alier–Vittas, 2001, p.
397 and endnote 13.)

"The all-equity portfolio achieves the highest capital accumulation ratio and the highest average [over the trials] individual replacement (60.5%) but also the highest volatility measured by the standard deviation (19.3%)... and the max/min ratio."

The gradual shift to bonds and the gradual purchase of annuities (not reported here) improve the performance of risky portfolios.

Operating costs

The computations reported above neglect the huge *operating costs* that are characteristic of such funds. We now turn to this issue (compare Diamond, 1998 and Murthi et al., 2001).

Individual pension assets at the end of year i are denoted by a_i. Operating costs during the accumulation stage will be modeled as proportional to assets and contributions, respectively. Denoting the pro rata costs of *assets management* as $1 - \vartheta_a$ and of *contribution management* as $1 - \vartheta_w$, the individual assets satisfy the following difference equation:

$$a_i = \vartheta_a r a_{i-1} + \vartheta_w \tau_w w_L \Omega^{i-L}, \qquad i = L, \ldots, R, \qquad a_{L-1} = 0. \quad (3.3)$$

We use the *net interest factor* $\tilde{r} = \vartheta_a r$ in the calculation of the present value of the net contributions paid during the accumulation period:

$$\tilde{r}^{1-T} a_R = \vartheta_w \tau_w w_L \sum_{k=0}^{T-1} \Omega^k \tilde{r}^{-k}, \qquad T = R - L + 1.$$

Using the notation I of (1.5), this directly implies

Theorem 3.1. *The total capital accumulated for retirement is equal to*

$$a_R = \tilde{r}^{T-1} \vartheta_w \tau_w w_R \Omega^{-(T-1)} I_{T-1}(\Omega/\tilde{r}). \quad (3.4)$$

We also want to know what annuity can be financed from the accumulated capital. In addition to the operating costs just analysed, we consider the money's worth ratio of annuity introduced in Chapter 2 and denoted here as ϑ_b, showing the ratio of actual to costless annuities. As a complement to Theorem 3.1, we have

Theorem 3.2. *The individual replacement rate is equal to*

$$\hat{\beta}_w = \frac{\vartheta_b r a_R}{w_R I_{D-R-1}(1/r)}. \quad (3.5)$$

Table 3.5. Operating costs, retirement capital
and replacement rate

Operating costs of		Assets per earning at retirement a_R/w_R	Individual replacement rate $100\hat{\beta}_w$
assets $100(1 - \vartheta_a)$	contribution $100(1 - \vartheta_w)$		
0	0	16.1	53.7
	5	15.3	51.0
	10	14.5	48.4
1	0	12.8	42.8
	5	12.2	40.7
	10	11.5	38.5
2	0	10.3	34.5
	5	9.8	32.7
	10	9.3	31.0

We illustrate the effects of these operating costs for the case in which $L = 20$, $R = 59$, $D = 79$ with growth factor of earnings $\Omega = 1.02$, contribution rate $\tau_w = 0.1$, money's worth ratio of annuity $\vartheta_b = 0.9$, and interest factor $r = 1.05$.

Table 3.5 shows that it is the operating costs on assets rather than on contributions that matter (the effect of the money's worth ratio on the annuity is simple). For example, if there are no operating costs, the individual replacement rate is 53.7%. This is reduced to 48.4% if there is no fee on assets but a 10% fee on contributions. On the other hand, if there are no operating costs on contributions but a 2% fee on assets, the individual replacement rate drops to 34.5%.

James et al. (2001) are much more optimistic. As they see it, with the maturation of these systems costs and fees can be dramatically diminished. For example, according to their Table 7.4 (James et al., 2001, p. 264), in Chile the pro-asset costs and fees fell from an initial (1982) 9.4% and 12.0% to a recent (1998) 1.36% and 1.13%, respectively.

Funded pension systems are often called *defined contribution* (DC) systems, because the pension is determined by the contributions. We have already seen that there is some deviation from this principle, stemming from life insurance, etc. We shall see that other factors, regulation for example, also weaken this principle (for details, see Diamond, 2002b, Chapter 1).

Under normal circumstances, individual accounts are somewhat insulated from political influence (compare Diamond–Valdés-Prieto (1993) on Chile). But Diamond (1997, p. 38) also argues that this insulation is generally far from perfect: the government can impose an additional tax on the savings, or allow owners to tap into them in response to events like unemployment and serious health problems.

Before turning to our case-study, we make a short detour. According to traditional microeconomics, every worker receives every year the value of his marginal product as his wage. Lazear (1979), however, argues that it may be rational for a firm to pay less than this to its younger workers and more to its older workers. This way, younger workers have strong incentives to work hard in order to keep their jobs, but older workers face reduced incentives to retire. As a result, the firm and the workers have to decide ex ante on the age of *mandatory retirement*. This problem is further aggravated by the surprising practice whereby so-called funded company pensions pay benefits proportional to final salary and length of employment (Economist, 2002, p. 7).

Chilean pension system

The Chilean pension system is the staple example of a mandatory pension system that relies almost exclusively on a fully funded pillar built on competing private pension funds. (From the rich literature on this topic, we refer to Diamond–Valdés-Prieto (1993), Valdés-Prieto, ed. (1997), Edwards (1998), Callund (1999), Hujo (1999) and Schmidt-Hebbel, 2001.) World Bank (1994) contains considerable information on other funded systems, notably government-owned provident funds.

The Chilean system, as a fully funded one, was inaugurated in 1981. The government of that era essentially closed down the dying unfunded system (for an analysis of the unfunded system, see Chapter 4), and within a decade almost every worker had joined the new system. (Paradoxically, the military, which had guided the whole transition, retained its unfunded pension system.) In addition, a very modest social assistance benefit amounting to 12.5% of the average wage is provided for the small fraction of the large population left out of the system (Hujo, 1999, p. 133.) Workers moving into the new system from the old one received so-called *recognition bonds* which transformed their contributions to the old system into capital (capitalized at an annual real interest rate of 4%). The new contributions to the funded system are added to this capital in individual accounts. Thus, for a given individual it makes no difference whether or not he had participated in the old system before entering the new one. (We shall see in Chapter 5 that this is not the case in the partially prefunded Hungarian system.)

Between 1981 and 1994 the real annual gross yields of the private funds were very high (13.8%) but approximately zero between 1994–1998, providing an average yield of 11.0% for the period 1981–1998. The high yields suggested that fair pensions could be assured with a modest contribution rate of 12.5%. Note, however, that "over the 1991–1997 period for which data is available, individual accounts yielded on average 8.3%, a figure which is 1.9%[point] lower—due to commissions—than the return on pension funds" (Schmidt-Hebbel, 2001, p. 150).

Objective analysts emphasize the darker features of the system: (i) given the volatility of the stock exchanges, the value of the pension is very sensitive to the timing of retirement (Callund, 1999, p. 531); and (ii) although indexed life annuities exist, over two decades the availability of accelerated withdrawal can reduce the real value of a pension by half (Diamond–Valdés-Prieto, 1993 and Example 3.1).

Chapter 4

Unfunded systems

The pension systems that had appeared in Europe by 1900 had largely begun as publicly run funded systems (Bod, 1995). Since life insurance had been born much earlier, there would have been no particular difficulty with funded pension systems had two world wars and the Great Depression not destroyed them. The new pension systems had to start from scratch.

The newly introduced *unfunded* pension systems are generally called *pay-as-you-go* systems. Their basic principle is simple: each generation pays the pension of its parents' generation. This implies, of course, that the first generation gets a free ride, that is, it is able to draw a pension at retirement without ever having made "contributions". (Before the reader turns green with envy, he should bear in mind the suffering of this 'free-rider' generation, its earlier contributions and its difficulties gearing up again after the wars and depression.)

After presenting the basic model of an unfunded system, we shall discuss its variants: the flat benefit system, the flat-rate benefit system, proportional systems, regressive link, and methods of indexation.

Basic model

As distinct from a funded system, an unfunded system must be mandatory and publicly managed. Indeed, the implicit social contract between successive generations requires government enforcement.

How does an unfunded system function? Assume that our would-be pensioner (born in year 0) or his employer pays every year (in fact, every month) a prescribed part of his total earnings to the agency administering social security. For some mysterious reason this contribution is generally divided into two parts, the *employer's contribution* and the *employee's contribution*. (In some countries, the government contributes a third part.) To add to the mystery, in practice a strange concept called *gross earnings* (v) plays a central role, which is equal to total earnings (w) less employer's contribution also expressed in terms of the gross earnings ($v\tau_1$). Therefore, the relation between total earnings and gross earnings is $w = v(1 + \tau_1)$. The employee in turn pays a contribution $v\tau_2$ from his gross earnings, assuming that it is less than a statutory limit, which is usually between double and triple the national average wage ($\mathbf{v}$), for example, $v_{\max} = 2\mathbf{v}$ in Hungary between 1997–2002. Let $\tau_v = \tau_1 + \tau_2$ denote the *total contribution rate* (or payroll tax rate). The contribution is then equal to $\tau_v v$. The gross wage is economically irrelevant, since the employee cares only about his net wage, while the employer is concerned only with the total wage.

At retirement an individual is entitled to or eligible for an *entry pension* which is an increasing (more precisely, a non-decreasing) function of his past contributions, or, equivalently for time-invariant contribution rates, of past earnings. To avoid notations for calendar years, wages and benefits are indexed by age rather than calendar year, at least at this stage of the exposition:

$$b_{R+1} = h(v_L, \ldots, v_R). \tag{4.1}$$

From a year after retirement until death, the individual receives a *continued pension* or pension in progress, which is a function of the previous pension:

$$b_{j+1} = H(b_j), \qquad j = R + 1, \ldots, D - 1. \tag{4.2}$$

Such systems are called *defined benefit* (DB) systems, suggesting that there is no, or only a weak, relation between contributions and benefits. We shall see in Theorem 8.1, however, that in a pure unfunded system there is a strict equality between aggregate contributions and aggregate benefits in each period, making h and H dependent on τ_v and other macroeconomic parameters (see for example, (15.1)).

The simplest measure of the efficiency of the unfunded system was introduced by Aaron (1966), the so-called *internal factor of return*, ρ, which is used as a discount factor to equalize expected contributions and benefits (compare with (3.1)), but total wage cost is replaced by gross wage. Formally,

$$\tau_v \sum_{i=L}^{R} l_i v_i \rho^{-i} = \sum_{j=R+1}^{D} l_j b_j \rho^{-j}. \tag{4.3}$$

Figuratively, if the pension contributions were earning interest at a rate of $\rho - 1$ in a fund, then the foregoing pension benefits could be financed from the fund.

In Chapter 8, we shall see that in a stable environment the internal factor of return is equal to the growth coefficient of the economy.

Problem 4.1. Prove that the net rate of return of the unfunded system is positive ($\rho > 1$) if and only if the sum of contributions is lower than the sum of benefits.

Although we generally restrict our attention to individuals, consider for a moment a widely disregarded feature of the unfunded system (already mentioned in Chapter 3), namely, survivors' benefits. It is true that, if a person dies close to retirement age, his adult children do not profit from their parent's contributions, and his well-to-do widow (or less frequently, her widower) may receive relatively little. However, if the worker dies at the beginning of his career, leaving behind a widow and children, then each dependent family member receives a rather generous monthly benefit, regardless of the length of the interrupted contribution period, the length of the remaining period foreshortened by death, the children's entry into the labor force, and the number of survivors. The disability pension is similarly structured (Bod, 2000; Réti, 2000 and Diamond, 2002a, Chapter 8).

Typically, the real value of continued benefits is constant (price-indexed):

$$b_{R+1} = \cdots = b_D. \tag{4.4}$$

Here we characterize a few typical unfunded systems. (For a more detailed description of the systems of five European countries, see Martos, 1997).

Flat benefit

In several countries, namely, the Netherlands (compare Bovenberg–Meijdam, 2001) and the Scandinavian countries, the unfunded pension is totally independent of individual contributions: it is *flat*. To be eligible, the beneficiary must have been a citizen or a resident of the country for a sufficiently long period. Flat benefit can be expressed in terms of national average gross earnings $\mathbf{v}_{R+1}$:

$$b_{R+1} = \beta_{\mathbf{v}} \mathbf{v}_{R+1}, \tag{4.5}$$

where $\beta_{\mathbf{v}}$ is the so-called *average replacement rate*. (From the point of view of the individual, however, what matters is the ratio of the benefit to final earnings, the individual replacement rate of (3.2): $b_{R+1} = \hat{\beta}_v v_R$.) In this case, the choice of (4.4) is almost inevitable.

Theorem 4.1. *With flat benefits, the higher the final individual earnings, the lower is the individual replacement rate.*

This system has the advantage that it achieves redistribution from rich to poor in the simplest way. It has drawbacks as well. Workers are incited to work in the hidden economy and report only a fraction of their earnings or of their employment.

In the countries listed above, the relatively small dispersion of earnings and the strongly progressive character of the personal income tax yield a relatively high average replacement rate. In the Netherlands in 1985, for example, we find 38% for a single worker and 54% for a couple (World Bank, 1994, p. 152).

Flat-rate benefit

In Great Britain (see Blake, 1997; Johnson–Rake, 1997; Budd–Campbell, 1998 and Disney, 2001) within wide limits the basic government benefit is also independent of contributions, but is proportional to the *actual* years of service, denoted by $T = R - L + 1$: $b_{R+1} = \alpha_1 T \mathbf{v}_{R+1}$, where α_1 is the *flat rate* or the *accrual rate*, determining the value of a year's service in terms of national average gross earnings. (Note that many experts blur the distinction between flat and flat-rate benefits.) For example, if $\alpha_1 = 0.005$ and $T = 30$, then $b_{R+1} = 0.15 \mathbf{v}_{R+1}$. To make this expression comparable to (4.5) for the flat benefit, we must rearrange it obtaining

$$b_{R+1} = \frac{T}{T^*}\beta_{\mathbf{v}}^*\mathbf{v}_{R+1}, \qquad (4.6)$$

where T^* is the *number of maximal years of service* and $\beta_{\mathbf{v}}^* = \alpha_1 T^*$ will be called *maximal average replacement rate*. In Great Britain, as the coefficient α_1 is declining inversely with respect to the national average wage, the real value of the basic pension is constant. Again, (4.4) holds.

The advantage of the flat-rate system over the flat system is that it creates an incentive to continue working as long as possible. This structure anticipates a move toward *earnings-related* pensions, to be discussed soon. Interestingly, in Great Britain the maximal average replacement rate was 20% in 1987, about 15% in 1996, and is expected to decline to 9% by 2030 (Budd–Campbell, 1998, pp. 101–102). Given such low replacement rates, the incentive effect in Great Britain might be rather weak. It is little wonder that this system does not function alone and needs, at the least, to be complemented by a system of social assistance.

Proportional benefit

In at least one country, Germany, (see Schmähl, 1999 and Börsch-Supan, 2000) the benefit is *proportional to lifetime contributions*, a system that achieves the highest degree of earnings-relatedness of pensions. At this point, we must introduce the growth factor of *average real earnings*: g, generally identified in this study with the *growth factor of labor productivity*. Rather than add up the real values of contributions, earnings-related pension systems typically *valorize* contributions according to national average earning dynamics; that is, earnings (v_i) at age i are multiplied by the growth factors of real earnings cumulated through date of retirement:

$$b_{R+1} = \alpha_2 \sum_{i=L}^{R} v_i g^{R-i}, \qquad (4.7)$$

where α_2/τ is a positive scalar multiplier transforming the accumulated *virtual pension capital* $\tau\sum_{i=L}^{R} v_i g^{R-i}$ into a life annuity b_{R+1}.

Example 4.1. For a person whose earnings have always been at the average national wage, the proportional pension is equal to the flat-rate benefit. Symbolically, for $v_i \equiv \mathbf{v}_R g^{i-R}$, $b_{R+1} = \alpha_2 T \mathbf{v}_R$. $\square$

To arrive at an individual replacement rate, we introduce the *average indexed (or valorized) annual (gross) earning*, corresponding to an individual earning path:

$$\bar{v}_R = \frac{\sum_{i=L}^{R} v_i g^{R-i}}{T}. \tag{4.8}$$

Then using the *individual lifetime replacement rate*, $\beta_v = \alpha_2 T$, we obtain

$$b_{R+1} = \beta_v \bar{v}_R. \tag{4.9}$$

Recall that the flat (rate) benefit was defined in terms of the current average earnings. Here, however, the past individual average indexed annual (gross) earnings is the base.

In Germany, the continued pensions also follow earnings dynamics:

$$b_{j+1} = b_j g, \qquad j = R+1, \ldots, D-1. \tag{4.10}$$

The German *point system*, it is worth noting, translates these complex mathematical expressions into human terms. Relate the individual earnings (v_i) to the national average ($\mathbf{v}_i$) every year and call the ratio $v_i/\mathbf{v}_i$ the number of *pension points* earned at age i. This value and the value of accumulated points up to age i could be reported to each contributor yearly. In this way every worker could know his or her standing at any point in time and, knowing the nominal point value, could compute the actual value of his entry pension were he to retire at that time.

Problem 4.2. Prove that the German point system is identical to (4.7).

In the proportional pension system, there is no *intracohort income redistribution*: rather, redistribution is achieved through other channels. (For completeness, let us add that, if an individual works for 35 years or more with lifetime earnings less than half the average, his total contribution is increased by 50% or to 75% of the average, whichever is less (Fehr, 2000, p. 421).) Of course, pension contributions of short-lived people can be used to finance the pensions of long-lived people; but I do not call such transfers 'income redistribution' except for the possible positive correlation between earnings and life expectancy. In Germany, the system ensures relatively high benefits to workers making regular contributions that amount to 70% of final earnings with a contribution rate of 21% plus a sizable government grant (Schmähl, 1999).

A further advantage of this system is that the retired cohorts share the fruits of the technological progress that occurs after their retirement. To illustrate this advantage, let us call two persons *similar* if they were born in different years and their earnings paths differ only by the cumulated growth factor of average earnings. For example, let the earnings path of the person born in year 0 be $v_L, \ldots, v_R$, then the earnings path of the similar person born in year 1 is $v_L g, \ldots, v_R g$. The proportional system has the following consistency property.

Theorem 4.2. *Consider a proportional pension system. For given years of service, (a) individual lifetime replacement rates are independent of lifetime earnings; (b) concerning the overlapping intervals, the pension paths of two similar persons are the same.*

Remark. The theorem remains valid if the growth coefficient is changing over time.

Proof. (a) By (4.9), it is trivial. (b) Introduce $S = D - R$ and consider the benefit paths of the persons born in years 0 and 1, respectively. By (4.9)–(4.10), the two paths are as follows:

$$
\begin{array}{cccccc}
\beta_v \bar{v}_R & \beta_v \bar{v}_R g & \ldots & \beta_v \bar{v}_R g^{S-2} & \beta_v \bar{v}_R g^{S-1} & \\
& \beta_v \bar{v}_R g & \beta_v \bar{v}_R g^2 & \ldots & \beta_v \bar{v}_R g^{S-1} & \beta_v \bar{v}_R g^S
\end{array}
$$

This proves the second statement. $\qquad\square$

Although the German pension system is very well-designed, long-run aging, high unemployment rates, and low activity rates may undermine its viability (see Schmähl, 1999 and Fehr, 2000, outlined in Chapter 16).

Until now the *retirement age* has been taken as given. In fact, the effective retirement age is much lower than the normal (statutory) retirement age. Today, in most developed countries, although people live longer and are healthier than in the past, they also retire younger (see Gruber–Wise, eds. (1999) for an international comparison). For example, Coile–Gruber (2000) report that 81% of the US male cohort of 62 year-olds worked in 1950; by 1995 this fraction had dropped to 51%. (In the US, the standard retirement age is 65, while early retirement comes at 62.)

Critics of the unfunded system (for example, Börsch-Supan, 1998) consider early retirement to be a major flaw of the system. Governments may well prefer early retirement to massive unemployment as a short-run (?) solution; but in the long run the demographic difficulties may overwhelm such policy efforts. On the other hand, it is conceivable that economic progress has diminished the quantity of lifetime labor as well as that of annual labor (but see Diamond (2002b, p. 4) and Chapter 12).

Table 4.1 displays only country-specific data on this phenomenon.

Table 4.1. Normal versus effective retirement age and expected duration of retirement for males (legislation in 1996)

Countries	Normal	Early	Effective	Duration
		retirement age		of retirement
Germany	65	63	60.5	13.8
Great Britain	65		62.7	13.6
Hungary	60	55–58	58.5	14.9
The Netherlands	65	58–63	58.8	14.4
US	65	62–64	63.6	14.9

Source: Columns 1–3: Blondal–Scarpetta (1999) as cited by Boeri et al. (2001a, p. 32), Table 2, except for Hungary. Column 4: at official retirement age, World Bank (1994, p. 371) Table A.10.

The problem of low effective retirement age can be mitigated by the system introduced in Sweden, referred to as *notional defined contribution* (NDC) which extends the capitalization implicit in valorization [(4.7)] to the calculation of entry annuities (compare Valdés-Prieto, 2000). Each year, the actual value of the annuity of the newly retired is set as the ratio of the notional capital to the remaining life expectancy of the cohort. If the latter increases, the entry annuity decreases proportionally (Diamond, 2002b, Chapter 1), fixing the contribution rate. It appears fair that a person retiring before (after) normal retirement age $R^* + 1$ at age $R + 1$, receives a proportionally reduced (increased) annuity—so-called *actuarially fair treatment* at *flexible (variable) retirement.* The factor of adjustment is given in

$$b_{R+1} = \frac{l_{R+1}E_{R+1}}{l_{R^*+1}E_{R^*+1}}b_{R^*+1}, \qquad (4.11)$$

where l_{R+1} and E_{R+1} stand for the survival probability and conditional life expectancy at age $R+1$, respectively.

In contrast, in Germany the replacement of the weak reward–no premium system of 1972 began only with a partially 'corrected' system in 1992. These two systems and the fair one are presented in Table 4.2.

Table 4.2. Adjustment of German pensions

Age (years)	60	61	62	63	64	65	66	67	68	69	70
Benefit-1972	88	90	93	95	98	100	110	120	123	126	129
Benefit-1992	70	76	82	88	94	100	109	117	126	134	143
'Fair'	66	72	78	84	92	100	109	120	131	144	159

Source: Börsch-Supan (2001, p. 21), Table 1.2 with a discount rate 3%. Note, however, that in calculating these rounded-off numbers it was assumed that everybody starts to work at the same time, so that later retirement automatically means longer service.

Unfortunately, traditional actuarial fairness itself may be unfair in that it (i) denies the principle of insurance by severely punishing those who are forced to retire before normal retirement age (Diamond–Mirrlees, 1986) and (ii) violates the principle of actuarial fairness by wrongly identifying the death risk of those retiring before, at, and after normal retirement age (Gruber–Orszag, 1999 and Simonovits, 1999, 2001). What happens in the likely case where life expectancy of late retirees is much higher than that of early retirees (Waldron, 2001)? Here, not only is the first group rewarded at the expense of the second, but the entire balance is upset (see Chapter 12 for details).

In this study, we generally ignore different treatments of males and females within social security systems. It is impossible to overlook, however, public pension systems' increasing intolerance of gender discrimination and the fact that it has always been forbidden to distinguish between the sexes in the calculation of life annuities. Although women generally retire much earlier than men and on average live much longer, the determination of pensions does not take account of their greater life expectancy.

Regressive formula and incomplete reference period

In a fourth group of countries, most notably the US (compare Stiglitz, 1988, Chapter 13 and Wise, 2001), benefits are based on a significant part of, rather than entire, life earnings (compare (4.8)). Correspondingly, the *estimated averaged indexed monthly (or annual) gross earning*, for short, AIME or *reference earning* v_R^* is defined on a long reference period:

$$v_R^* = \frac{\sum_{i=L^*}^{R} v_i g^{R-i}}{R - L^* + 1}, \quad \text{where} \quad L < L^* < R. \qquad (4.12)$$

More precisely, in the US the best 35 years count. Assuming that individual earning increases with age (and time), $R = 64$ implies $L^* = R - 35 + 1 = 30$.

We have already mentioned that governments revalue individual earnings by the national averages rather than by the price index. Nevertheless, Gokhale–Kotlikoff (1999) consider price valorization an instrument for affecting a disguised reduction of unfunded pensions. In comparison with the traditional method it is easy to see that for increasing average earnings this solution decreases lifetime average earnings and (with an unchanged replacement rate) the entry pension as well. However, it has an unpleasant side-effect: the relative values of different contribution paths change too. The flatter the individual earnings path, the larger is the proportional reduction in the pension. (It is noteworthy that this technique was proposed by the Commission to the President (2002) and justly criticized by Diamond–Orszag (2002).)

The entry pension is not proportional to but is a *regressive function* of v_R^*, that is, φ is an increasing concave function:

$$b_{R+1} = \varphi(v_R^*). \qquad (4.13)$$

Defining φ in (4.13), we can ignore the asterisk referring to an estimated average. Assume that there exist K earning classes (brackets) and the benefit function is a piecewise linear function. Let

v^k be the *lower bending point of bracket* k, $k = 0, 1, \ldots, K - 1$ and let φ^k be the corresponding regression coefficient, concavity implies $0 = v^0 < \cdots < v^{K-1}$, $1 \geq \varphi^0 > \cdots > \varphi^{K-1} > 0$ and let $v^K = \mathbf{v}_{\max}$. Then we determine the pension switching points: $b^{k+1} = b^k + \varphi^k(v^{k+1} - v^k)$, $b^0 = 0$. Hence the general pension function is

$$\varphi(v^*) = b^k + \varphi^k(v^* - v^k) \text{ if } v^k \leq v^* < v^{k+1}. \qquad (4.14)$$

In 2000, the US parameters had the following values: $K = 3$, $v^1 = 531$, $v^2 = 3202$, $v^3 = 6050$ \$/month and $\varphi^0 = 0.9$, $\varphi^1 = 0.32$, and $\varphi^2 = 0.15$.

Problem 4.3. Determine the monthly pension of a US citizen who retired in 2000 after working at least 35 years and whose earnings were always equivalent to \$2000.

This system is further refined by the principle of flexible retirement (4.11). In fact, (4.13) gives only the *primary insurance amount* (PIA) which is adjusted down for early retirees and up for late retirees: *delayed retirement credit*. As a nuance, it is also possible to *delay claiming benefits* but very few people do so (Coile et al., 1999).

In the US, for an individual with average earnings and full work time, both the contribution rate (12.4%) and the average replacement rate (53%) are much lower than in Germany. The effect of redistribution is illustrated in Table 4.5 below.

In the US, national average gross wages have been increasing very slowly in real terms since World War II (compare with Table 8.4), so the indexation issue is not very pressing: (4.4) holds.

Obviously, the length of the reference period matters. The longer the period, the more proportional is the benefit to lifetime contribution. The exclusion of few years can be justified as an insurance device but it can also be criticized as a subsidy for people writing Masters and Ph.D. dissertations. Regression is a compromise between flat benefit and proportional benefit. The principle of regression is an extension of the progressive income tax to pensions and we shall see later (Example 10.1) that it can be justified to a certain extent. It seems likely, however, that a flat benefit in combination with a proportional benefit could accomplish the same ends (compare with (17.1) below).

Short reference period and other imperfections

The reader has already encountered passing references to the Hungarian pension system. Here I discuss it in greater depth. In this rather lengthy section I broaden the focus beyond the short reference period to include additional interesting specifics, namely, the deficiency in valorization, the regressivity in earnings and years of service, and the effect of the date of retirement on the benefit and price-wage indexed benefits. It will turn out that over time Hungarian governments 'succeeded' in creating complex but dysfunctional pension formulas (see Augusztinovics, 1993; Antal et al., 1995 and Martos, 1995).

Before we turn to the details, the complications regarding *personal income tax* must be mentioned. Rather than working with gross wages and gross benefits, the Hungarian pension is tax-free and is based on *net-gross earnings*. To understand this concept, remember that both the employee's contributions and personal income tax are based on gross earnings, which implies that the employee is formally taxed twice: if ι is the progressive personal income tax function, then the net earning is equal to the gross earning less employee's contribution less personal income tax: $u = (1 - \tau_2)v - \iota(v)$. As compensation for double taxation, the pension benefit depends on the net earnings plus the employee's contributions, the *net-gross earnings*: $z = u + v\tau_2$.

A distinctive feature of the Hungarian (and some other) pension system(s) is that the reference period for which the estimated averaged indexed annual net-gross earnings is calculated is rather short, just a few years. If the number of years of service is still taken into account (as in the British system), one has to calculate the entry benefits as the product of a uniform accrual rate (α_3), years of service (T), and reference earnings (z_R^*) or of its regressive function ψ:

$$b_{R+1} = \alpha_3 T \psi(z_R^*). \qquad (4.15')$$

But since this formula would still be 'too simple' for Hungary, the product of the first two factors is replaced by an increasing function of the years of service, the so-called *statutory replacement rate*: χ_T. Symbolically,

$$b_{R+1} = \chi_T \psi(z_R^*). \qquad (4.15)$$

Table 4.3. Statutory replacement rates in Hungary, χ_T

Years of work	10	25	32	36	42
Rate until 1996 %	33	63	70	72	76
Rate from 1997 %	33	63	70	74	83

For decades, the statutory replacement rate was very regressive, with a value of 0.33 for 10 years of service, increasing by 0.02 per year until 25 years of service, then by 0.01 between 26 and 32 years, and 0.05 for the remaining years. In 1996 the government suddenly realized that this formula almost punished late retirement and introduced a hybrid function, replacing 0.05 by 0.01 before 36 years of service and 0.015 after. The bending points of the two functions are displayed in Table 4.3.

Until 1992 *reference* (net-gross) earnings were essentially calculated as the average of the unvalorized earnings of the last three years before retirement. This method was very rough and easy to manipulate. For example, if the earnings in the last year before retirement were much lower or, more likely, much higher than in an average year, then the reference wage was also much lower or much higher than the life-path average. For the time being, we shall ignore the other aspects of calculating the entry pension. The continued pensions were raised in a modest and *ad hoc* way until 1992.

Since 1992, all earnings (below the ceiling) from 1988 have been taken into account. Presently (2002) the reference period already comprises 14 full years. As a historical fossil, the valorization leaves out the last three years (following the 'progressive' traditions of the pre-indexation stage). As a rule, continued benefits have been indexed to national net average earnings:

$$\text{either} \quad b_k = b_{k-1}\frac{u_k}{u_{k-1}} \quad \text{or} \quad b_k = b_{k-1}\frac{u_{k-1}}{u_{k-2}}. \tag{4.16}$$

The first, forward-looking version was used in 1992–1995 and from 1999 on; a variant of the second, backward-looking version was used in 1996–1998 (see Chapter 6 on the direct effect of inflation). Note that in (4.16) we had to relax the constancy of earnings growth factor to bridge the gap between the model and reality (compare with Figures 4.1–4.2).

It has quite often happened that a worker who retired after the normal retirement age was disadvantaged by a reduction in his monthly pension benefit (which was not properly indexed) in comparison with another person who retired at the normal age (whose benefit was properly indexed). Contrast this madness with the logic of Theorem 4.2.

Réti (1997, pp. 39–41) reports that partial valorization of earnings diminished entry pensions by about 8–10% for a long time. The impact of regression has been changing continually, but since 1998 it has been weakening rapidly (Table 4.5).

According to the original framework, by 2013 regressivity will be eliminated from the pension formula, and both wages and benefits will be gross rather than net, leading to $b_{R+1} = \alpha_2 v_R^*$, where v_R^* is given by (4.12) and $\alpha_2 = 0.0165$.

The indexation of continuing benefits has already changed. Since 2001 continuing pensions are to be indexed by a combined wage and price rule like that of Switzerland (see also World Bank, 1994, pp. 151–157 and Table A.7, p. 368):

$$b_{j+1} = b_j g^{1/2}, \qquad j = R+1, \ldots, D-1. \tag{4.17}$$

(In fact, the arithmetic $[(1 + g)/2]$ rather than the geometric $[g^{1/2}]$ average is used, but the difference is not significant.)

Figure 4.1 shows the earning and pension dynamics of the years of economic transition in Hungary.

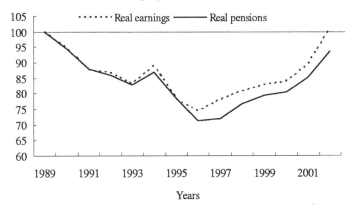

Figure 4.1. The real net earnings and pensions: Hungary, 1989 = 100

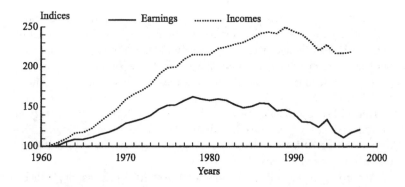

Figure 4.2. Real earnings and incomes: Hungary, 1960 = 100

Figure 4.1 shows the earning and pension dynamics of the years of economic transition in Hungary.

From Figure 4.2, which reports earnings for a much longer period, 1960–1998, and compares them with personal incomes, we see that real net earnings have lagged behind real incomes. Beginning in 1978, the former started to diminish dramatically while the latter

Table 4.4. Dependence of Hungarian pensions on date of retirement, 1996:11

Date of retirement	Distribution of number of pensioners %	Pension in terms of the average %
until 1970	2.2	95.7
1971–75	4.8	99.6
1976–80	11.4	98.5
1981–85	17.7	101.8
1986–89	18.1	105.8
1990	7.9	113.2
1991	8.3	98.1
1992	6.8	94.0
1993	6.7	93.3
1994	6.2	90.4
1995	6.8	93.9
1996	2.9	97.0

Source: Réti (1997, p. 42) Table 9 with corrections.

incomes, and this contraction has frequently been absolute (see also Augusztinovics, 1999c, p. 355).

Table 4.4 shows how strongly the value of the pension in a given month (November 1996) depends on the *date of retirement.* The contrast between the peak in 1990 (113%) and the trough in 1994 (90.4%) shows pathological sensitivity to retirement date and lack of consistency in the formula.

Summary with a table

Having analyzed various unfunded pension systems, we return to first principles. Unfunded systems are generally defined-benefit systems, and most people suppose that in such systems there is no, or only a weak, relationship between contributions and benefits. Our detailed case studies demonstrate that this is not universally the case. There are systems like the German one, where the benefit is proportional to the whole contribution path. In such systems it is the average real earnings growth rate rather than the interest rate which capitalizes savings. The system of notional defined contribution is adjusted to changing demographic parameters as well. On the other hand, in the Netherlands the bulk of the funded pension schemes provide defined benefits, proportional to the last year salary rather than lifetime earnings (Bovenberg–Meijdam, 2001, pp. 47–48).

Table 4.5 characterizes the redistribution and (for later use) the size of the public system in a few mandatory public systems.

We see from Table 4.5 that, regardless of the system, people earning at the poverty threshold (that is, earning half the average) receive about 3/4 of their earnings as pension. The individual replacement rate of the average worker remains 3/4 in proportional systems, drops to half in regressive systems, and sinks to 43% in the Netherlands. Finally, the benefits of contributors near the upper limit drop from a high of 75% in Germany to 32% in the US and to 25% in the Netherlands. In the next chapter we shall see the other side of the coin: with the exception of the Czech system (soon to be made less regressive), the more regressive the system, the larger is the role of the private pillars. If it were not so, then the living standard of a just-retired Dutch professor would suddenly drop to a third of that of his German colleagues.

Table 4.5. Size and redistribution of public systems in OECD countries, %

Country	Replacement rate for earning			Type	Aggregate pension per GDP
	Half the	Double the			
		Average			
France	84	84	73	proportional	12.5
Hungary (2000)	78	79	73	regressive?	9.5
Germany	76	72	75	proportional	12.8
US	65	55	32	regressive	4.6
Great Britain	72	50	35	regressive	4.4
Czech Republic	81	49	28	degressive	9.6
The Netherlands	73	43	25	flat	5.2

Source: Johnson's unpublished but recent data cited by Casamatta et al. (2000, p. 504), Table 1. The corresponding Hungarian numbers were provided by J. Réti. The Czech data are taken from Mácha (2002, p. 82), Table 4.

The reader may have noticed that we have not dwelt on the operating costs of public pension systems. The reason is quite simple: they are typically negligible, amounting to 1–4% of contributions (Mitchell, 1998), at least in developed countries.

Chapter 5

Mixed systems

In reality, most pension systems are mixed. We shall discuss mixed pension systems in general and outline a new, mandatory mixed system, that of Hungary.

Mixed systems in general

Following the World Bank (1994) and oversimplifying reality, we distinguish three *pillars* (or tiers) of the pension system: (i) the *mandatory public pillar*, which is generally unfunded; (ii) the *mandatory private pillar*, which is funded and typically pays a life annuity; and (iii) the *voluntary private pillar*, which is also funded but does not provide a life annuity. According to the World Bank's master plan, the optimal pension system should be based on all three pillars. Furthermore, the first pillar should pay a relatively modest flat or flat-rate benefit, and the second pillar should provide the bulk of benefits with individual accounts managed by competing private funds. The third pillar satisfies the needs of wealthier or more prudent workers. The basic notion is that insurance is efficient if it stands on several legs.

In principle, there is no reason to discuss the third pillar since it does not differ from ordinary savings, apart from the tax-exemptions that sweeten the long-term engagement. In certain countries, however, it is so widespread (most notably in the US), enjoys such visible tax exemptions, and promises such fabulous benefits that it is difficult to gloss over it. Moreover, in the US it has some of the character-

istics of a mandatory system insofar as it is obligatory in a wide
band of the economy; in 1998 about 22% of workers participated in a
defined benefit system and 50% in a defined contribution system,—
both private—paying out about 10% of their earnings (Blake, 2000
and Economist, 2002, p. 13).

Surprising as it may seem, a decade ago mandatory mixed systems existed in only a few countries: for example, Great Britain, the
Netherlands, Switzerland (for details, see Brombacher Steiner, 2001),
and Scandinavia. (Chile's is practically a one-pillar system.) In most
developed countries (for example, France, Germany, the US, Italy),
the *mandatory* pension system is basically unfunded and the public
pension is more or less earnings-related. (The new subsystem taking
effect in Germany from 2002 is apparently voluntary but, with the
reduction of replacement rates from 70% to 64%, about 80% of the
workers were expected to join (Economist, 2002, p. 9). According to
the latest reports, however, the voluntary system is so unpopular or
so complex that there is a temptation to make it mandatory.) The
British pension system is not only an example for a multipillar system but its very structure is in permanent flux; for example, a public,
earnings-related pillar was introduced in 1975 downsized and frozen
in 1986 (Blake, 2001, pp. 89–93).

The *zero pillar* provides modest social assistance. Such a supple-
mentary pillar functions in many countries and is usually financed
from general tax revenues rather than contributions. Here we introduce the concept of a *means-tested* pension: the government sets
an amount b_m and raises to that amount the income of any person
whose total income falls below it. This means-tested support can be
confined to the elderly or it can be universal.

Problem 5.1. (a) In an idealized version of the Dutch pension
system (for the real one, see Bovenberg–Meijdam, 2001), the citizen's pension b_m is given to a person only if his labor benefit $\beta_v v$,
proportional to his gross earnings, is less than b_m. What is the critical value of gross earnings at which the two types of benefit are
equal? (b) In an idealized version of the Swiss pension system (for
the real system, see Brombacher Steiner, 2001), the citizen's contributions are proportional to gross earnings, and the benefit consists
of two parts: (i) the flat benefit and (ii) the proportional benefit. For
average earnings, the two parts are equal. What is the Swiss benefit
formula? (c) Compare the two systems.

We present Table 5.1, illustrating the benefit structure of certain mixed systems. Note the modest replacement rates of the two 'model' countries of the World Bank: Great Britain (34%) and Chile (42%):

Table 5.1. Benefit structure of average workers
in certain mixed systems, %

Country	First pillar	Second pillar	Total
Chile	–	42	42
Hungary	43	27	70
The Netherlands	35	35	70
Switzerland	30	30	60
Great Britain	17	17	34

Source: James–Brooks (2001 p. 138), Table 4.1

Remarks. 1. The (entry) benefits are calculated in terms of final gross earnings.

2. As far as I can judge, the Hungarian number is very optimistic if one compares the ratio of private to public pillar benefits ($27/43 = 0.63$) with that of contributions ($8/23 = 0.35$).

We can compare the means-tested pension with the flat benefit in a nutshell (Feldstein, 1987 and Diamond, 2002b, p. 39). The literature attributes two related advantages to means testing: (i) there is no need to tax the public to provide public pensions to the wealthier part of the population and (ii) the remaining pillars can function more freely, with a stronger link between contributions and benefits. Its disadvantages are also multifaceted: (i) means testing may stigmatize recipients; (ii) the poorest may not receive the benefit; and (iii) people just above the threshold have an incentive to deplete their wealth just before retirement in order to qualify for eligibility (Hubbard et al., 1995). In this regard it is interesting that, in Great Britain in the period from 1999 to 2003, the Minimum Income Guarantee is increasing by 33%, undermining incentives for lower-income people to engage in private pension saving (Economist, 2001).

These complications necessitate a much more precise classification, given by Augusztinovics (1997a; 1999c, pp. 356–357). We list her seven criteria without explanation.

1) *Risk community:* comprehensive, for members, depending on employment, only for buyers.

2) *Participation*: mandatory, mandatory for above-minimum earning, mandatory selection.

3) *Entitlement*: flat benefit, flat-rate benefit, regressive earnings-related, proportional.

4) *Indexation*: price, earning, combined, changing.

5) *Contributions*: employer, employee, government budget, yield of capital.

6) *Financing*: pure unfunded, pure funded, partially funded.

7) *Management*: government budget, elected self-government, separate government institution, non-profit fund, private fund.

Hungary: 1998–

Hungary introduced a mandatory mixed system in 1998. Here we outline its individual aspects and in Parts II and III we shall deal with its macro view. (The most up-to-date account is provided in Augusztinovics et al. (2002).) We distinguish three types of worker: (i) a worker who remained in the pure system; (ii) a worker who entered the labor force after 1 July 1998 and who had to start his contributory career in the mixed system and (iii) a worker who started working before 1 July 1998, began his contributory career in the pure system, but chose the second pillar voluntarily.

(i) The current worker who remains in the pure system retains his public pension rights and will not benefit (suffer) from the higher (lower) yields expected from the funded pillar. After retiring, his benefit will be 1.65% of gross reference earnings for every year he contributed to the mandatory system.

(ii) Every new worker must choose a private pension fund and his employer must transfer to that fund roughly one quarter of his total contribution (that is, 8% out 31% of gross earnings). More precisely, to ease the transition, about a fifth of the total contribution (6% and 7% of his gross earning) was to be paid to the second pillar in 1998 and 1999, respectively. After retiring, his public benefit will be 1.22% of gross reference earnings for every year he contributed to the mandatory system. The savings accumulated on the individual account earn interest and can be freely transferred among various pension funds. At retirement the pensioner must buy a unisex life annuity that is to be indexed in approximately the same way as the first pillar benefit. If the worker works at least 15 years in the mixed system and his resulting private life annuity does not reach 25% of the first pillar benefit, then a guaranty fund tops up his second pillar annuity to that value, that is, 93% of the pure unfunded pension.

(iii) Every current worker was allowed to enter the mixed system, but he lost about 1/4 of the entitlement he had obtained under the old system (as if he had paid his 8% contributions to his private account even before it was set up). The longer a worker has participated in the old system, the greater is the loss incurred by entering the new system.

Table 5.2. Relative gain (loss) due to
entering the mixed system: Hungary

Relative interest	Years of service in the old system $(\overline{T})$			
factor (r/Ω)	0	10	20	30
1.00	0	−6.3	−12.5*	−18.8
1.02	12.8	4.0	−9.8*	−18.2
1.04	34.4	10.1	−6.4	−17.5

In Table 5.2, the transition gain (loss) is expressed in relation to the old (pure) unfunded pension. It is assumed that the individual will work 40 years; we change the number of years spent in the old system and the *relative interest factor*, the ratio of the interest factor to the growth factor of real earnings. In order to make clear the significance of the government guaranty, we deliberately omit the lower bound of −7% for people serving at least 15 years in the mixed system, and mark cases where the bound is effective with an asterisk. In the last column there are no asterisks because in these cases our individual will serve only 10 = 40 − 30 years in the mixed system, excluding the guaranty. Was this the reason that the original upper bound on the age of entrance (47 years) was eliminated? Or did the government of the period 1994–1998 receive such a pessimistic forecast of the benefits under the unfunded system that any transition was seen as advantageous? In any case, under the original laws it is clear that, even after 20 years of service in the new system, even with a rather optimistic relative interest rate of 4%, the transition loss approaches the guaranty. Note that between 1998 and 2000 the average real yield of the Hungarian second pillar was −3.7% (Augusztinovics et al., 2002, p. 81), while the internal rate of return of the first pillar was about 3%.

Problem 5.2. Distinguish individual and average wage dynamics and recalculate Table 5.2.

Further serious problems arise as a result of inconsistent treatment of survivor and disability benefits in the mixed system. In cases where either the private disability or the survivor's benefit is insufficient, the disabled or the survivors of the deceased are simply returned to the pure unfunded system. That is, the costs of their benefits are shifted to the unfunded pillar (Bod, 2000 and Réti, 2000). Of course, in a system which relies predominantly on the unfunded pillar this shift is less serious than it would be otherwise.

In the fifth month of the pension reform (May 1998), a conservative political coalition opposed to the pension reform just introduced came to power. It was too late to cancel the reform, but the then new government introduced measures unfavorable to members of the mixed system. Most notably, the contribution rate to the second pillar was frozen at 6% rather than raised to 8%, without any adjustment to the accrual rates. To signal the government's antipathy to the mixed system, at the end of 2001, the mixed system ceased to be mandatory; the pure system, moreover, became the default option, and the benefit guarantee was withdrawn. In April 2002 the political coalition that introduced the original reform returned to power. It raised the contribution rate to the second pillar from 6% to 7% in 2003, made the mixed system mandatory for beginners and opened the mixed system to workers younger than 30. No proposals have yet been put forward to deal with the other anomalies of the mixed system.

Chapter 6

Contributions, taxes and inflation

For the sake of simplicity, we have largely abstracted from the details of contributions, taxes, and inflation. Nevertheless, in this chapter, we must deal with them.

Contributions and taxes

As a first approximation, contributions yield proportional service (for example, earnings-related pensions), and taxes yield uniform service (for example, flat pensions). What should we call a pension contribution (tax) which provides a mixture of earnings-related and flat benefits?

We must distinguish between health-care premiums and pension contributions, between employees' contributions and employers' contributions, and the personal income tax. Clearly, health-care premiums are a tax, whatever we may call them.

Some critics of the public pension system oppose the existence of a ceiling on contributions. Their argument is simple: the ceiling contributes to the perversity of lifetime redistribution from the poor to the rich (see Example 10.1 below) since the contributions of the rich constitute a smaller fraction of their earnings than those of the poor. This argument is debatable. On the one hand, there is no reason to compel the rich to insure their old-age incomes above a relatively modest level; on the other hand, if the rich live longer than the poor, then more ample insurance increases the perversity of the redistribution.

In many developed countries, the employer's and the employee's social security (health and pension) contribution rates are equal: $\tau_1 = \tau_2$ (World Bank, Table A.7, pp. 364–368). (Note that, in the US, 'social security' refers mainly to pensions, since only a part of health insurance is mandatory; see Chapter 10). In contrast, in Hungary and in other ex-socialist countries, the employee's rate (if exists at all) is much lower than the employer's rate. For example, in Hungary in 1998, $\tau_1 = 35\%$, $\tau_2 = 10\%$. In itself, the distribution of the total rate is arbitrary (Stiglitz, 1988, p. 421), but any deviation from the international standard causes confusion: the East European practice makes gross earnings *appear* lower and the contribution rates and the personal income tax rates higher than they really are. Moreover, this practice diminishes the worker's awareness and appreciation of the sources of his future pension (Csontos et al., 1998).

As mentioned before, the Hungarian social security contribution rates (total, employee's and employer's) are also divided into two parts, pension and health-care premium rates: $\tau = \tau_P + \tau_H$, $\tau_1 = \tau_{1,P} + \tau_{1,H}$ and $\tau_2 = \tau_{2,P} + \tau_{2,H}$, respectively. In other readings, the pension contribution rate is $\tau_P = \tau_{1,P} + \tau_{2,P}$ and the health-care premium rate is $\tau_H = \tau_{1,H} + \tau_{2,H}$. As of 1998, $\tau_{1,P} = 24\%$, $\tau_{2,P} = 7\%$, $\tau_{1,H} = 11\%$, $\tau_{2,H} = 3\%$. A lump sum of about 6% of the average gross wage is added as a health-care tax. According to international standards, the two pension rates could be made equal. With equality—$93 + 7 + 24 = 93 + 15.5 + 15.5$—the total pension rate would drop from 31% to 28.6%. A similar reduction applies to health-care premiums, further diminishing the total contribution rate to 26.4%.

In the US, as "a good way to integrate [the social security system and income tax system] is ... mandated contribution is tax-deductible, and all benefits are taxed" (Diamond, 2002b, p. 58). Furthermore, between the early and the normal retirement ages, an earnings test applies: those who have additional earnings lose $1 of benefits for each $2 of earnings above a limit.

Problem 6.1. (a) Write down the simplest pension system where there is no employer's contribution and pensions are taxed. (b) Show that such a system requires no modifications with respect to a situation where everybody cares for his old age, consumption is taxed, and savings are not.

Taking several European countries as examples, we show the dispersion of the ratios of net to total earnings in Table 6.1.

Table 6.1. The ratio of net to total earnings ($100\mathbf{u}/\mathbf{w}$), 1997, %

Low		Middle		High	
Germany	47.7	Poland	56.1	Portugal	66.1
Hungary	48.0	The Netherlands	56.4	Great Britain	68.0

Source: OECD.

To return to the earlier relations: $\tau_w w = \tau_v v = \tau_v w/(1 + \tau_1)$ and $b = \beta_u u$.

Changing contribution rates of the two mandatory pillars are a source of problems in the calculation of benefits. Theorem 6.1 shows the theoretical superiority of the notional defined contribution over the traditional accrual rate (though Valdés-Prieto, 2000 also discusses the problems with the former approach).

Theorem 6.1. *Suppose that the contribution rates in pillars 1 and 2 are time-variant: $\tau_{1,i}$ and $\tau_{2,i}$, $i = L, \ldots, R$. Denote the time-variant gross earnings' growth coefficients and the interest factors by g_i and r_i, respectively. The following rule then assures a fair combination of the benefits in a mixed system:*

$$b_{R+1} = \alpha \sum_{i=L}^{R} \left(\tau_{1,i} g_{i+1} \cdots g_R + \tau_{2,i} r_{i+1} \cdots r_R \right) v_i,$$

where the coefficient α determines the annuity value of the total capital accumulated in a virtual and a real asset.

Some authors argue that the presence of social security contributions weakens work incentives. To measure this effect, we need *deadweight loss*, defined by Varian (1992, Section 13.12, p. 229) as "the difference between the surplus achieved by the tax and the welfare achieved in the original equilibrium.... The deadweight loss measures the value to the consumer of the lost output." Browning (1987) (see, Feldstein, 1998b, ftn. 17 on p. 6) reports the following formula of the deadweight loss on a wage base due to taxation. Let ε

be the compensated elasticity of the tax base W with respect to the marginal net of tax share $1 - \tau$: $DWL = \varepsilon\tau^2 W/(2(1 - \tau))$. Since the contribution rate is added to the income tax, the DWL increases as follows: $\Delta DWL = \varepsilon((\iota + \tau)^2 - \tau^2)W/(2(1 - \tau))$.

Consider, for example, the US case: $\iota = 0.33$, $\tau = 0.105$ (dropping the disability contribution rate). $DWL = 0.0053\varepsilon W$ is replaced by $\Delta DWL = 0.046\varepsilon W$.

Other authors, like Diamond (1998) and Orszag–Stiglitz (2001), emphasize counteracting tendencies. For example, the highly redistributive character of the US Social Security system creates strong incentives for low earners to contribute to the system.

Before completing this analysis, we must refer to the *hidden economy* (for example, Tanzi, eds. 1983 and Lackó, 2000). In the hidden economy, participants do not report their total incomes and thus pay only a portion of the personal income tax and social security contributions they would otherwise pay. The hidden economy exists everywhere, although its size may vary. It is widely believed that, if it were possible to reduce tax and contribution rates significantly, then the size of the hidden economy would diminish and the competitiveness of the economy would improve in a spectacular way. As we shall see in the analysis of the Chilean pension system, this view is too simple (Chapter 9). Even a 'perfect' pension system cannot attract the 'working poor' if they can avoid paying contributions they cannot afford.

Although our focus is on mandatory pensions in general, here we look again at *voluntary pensions* because of the tax exemptions they enjoy. In Hungary voluntary pension funds were set up in 1993 and half the employee's voluntary contribution was immediately returned by the government within quite generous limits (roughly, the minimum wage in 1998). The employer who paid the contribution to this pillar received a different but generous reduction in personal income tax and social security contributions. In 2000 the system was made less generous for the employee but more generous for the employer.

In the US, where the voluntary pension pillar plays an important role, tax exemption consists of delayed taxation.

Inflation

One of our reasons for ignoring inflation in this study is that nominal time series are meaningless in themselves. In 2001, data on 1970 wages or pensions tell us nothing if we do not know the subsequent change in the price level. Of course, it is quite pleasant to work with constant price data in a model, but in real life it is frequently impossible. Moreover, not all workers understand the impact of inflation; and those who do may find it difficult or impossible to protect themselves from its ravages. We might note parenthetically that, for many years and in many countries, pensions, both public and private, were not properly indexed. Here we return to several issues connected to inflation.

• To return to the annuity calculations of Chapter 3, note that the authors omit treatment of the utility provided by insurance. Mitchell et al. (1999b), for simplicity, studied the case where an individual of age 65 buys a nominally fixed annuity. The interesting question is this: is it worthwhile for an individual to buy an annuity if in so doing he maximizes his utility function under his intertemporal budget constraint (Chapter 11)? To avoid the complications associated with the cardinality of the utility function, Mitchell et al. determined what fraction of the original wealth spent on insurance yields the same utility as the original wealth without insurance. If the annual inflation rate is time-invariant (and is equal to 3.2%), then "individuals would accept a reduction of between 30 and 38 percent in their wealth at age 65 if they were able to purchase actuarially fair nominal annuities rather than pursue an optimal consumption strategy without annuity contracts.... [I]f half of an individual's wealth at retirement were held in an annuitized form (similar to Social Security), the share of non-annuitized wealth that he would be prepared to relinquish would [be] between 23 and 31 percent" (Mitchell et al., 1999b, pp. 1314–1315).

• The annuity problem arose in connection with Table 3.1: if the annual inflation rate is 5% and the benefits are unindexed, then the real and the relative pensions at death may fall distressingly to 15% and 10%, respectively.

• The Hungarian student loan program, introduced in 2001 (see around Problem 3.2) set only the nominal value of the initial interest rate; for political reasons it was subsequently reduced. On the assumption of an annual inflation rate of 9% for 2001, the planned and the actual real interest factors are roughly $r = 1.06$ and $r = 1.00$, respectively.

• Interestingly, unindexed mortgage repayments are much more common than unindexed pension benefits (compare Modigliani, 1976, which suggests *dual indexed mortgages* in which not only the interest rate but also the annual payment follows inflation; also Simonovits, 1992).

• While the volatility of annuity values can be mitigated, it is in practice rather costly to insure their real value (Barr, 1987 and Stiglitz, 1988, pp. 331–332). Some analysts see a solution in providing inflation-proof government bonds; others (identifying insurance with redistribution) prefer unindexed annuities with the elimination of inflation up-front.

• The effects of inflation are not eliminated in public pension systems either (Chapter 4). We mention here that, at valorization, most pension systems leave out the preceding year's real and nominal changes. Therefore, the real value of entry pensions depends on the inflation rate of the previous year: the higher the inflation rate, the lower is the real value of the entry pension. This distortion (as well as others) could be eliminated without raising the real values of the benefits, but these efforts have often failed, at least in Hungary.

• Politically, it is much easier for government to diminish the real value of pensions by 10% when the inflation rate is 20% than to make the equivalent reduction (8.3%) in an inflation-free environment (Shafir et al., 1997). Behind the smokescreen of complex pension formulas it is easier to 'modify' the pension system than to announce openly that both individual and average replacement rates are too high and should be reduced. For decades, this is precisely what has been taking place in Hungary under 'stealth reform'. While delayed upward shifts of bracket boundaries may be especially helpful to governments seeking ways to trim outlays, the reductions associated with delayed valorization of contributions should not be underestimated.

• At this point we have to admit that, as we had not yet introduced inflation, in (4.16) we had to idealize the indexation rules. Here we rectify this omission. To get off the ground we revise the calculations in nominal rather than real terms. We shall show that this complication does not affect forward-looking indexation but significantly modifies the backward-looking version. Here we replace the artificial age index k with the more natural time index t.

Let $\mathcal{P}_t$ be the *price level* and π_t the inflation factor in year t. By definition, $\mathcal{P}_t = \mathcal{P}_{t-1}\pi_t$. Mark with the tilde the nominal value of the corresponding variable. Then the nominal benefit and the nominal average net earnings are respectively

$$\tilde{b}_t = \mathcal{P}_t b_t \quad \text{and} \quad \tilde{u}_t = \mathcal{P}_t u_t.$$

The backward-looking indexation rule is

$$\frac{\tilde{b}_t}{\tilde{b}_{t-1}} = \frac{\tilde{u}_{t-1}}{\tilde{u}_{t-2}}. \tag{6.1}$$

Substituting the price level and the inflation factor in (6.1) yields

$$\frac{\pi_t b_t}{b_{t-1}} = \frac{\pi_{t-1} u_{t-1}}{u_{t-2}}, \quad \text{that is,} \quad \frac{b_t}{b_{t-1}} = \frac{\pi_{t-1}}{\pi_t} \frac{u_{t-1}}{u_{t-2}}.$$

This implies

Theorem 6.2. *Under the backward-looking nominal indexation rule (6.1), if inflation accelerates ($\pi_t > \pi_{t-1}$), then the rule under-indexes:*

$$\frac{b_t}{b_{t-1}} < \frac{u_{t-1}}{u_{t-2}};$$

if inflation decelerates ($\pi_t < \pi_{t-1}$), then the rule overindexes:

$$\frac{b_t}{b_{t-1}} > \frac{u_{t-1}}{u_{t-2}}.$$

Problem 6.2. Prove that, with forward-looking indexation, the value of the inflation factor does not influence the real value of the benefits.

As a useful complement to Figure 4.1, Figure 6.1 depicts the rates of nominal increases in the average earnings and benefits as well as the inflation rates for the Hungarian transition.

These time-series on nominal earnings, consumption and inflation may help the reader understand the anomalies in the indexation of benefits in Hungary.

Comparing this figure with Figure 4.1 clarifies the underlying dynamic. The deviation observed for 1994–1995 finds additional explanation in temporary changes in the Hungarian tax rules. Note that in

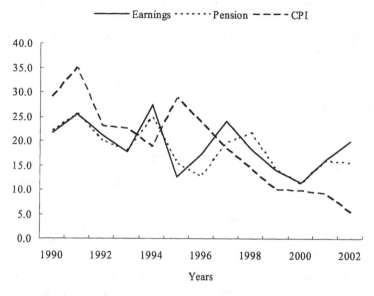

Figure 6.1. Change in nominal net earnings,
pensions and prices in Hungary, %

1996, with the introduction of backward-looking indexation, average
nominal benefits increased almost 5% points more slowly than average nominal earnings. On the other hand, in 1999, with the return to
forward-looking indexation, benefits increased only in parallel with
current rather than past wages. In both cases, it was the pensioners
who suffered.

Part II

Macro level

In Part I we confined our attention mostly to the individual (the micro level). In Part II we extend our analysis to encompass a large set of individuals (the macro level). We shall encounter the importance of demographic and macroeconomic factors. We shall also deal with the transition between different pension systems, and give special attention to the present Hungarian reform and the distribution of pensions.

Chapter 7

Demographic processes

In Chapters 1–3 we have already discussed the influence of demographic processes on the life cycle in general and pension systems in particular. Here we continue the demographic analysis as a basis for macro-analysis of the pension system. We first introduce the notion of stationary and stable populations, then go on to outline actual demographic processes. Hinde (1998) is an excellent textbook on demography, Keyfitz–Beekman (1984) is an unequaled study of problems and solutions on the subject, while Hablicsek (1999) and Hablicsek et al. (2000) give good accounts of Hungarian demographic issues. For the sake of simplicity, we generally adhere to unisex populations but, for the differing male and female survival curves, see Figure 2.1.

Stationary or stable population

Our starting point is the counterpart of Example 1.1.

Example 7.1. If everybody dies at the same age $(D+1)$, if everybody retires at the same age $(R+1)$ and if the number of annual births is constant, then the share of children in the population is $L/(D+1)$, the share of workers is $(R-L+1)/(D+1)$ and the share of pensioners is $(D-R)/(D+1)$. In this case, individual (longitudinal) and societal (cross-sectional) shares are identical. □

This set of assumptions is too restrictive. Rather, we shall work with the notion of *stationary* or *stable populations*. In the former case, the size of each cohort is time-invariant; in the latter case, only their proportions are time-invariant.

Let $n_{k,t}$ denote the number of people of age k in year t. Assume that the number of newborns is increasing at a rate $\nu - 1$ and age-specific mortality (survival) rates are time-invariant. To recapitulate Chapters 1 and 2, let q_k be the probability that somebody dies at age k and l_k be the probability that somebody survives until age k.

Then by definition we have the following equations:
Number of births

$$n_{0,t} = \nu n_{0,t-1}. \tag{7.1}$$

Size of cohorts

$$n_{k,t} = l_k n_{0,t-k}, \qquad k = 1, 2, \ldots, D. \tag{7.2}$$

The number of k-olds can be expressed in terms of that of current newborns:

$$n_{k,t} = n_{0,t} l_k \nu^{-k}. \tag{7.3}$$

The series $\{n_{k,t}\}_{k=0}^{D}$ forms the (half) *age-tree*.

For a stationary population, $\nu = 1$; for a stable one, ν is arbitrary. (7.3) implies

Theorem 7.1. *Stable population. (a) Each period, the number of k-aged is equal to ν-times that of the previous period: $n_{k,t} = \nu n_{k,t-1}$. (b) The greater the population growth factor, the higher is the share of the young in the population.*

We shall illustrate the statements above with three simple examples.

Example 7.2. No death risk. Assume that everybody lives for $D + 1$ years, and the number of births increases by a factor ν. Then the number of k-aged is $(1/\nu)$-times that of $(k - 1)$-aged: $n_{k,t} = n_{k-1,t}/\nu$. □

Example 7.3. No growth. Assume that the number of births is constant but the survival probabilities are less than 1. Then the number of k-aged is (l_k/l_{k-1})-times that of $(k - 1)$-aged: $n_{k,t} = (l_k/l_{k-1})n_{k-1,t}$. □

Example 7.4. Growth and survival. As a combination of the previous two examples, consider the following. Let K be an integer (the half lifespan) and $D = 2K - 1$. Consider a stylized survival function:

$$l_k = 1 \qquad\qquad \text{if} \quad k = 0, \ldots, K - 1 \text{ and}$$

$$l_k = \cos\left(\frac{k - K}{2K}\pi\right) \qquad \text{if} \quad k = K, \ldots, 2K - 1.$$

Using continuous approximation, the life expectancy at birth is

$$E_0 \approx \int_0^D l(t)\, dt = K + \frac{2K}{\pi} \approx 1.637K.$$

For $K = 45$ years, $E_0 = 73.6$ years. The increase in life expectancy (with minimal infant mortality) can be most easily described by the increase of K. □

Problem 7.1. Using a computer, calculate the discrete-time value of E_0.

Figure 7.1 displays three variations for half age-trees: the number of newborns is (a) constant, (b) grows and (c) decreases, by the rate 1% per year in cases (b)–(c). It is obvious that, for a growing population, the size of the older cohort relative to the youngest cohort's falls, for two reasons: the initial size of an older cohort was smaller, and fewer and fewer people survived from it into the present. For a

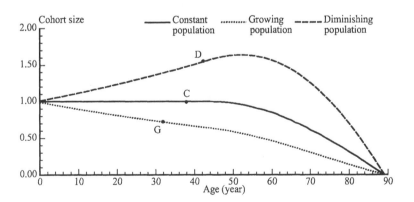

Figure 7.1. Half age-trees

decreasing population, the situation is even more interesting: with age, the relative cohort size first grows, then drops.

A simple statistics for the age of population is the *mean age of population* in year t, defined as follows:

$$X_{n,t} = \frac{\sum_k k n_{k,t}}{\sum_k n_{k,t}}.$$

Problem 7.2. (Keyfitz–Beekman, 1984, Problem 3.32.) (a) Determine the mean age of population for a stable population. (b) Demonstrate that the derivative of the mean age of population with respect to the population growth factor is equal to the minus of the variance of the age distribution over the population growth factor:

$$X'(\nu) = \frac{1}{\nu} \left[-\frac{\sum_k k^2 l_k \nu^{-k}}{\sum_k l_k \nu^{-k}} + \left(\frac{\sum_k k l_k \nu^{-k}}{\sum_k l_k \nu^{-k}} \right)^2 \right],$$

implying the apparently obvious statement: The mean age is a decreasing function of the growth rate of the number of births.

(c*) Prove this obvious statement also with the help of Chebysev's algebraic inequality (see Simonovits, 1995a).

We marked the corresponding points of Example 7.4 in Figure 7.1: C(onstant) = 36.9; G(rowing) = 32.0 and D(iminishing) = 41.9 years.

To evaluate the demographic situation of a pension system, the *old-age demographic dependency ratio*, defined as the ratio of the size of old-aged population to that of working-age population, is used:

$$\pi_t^* = \frac{\sum_{j=R+1}^{D} n_{j,t}}{\sum_{i=L}^{R} n_{i,t}}.$$

We shall also meet *total demographic dependency ratio*, defined as the ratio of the size of the young *and* the old population to that of working-age population:

$$\Pi_t^* = \frac{\sum_{j=0}^{L-1} n_{j,t} + \sum_{j=R+1}^{D} n_{j,t}}{\sum_{i=L}^{R} n_{i,t}}.$$

Problem 7.3. (Keyfitz–Beekman, 1984, Problem 3.38.) (a) Determine old-age demographic dependency ratio for a stable population.

(b) Prove the following formula:

$$\pi^{*\prime}(\nu) = \frac{\pi^*(\nu)}{\nu}(X_W - X_P),$$

where X_W and X_P are the mean ages of working and retired populations, respectively. This implies that the old-age demographic dependency ratio is a decreasing function of the growth factor of the population. (c) Calculate the approximate and the exact values of the dependency ratio for $L = 20$, $R = 59$, $D = 79$, $l_k \equiv 1$ and $\nu = 0.99$. (d) Prove that, in a stable population,

$$\Pi^{*\prime}(\nu) = \frac{\Pi^*(\nu)}{\nu}(X_W - X_D),$$

where X_D is the mean age of the dependent population. Note that the total demographic dependency ratio is not necessarily a decreasing function of the growth factor of the population.

What determines the number of births and its growth rate? The birth equation (7.4) below assumes that the number of children born to a given cohort k in a given year is proportional—*age-specific fertility rate f_k*—to the size of the given cohort:

$$n_{0,t} = \sum_{k=K_1}^{K_2} f_k n_{k,t}, \tag{7.4}$$

K_1, K_2 are *minimum* and *maximum fertility ages*, respectively: $1 \leq K_1 \leq K_2$. For a stable population, the growth factor of population is determined by the age-specific fertility and survival rates: $\{f_k\}$ and $\{l_k\}$, respectively. Various statistical sources present data on these rates. We present

Theorem 7.2. *For a stable population, the growth factor of population is determined as the unique positive root of the K_2-degree polynomial*

$$\sum_{k=K_1}^{K_2} f_k l_k \nu^{-k} = 1. \tag{7.5}$$

This root is greater than 1 if and only if the number of births per person is larger than 1:

$$\sum_{k=K_1}^{K_2} f_k l_k > 1.$$

Proof. Substitute (7.3) into the birth equation (7.4):

$$n_{0,t} = \sum_{k=K_1}^{K_2} f_k l_k n_{0,t} \nu^{-k}.$$

By simplifying with $n_{0,t}$, (7.5) obtains. Since the left-hand side of (7.5) is a decreasing function of ν, there is at most one root. Since the limit at 0 is infinity, and the limit at infinity is 0, there exists exactly one root. The root is greater than 1 if the value of the left-hand side at $\nu = 1$ is also greater than 1. □

Equation (7.4) is also useful in more general cases, where the initial values of cohort sizes are arbitrary.

Theorem 7.3. *(Lotka–Sharpe, 1911.) For time-invariant age-specific fertility and survival rates, and at least two subsequent fertile cohorts, the actual population shares and the population growth rate converge to the values of the corresponding stable population.*

Remark. This statement is a special case of the ergodicity of Markov-chains.

Sketch of the proof. Substituting (7.1) into (7.4) yields

$$n_{0,t} = \sum_{k=K_1}^{K_2} f_k l_k n_{0,t-k}, \tag{7.6}$$

a K_2-order linear scalar difference equation, with initial conditions $n_{0,t-K_2}, \ldots, n_{0,t-1}$. Introducing the state-vector of $K_2(> 1)$ subsequent standardized birth numbers $n_{0,t}/\nu^t$,

$$\mathbf{x}_t = \left(n_{0,t-K_2+1} \nu^{-t+K_2-1}, \ldots, n_{0,t} \nu^{-t} \right),$$

the transition matrix

$$\mathbf{M} = \nu^{-1} \begin{pmatrix} 0 & 1 & \ldots & 0 \\ 0 & 0 & \ldots & 0 \\ \ldots & \ldots & \ldots & \ldots \\ 0 & 0 & \ldots & 1 \\ f_{K_2} l_{K_2} & f_{K_2-1} l_{K_2-1} & \ldots & 0 \end{pmatrix}$$

transforms every state vector into the next one: $\mathbf{x}_t = \mathbf{M}\mathbf{x}_{t-1}$.

With its non-negative, irreducible and (probably primitive) coefficient matrix, the Perron–Frobenius-theorem guarantees the positivity of the dominant characteristic root and vector (Berman–Plemons, 1979). The standard stability theorem of linear difference equations yields the result. □

Example 7.5. Working with (at least) a three-generation model ($D \geq 2$), assume that only the third generation is fertile ($K_1 = K_2 = 2$). According to (7.6), $n_{0,t} = f_2 l_2 n_{0,t-2}$, hence $n_{0,t+1} = f_2 l_2 n_{0,t-1}$, that is, the birth numbers of odd and even periods follow two independent dynamics. □

The concept of *life expectancy at birth* also builds on the stable population. Assume that the current age-specific fertility and survival coefficients remain valid in the future. Calculate the corresponding stable population and the expected value of age at death:

$$E_0 = \text{LEXP} = \sum_{k=0}^{D} q_k (k + 1).$$

(2.1) generalized this notion to the remaining lifetime at age i.

Actual populations

Of course, actual populations are seldom stationary or stable. (This is a central topic of Augusztinovics, 2000b.) For example, cohort-specific fertility rates change quite abruptly (think of the postwar baby boom generation in the US) and mortality rates generally (but not always or everywhere) diminish. For illustration, we present some data on the fluctuation of *total fertility rate*, TFR$= \sum_{k=K_1}^{K_2} f_k$ in the US, 1910: 3.5, 1935: 2.2, 1955: 3.5 and since 1975: below 2 (Anderson et al., 2001, p. 16).

Example 7.6. Demographic transition. Working with a three-generation model ($D = 2$), we assume that only the second generation is fertile ($f_0 = f_2 = 0$). (a) (7.4) reduces to $f_1 l_1 \nu^{-1} = 1$, hence $\nu = f_1 l_1$ provides the steady state growth coefficient of the population is. (b) Assuming that everybody lives until the maximal age, the corresponding age distribution is given in row 1 of the table below. (c) Assume that the birth size was originally growing: $\nu = 2$, but from

Table 7.1. Scheme of demographic transition

| Time | Number of | | | Total | |
	children	workers	elderly	population	dependency rate
(b) $f_1 = 2$					
0	4	2	1	7	2.5
1	8	4	2	14	2.5
(c) either $f_1' = 1$					
2	8	8	4	20	3
3	8	8	8	24	2
(d) or $f_1'' = 1/2$					
2	4	8	4	16	1
3	2	4	8	14	2.5

period $t = 2$ the fertility rate diminished to 1 or (d) to the reciprocal of the original value. Then we can construct the age-distribution of the population in both cases for four periods.   □

Example 7.6 can be used to explain the Chinese family policy practiced from the late 1970s. In a country where the number of births increased very fast for decades, the number of daughters can be double that of mothers. If a government wants to limit the population size effectively, then temporarily the number of newborns per family should be much fewer than 2. Moreover, the total dependency rate changes abruptly: in the less drastic slowdown, it first jumps from 2.5 to 3 and then drops to 2. In the more drastic slowdown (representing Japanese developments between 1950 and 2050), the rate sinks to 1 and then jumps to 2.5.

As a result of dropping fertility rates and increasing age-specific mortality rates, the population sizes of several East European countries are already sharply decreasing.

We sketch here the history of the size of the Hungarian population. Figure 7.2 shows the developments of numbers of births and infant mortality between 1911–1995 within the present borders (CSO, 1996, Table 1, p. 65) and the forecast data until 2050 (Hablicsek, 1999, p. 405). It is noteworthy that both time series started from very high levels and converge to very low values. Skipping the mortality time series, Figure 7.3 presents the actual and forecast time series of the

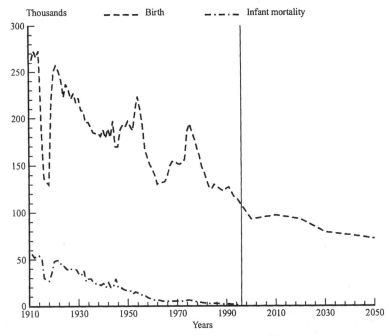

Figure 7.2. Number of births in Hungary

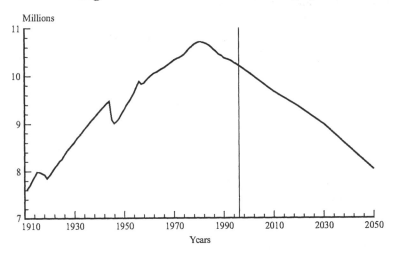

Figure 7.3. Size of population in Hungary

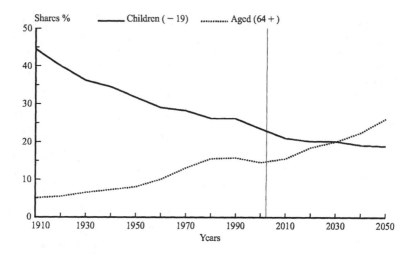

Figure 7.4. Proportions of age groups in Hungary

size of the Hungarian population. Apart from the two world wars and the exodus in 1956–1957, note how fast the size of population increased until 1980 and how quickly it has been diminishing since then (CSO, 1996, Table 4, p. 43 and Hablicsek, 1999, p. 405).

Figure 7.4 displays the actual and forecast shares of youngsters (below 19 years) and of aged (above 64 years) (CSO, 1996, Table 5, pp. 44–45 and Hablicsek, 1999, p. 405). Of course, the limits of childhood and old age historically change but we do not consider that process here (Chapter 1).

Table 7.2 provides a sample of international forecasts of aging, using the old-age dependency ratio as the single best measure of aging from the point of view of the pension system.

We emphasize that a decrease in the age-specific mortality rates can delay the drop in the size of the population owing to the drop in fertility rates, but only to a limited degree.

We only mention the problem of *international migration*, which helps to solve the problems of the demographic and pension systems of the host country at the cost of the countries of origin (for example, Börsch-Supan et al., 2001).

Table 7.2. Population aging: old-age dependency ratio, %

Country	1995	2010	2030	2050
Chile	18.3	24.4	40.9	56.3
Germany	36.2	46.5	82.5	101.7
Great Britain	38.0	42.3	62.1	72.3
The Netherlands	30.6	40.3	70.7	85.3
Switzerland	33.4	44.5	78.3	89.1
US	30.3	34.6	52.8	52.9

Source: Börsch-Supan (2001a, p. 8), Table 5. The old-age dependency ratio is given by the ratio of the size of the population aged over 60 to that of the population aged 20–59.

Chapter 8

Macroeconomics of pension systems

To begin with, we present some statistics on the share of various types of pension subsystems (pillars) in various countries, then turn to the macroeconomics of pure unfunded systems.

Shares of subsystems

To get a feeling for the order of magnitudes of various pension subsystems, we present Table 8.1.

These numbers tell us that, whereas in Switzerland the share of the public pillar was only about 45%, in the other three countries the

Table 8.1. Share of three pension subsystems in selected countries around 1985, %

Country	Mandatory public	Occupational saving	Personal saving
Switzerland	45	14	41
The Netherlands	75	21	4
US	75	6	19
Germany	93	2	5

Source: World Bank (1994, p. 250) Figure 7.1.

public pillar was dominant, with a share at least 75% of the pension incomes.

Note that the table's division of pension expenditures does not reflect the three-pillar principle, because it is unclear whether occupational savings are mandatory or voluntary. Furthermore, if recent trends follow in the US, "average 401(k) balances in 2025 will be between five and ten times as large as they are today, and would represent one-half to twice Social Security wealth depending on investment allocation and based on current Social Security provisions" (Poterba et al., 1999, Abstract; see also Wise, 2001, pp. 127–128).

Pure unfunded systems

We have almost nothing to say on the macroeconomics of funded systems. If we neglect the longevity risk and lifetime annuities (Chapter 2), the difference between funded pensions and normal saving is minimal.

We shall analyze the macroeconomics of pure unfunded systems. We confine our attention to a given year and present apparently trivial identities. We shall soon see, however, that these identities are very useful for identifying causal relationships and for understanding the quantitative connections among important characteristics of the 'pension economy' (for example, Augusztinovics, 1999a,b).

In a pure unfunded system, the workers' aggregate pension contribution is equal to the pensioners' aggregate pension benefit. If we neglect the upper bound on contributions, the following relation holds by definition: number of pensioners · average pension = contribution rate · number of workers · average earning. Introducing notations for the number of workers (M) and the number of pensioners (P), the value of an average pension $(\mathbf{b})$ and the value of an average net wage $(\mathbf{u})$, we arrive at the formula

$$P\mathbf{b} = \tau_u M \mathbf{u}.$$

Rearranging the identity:

$$\tau_u = \frac{P}{M} \frac{\mathbf{b}}{\mathbf{u}}. \tag{8.1}$$

This new identity contains the *average replacement rate* $\beta_{\mathbf{u}} = \mathbf{b}/\mathbf{u}$ and it suggests the introduction of the *system dependency ratio* as the ratio of the number of pensioners to that of workers: $\pi = P/M$. Hence follows

Theorem 8.1. *In a pure unfunded system, the contribution rate is equal to the product of the system dependency ratio and the average replacement rate:*

$$\tau_u = \pi\beta_u. \tag{8.2}$$

For example, in a *mature* pension system, where the bulk of pensioners have full contribution histories, we can illustrate the situation with $\pi = 0.5$, $\beta_u = 0.6$, yielding $\tau_u = 0.3$. In general, the more pensioners 'supported' by every worker and the higher the relative level of pensions, the higher is the contribution rate.

We shall now refine identity (8.2). We shall take into account the fact that the number of workers (M) depends not only on the number of working aged (M^*) but also on the participation rate. Similarly, the number of pensioners (P) depends not only on the number of old people (P^*) but also on their eligibility. We shall introduce the *participation rate* as a ratio of the number of workers to the number of working age population: $\mu = M/M^*$. We shall use the *eligibility rate* as a ratio of the number of pensioners to the number of pensionable population: $\zeta = P/P^*$. Finally, to distinguish the actual from the potential dependency ratio, we shall call the latter the *demographic dependency ratio* and denote it by π^* (see Chapter 7). With the help of these variables, the first factor in (8.1) can be rewritten as follows:

$$\frac{P}{M} = \frac{P}{P^*}\frac{P^*}{M^*}\frac{M^*}{M}.$$

Using our notations, we arrive at

Theorem 8.2. *In a pure unfunded pension system, the system dependency ratio is equal to the eligibility rate times the demographic dependency ratio divided by the participation rate:*

$$\pi = \frac{\zeta\pi^*}{\mu}.$$

In other words, the higher the demographic dependency ratio, the more pensionable persons retire and the fewer working age persons work, the higher is the ratio of the number of actual pensioners to that of actual workers.

Stiglitz's (1988, p. 337) Figure 13.3 provides a very vivid picture of the rise of the US system dependency ratio: it rose from 0.06 in 1950 to 0.3 in 1980 and is forecast to jump to 0.5 by 2035.

Let us introduce the following notations: Y for the GDP and $B = Pb$ for aggregate pension benefits and define indicators; *GDP/workers*: $\mathbf{y} = Y/M$, *efficiency of net earnings*: $\eta_{\mathbf{u}} = \mathbf{y}/\mathbf{u}$. In the usual analysis, the share of pension expenditure in GDP plays an outstanding role (for example, World Bank, 1994 and Table 4.5 above—showing a strong correlation between proportionality and size—Tables 8.2 and 15.1 below), although it does not reflect the ratio of per capita consumption of the old to that of the population (Augusztinovics, 1999c). According to $B/Y = (Pb)/(M\mathbf{y})$, we arrive at

Theorem 8.3. *The share of pension expenditure in the GDP is equal to the system dependency ratio times the average replacement rate divided by wage efficiency:*

$$\frac{B}{Y} = \frac{\pi\beta_{\mathbf{u}}}{\eta_{\mathbf{u}}}.$$

Table 8.2 displays these relations using the example of Hungary. (Gál (1999) extends the analysis in other directions.)

Table 8.2. Pensions in the Hungarian economy, 1970–1996, %

Year	Pension expenditure/GDP	Eligibility	Dependency	Net replacement	Participation	Net efficiency of earnings
				rates		
	$100\overline{B/Y}$	100ζ	100π	$100\beta_{\mathbf{u}}$	100μ	$100\eta_{\mathbf{u}}$
1970	3.5	66.7	38.7	37.5	91.2	305.1
1975	5.0	82.1	37.3	45.4	87.8	315.1
1980	6.9	93.0	38.2	54.7	87.3	320.1
1985	7.9	100.0	40.4	61.2	86.9	358.7
1990	8.8	109.9	41.8	66.2	86.4	398.4
1996	8.9	119.2	40.7	58.9	64.0	504.5

Source: Réti (1997, p. 9) Table 3/1.

Note in column 4 how dramatically the ratio of the pension to net earnings increased between 1970 and 1990: from 37.5% to 66.2%. Take into account Figure 4.2 and the last column, however, and check how much the average real net earning lagged behind the average real income.

Example 8.1. Theorem 8.2 and Table 8.2 provide the following system dependency rates: $\pi_{1970} = 0.283$ and $\pi_{1996} = 0.758$.   □

We shall display similar data on selected countries in Table 8.3.

Table 8.3. Macro characteristics of (public) pension systems about 1990, %

Country	Partici-pation	Eligi-bility	System de-pendency	Covered wage bill	Total* pension
		ratios		/GDP	
Germany	93.6	88.0	–	36.3	10.8
Great Britain	94.2	83.6	–	–	9.5
The Netherlands	93.6	80.7	–	49.3	9.8
Switzerland	99.4	98.0	41.7	60.0	9.9
US	96.7	82.9	30.3	38.5	6.5

Source: World Bank (1994, pp. 356–360) Tables A.4–5. Eligibility rate = Number of pensioners/number of persons over 60.
*Contrary to its title, Table A.5 contains total (mandatory?) rather than public pension expenditures.

Since in an unfunded system every generation takes care of the previous generation, setting the contribution rate τ_u or the average replacement rate β_u in different years to achieve intergenerational equity is a very delicate issue.

Under certain demanding assumptions, the efficiency of the unfunded system can be measured in several ways (Geanakoplos et al., 1998). For this purpose, Aaron (1966) used the internal factor of return, ρ, defined in

$$\tau_v \sum_{i=L}^{R} l_i v_i \rho^{-i} = \sum_{j=R+1}^{D} l_j b_j \rho^{-j}. \qquad (4.3)$$

It is relatively easy to prove

Theorem 8.4. *(Aaron, 1966.) If the population is stable, the participation and eligibility rates are time-invariant, and age-dependent earnings and benefits increase by a time-invariant and common rate, then the internal factor of return of the unfunded system is equal to* *the growth factor of aggregate real earnings, which in turn is equal to the product of the growth factors of population and of average real earnings:* $\rho = \nu g$.

Remark. If the growth rate of average real earnings is equal to that of labor productivity, then the growth rate of aggregate real earnings is equal to that of output.

Proof. For simplicity, assume full employment and eligibility. Denote v_i the average earning of the aged i, and b_j the average pension of aged j. Let the number of persons born in year 0 be equal to 1. Then by (7.3), the number of persons of age k in year 0 is equal to $l_k \nu^{-k}$. The earning of a person starting to work i years earlier is equal to $v_i g^{-i}$ and the pension of a person retired j years earlier is equal to $b_j g^{-j}$. That is, the cross-section balance condition at year 0 is

$$\tau_v \sum_{i=L}^{R} l_i \nu^{-i} v_i g^{-i} = \sum_{j=R+1}^{D} l_j \nu^{-j} b_j g^{-j}. \tag{8.3}$$

Comparing (4.3) and (8.3) yields the theorem. $\qquad\square$

Aaron based his famous theorem on Theorem 8.4 (see also Theorem 11.2 below).

Theorem 8.5. *(Aaron, 1966.) Under the assumptions of Theorem 8.4, the unfunded system is welfare-superior to the funded system if and only if the growth factor of the economy is higher than the interest factor:* $\nu g > r$.

It is noteworthy that in the golden age of economic development between 1950 and 1970, economists took it for granted that the long-term growth rate was higher than the real interest rate: that is, the unfunded system was welfare-superior to the funded system. Since 1970 a U-turn has occurred: it has become axiomatic that the growth rate is lower than the interest rate: *dynamic efficiency* (Blanchard–Fischer, 1989, Chapter 3), otherwise the introduction of an unfunded system would be welfare-improving. A serious limitation of Aaron's theorem is that it assumes that both systems have been working since the beginning of time, with identical eligibility and consumption dynamics. Note that, in reality, none of the assumptions holds, even approximately.

Table 8.4. Average real growth rates/yields: 1953–1995, %

Country	Germany	Japan	Great Britain	US
Earning growth rates	4.8	5.2	3.6	1.0
(variance)	11.8	37.7	8.8	6.0
Government bond yields	3.9	3.8	1.0	2.3
(variance)	1.3	5.4	9.3	8.2
Stock yields	10.1	10.8	10.8	9.8
(variance)		several hundreds		

Source: Thompson (1998) Table A from the Appendix, cited in Holzmann (1998, p. 13, ftn. 7).

Further complication arises from the multiplicity of interest rates with various risks, as shown in rows 3–6 of Table 8.4.

As a bridge to the next section, Table 8.5 is presented, showing the decline of average real rates of return to US Social Security for several subsequent cohorts.

Table 8.5. Average real rate of return to the US Social Security by cohorts, %

Year of birth	Average real rate of return
1876	36.5
1900	11.9
1925	4.8
1950	2.2

Source: Leimer (1995) Table 3 as cited by Orszag–Stiglitz (2001, p. 29), Table 1.2.

Note that this decline has nothing to do with the alleged crisis of the unfunded system. It is an inevitable consequence of its setup: the early beneficiaries have hardly contributed to the system, imposing an additional burden on later contributors.

Problem 8.1. Consider a stable economy with a stable population, where the growth rates of population and productivity are constant, and people enter the labor force at age 0 earn in accordance with an age-dependent profile until they retire at age $R + 1$ and die at age $D + 1$. Suppose that an unfunded pension system is introduced with an age-dependent benefit profile and a constant contribution rate τ in year $t = 0$. Suppose that the mature system is in equilibrium. Determine the internal rate of return of the first $D + 1$ cohorts.

With the Aaron-paradox, we also encounter a logical confusion. During a discussion with Johann Brunner, we realized that, since Aaron's paper was published, two approaches have been confused in the literature. Two unfunded systems have been analyzed without any understanding that they are different. In the first, the size and the structure of the system are given from outside, but the consumer can freely save and borrow (PAYG1). In the second, the size and the structure of the system are determined by optimization, but the consumer cannot save or borrow (PAYG2). It turns out that, following Aaron's verbal introduction, the traditional literature (for example, Blanchard–Fischer, 1989 and World Bank, 1994, Issue Brief 2, pp. 297–302) considered the first, while in pursuit of Aaron's model I originally considered the second.

If Aaron's stringent assumptions (earnings are independent of age, there is no credit constraint, the structures of the consumption paths are identical in both pension systems, and there are no costs of raising children) are relaxed, the message of Theorem 8.5 loses its validity in both cases (Simonovits, 1996).

Problem 8.2. How does the lifetime budget constraint of a PAYG1 system depend on the growth factor of the economy?

Problem 8.3. Analyze the dependence of the optimal consumption path of a PAYG2 system on the growth factor of the economy.

There is another efficiency indicator of an unfunded system, more general than the internal factor of return: the *present value* of the net contributions of the cohort born in year 0 discounts the contributions and the benefits with a suitably chosen interest factor:

$$\text{NPV} = \tau_v \sum_{i=L}^{R} l_i v_i r^{-i} - \sum_{j=R+1}^{D} l_j b_j r^{-j}. \tag{8.4}$$

It is obvious that, if the internal factor of return is taken as the interest factor, then the net present value is equal to zero: (4.3).

Feldstein's (1974) claim that the introduction of the unfunded pension system decreases savings has stimulated much debate (for a naive theoretical explanation, see Theorem B.9 below). Leimer–Lesnoy (1982) have found errors in Feldstein's computer calculations and demonstrated that the results are sensitive to the method of expectations (Barr, 1987). The role of expectations is analyzed in Chapter 13. Vittas (1997, p. 19) emphasizes that Feldstein's claim is generally not true, *everything goes*. Indeed, there are countries with significant funded pillars and high saving rates (for example, Switzerland) and no funded pillar and no savings (poor countries). But there are other countries with significant funded pillars and low saving rates (for example, the US and the Scandinavian countries), and there are still other countries with dominant public pillars and high saving rates (Southern Europe). The development of the credit system and changes occurring simultaneously with pension reforms make these relations rather complex. For example, in the US it is possible to finance private funded pension contributions from refinanced mortgages, both enjoying tax advantages. For the debate on the role of contributions to voluntary funded pension in raising savings, see for example, Engen et al. (1996) and Poterba et al. (1996).

For illustration, Table 8.6 presents an international comparison on the dynamics of household saving rates.

Table 8.6. Household saving rates in selected years for selected countries, %

Country	1982	1990	1995	1999
Germany	10.9	16.1	10.3	8.6
Great Britain	10.8	7.7	10.5	6.2
The Netherlands	9.5	11.9	9.9	2.8
US	10.9	7.8	5.6	2.4

Source: OECD (2000) Table 26.

Modified unfunded system

Before becoming despondent about the difficulties of the pure unfunded system, we should note that the system can be simply modified. There is no special difficulty in accumulating a *trust fund* in good years to be used up in bad years, and only a part of the fund is to be paid out immediately. This happens in the US, where about 3/4 of the contributions are paid out and 1/4 are accumulated.

The Board of Trustees of the US Social Security forecasts the dynamics of the trust fund for the next 75 years. According to the 1996 (already outdated) medium-case forecast, the trust fund disappears by 2029. (Note that the 2002 forecast pushed that date back to 2041.) The forecasts are uncertain: the pessimistic 1996 forecast put this event at 2017, while the optimistic 1996 forecast maintained that the trust fund would remain higher than 3-year expenditure for ever. The same uncertainty is reflected in a different way in Lee–Tuljapurkar (1998): the balancing contribution rate in 2070 will be between 16% and 34%.

Supporters of the funded system oppose the accumulation of a trust fund, arguing that the government diverts savings from the fund. Indeed, there is a permanent dispute over whether to take the temporary Social Security surplus into account in the government budget. If the surplus is taken into account, then it is possible to overspend in other areas. If the surplus is excluded, then one has to find a niche in which to place it (compare with Elmendorf–Liebman, 2000).

Generational accounting

A basic complaint about the unfunded system is that it achieves strong and unsustainable intergenerational redistribution. In fact, Auerbach et al. (1991, 1994) developed *Generational Accounts* to measure the extent of intergenerational redistribution. The core of the method is as follows: pick a base year (denote it 0) and, by fixing distributive trends and projecting productivity trends, determine the net present value (NPV) for each generation already born or yet to be born:

$$\text{NPV} = \tau_v \sum_{i=L}^{R} l_i v_i r^{-i} - \sum_{j=0}^{D} l_j b_j r^{-j}. \tag{8.4'}$$

Long-time government budget constraint (8.7) can necessitate a uniform correction for the net contributions and NPVs of all future generations. By using this method, it can be shown that in most countries the correction factor is much greater than 1, that is, future generations have to pay a much higher detrended lifetime net contribution than the newborn generation pays. In general, the net contributions comprise all social expenditures but it is possible to confine the examination to pensions (Chapter 18 below).

We try to describe the mathematics of the method in a nutshell. We distinguish between already born cohorts $(i = 0, 1, \ldots, D)$ and unborn cohorts $(t = 1, \ldots, \infty)$. We proceed from the profile of age-specific net contributions in year 0: N_i, $i = 0, 1, \ldots, D$. It is assumed that the net contributions of the already born cohorts grow according to the long-run productivity growth factor: each surviving person of age i at date 0 will pay a net contribution $N_k g^{k-i}$ at age k. In contrast, each surviving person to be born at date t will pay a net contribution $\varepsilon N_k g^{k+t}$ at age k, where ε is the correction factor.

In accordance with the logic of present-value calculations, we discount all net contributions to year 0 (now): the net contribution of the originally k year-old who is now i year-old should be multiplied by r^{i-k}, the net contribution of the would-be k year-old who will be born in t years should be multiplied by r^{-t-k}. Taking into account the projection of future net contributions g^{t+k}, finally the reciprocal of the relative interest factor $(\hat{r} = r/g)$ will be the discount factor.

Denoting by $n_{k,t}$ the number of people of age k at year t, we have the following two sets of equations.

The present value of the future net contributions of the cohort born in year $-i$:

$$J_i = \sum_{k=i}^{D} n_{k,k-i} N_k \hat{r}^{i-k}, \qquad i = 0, 1, \ldots, D. \qquad (8.5)$$

The present value of the unrevised net contributions of the cohort to be born in year t:

$$J_t^* = \hat{r}^{-t} \sum_{k=0}^{D} n_{k,k+t} N_k \hat{r}^{-k}, \qquad t = 1, 2, \ldots. \qquad (8.6)$$

We assume that the government is unable to service its debt in the long run without correcting the net contributions of future cohorts by a factor of ε: $J_t = \varepsilon J_t^*$. Denoting the present value of government debt plus the present value of undivided future government expenditures by G^*, we have

The zero-sum budget constraint of the government:

$$\sum_{i=0}^{D} J_i + \varepsilon \sum_{t=1}^{\infty} J_t^* = G^*. \qquad (8.7)$$

Inserting (8.5)–(8.6) into (8.7), yields

Theorem 8.6. *The correction factor is equal to*

$$\varepsilon = \frac{G^* - \sum_{i=0}^{D} \sum_{k=i}^{D} n_{k,k-i} N_k \hat{r}^{i-k}}{\sum_{t=1}^{\infty} \hat{r}^{-t} \sum_{k=0}^{D} n_{k,k+t} N_k \hat{r}^{-k}}. \qquad (8.8)$$

It is obvious that, in addition to the correction factor, the size of the imbalance is also interesting. For example, if both the numerator and the denominator are small, then the value of the correction factor is uncertain and irrelevant (compare with (8.8)).

The critics of the method (for example, Haveman, 1994) also admit the virtues of Generational Accounting, but point out serious shortcomings, which prevent direct applications. To give two examples: (i) there are benefits which cannot be properly distributed among generations; (ii) it is artificial to assume that a person born in year 0 can retain all his benefits until his death, while another person born in year 1 has to accept sharp reductions immediately. (For a relaxation of this restriction, see Chapter 18.)

Table 8.7 shows an international comparison for generational accounts.

Table 8.7. Generational accounts in international comparison

Country	Newborn generational account	Future	Absolute generational imbalance	Relative
	US dollars			%
Canada	113.8	114.0	0.2	0.0
Germany	165.0	316.8	151.8	92.0
The Netherlands	110.0	193.8	83.7	76.0
US	86.3	130.4	44.1	51.1

Source: Kotlikoff–Leibfritz (1998/1999) Table 2.

Notice that these calculations treat educational expenditures as government consumption. If these expenditures, however, are considered government transfers and are distributed among the cohorts, then the results are quite different: for example, the relative imbalance $(\varepsilon - 1)$ of the US jumps from 51% to 159%.

Chapter 9

Transition between pension systems

Because of worldwide aging and slowdown of productivity increase, most experts consider the pension problem as threatening or even critical. (There are few economists—for example, Razin et al. (2002) —who claim that aging will diminish rather than increase social transfers!) Most experts see the solution in the revival of the funded system, if not fully then at least in part (for example, Feldstein, 1974; Auerbach et al., 1989; Feldstein–Samwick, 1998 and Disney, 2000). Other economists (for example, Augusztinovics, 1995; Diamond, 1997 and Orszag–Stiglitz, 2001), disagree with the pessimists and seek to mend rather than replace the existing unfunded public pension systems. I too belong to this group. This chapter starts with the general argument, then illustrates its points using the examples of two countries, Chile and Hungary. Chapter 15 supplies the details.

The general problems of transition and revival

As was already mentioned in Chapter 4, the transition from a funded system to an unfunded one was relatively simple because the members of the first generation of the unfunded system need not have paid anything for their pensions, apart from their unimaginable losses (including previously accumulated pension capital) during the world wars and the Great Depression. (The step-by-step introduction of the unfunded system, that is, the smooth increase of the eligibility ratio and the average replacement rate—see Table 8.2 for Hungary—made the transition even smoother at the macro level.) The latest introduction and extension of a new pay-as-you-go system occurred in East Germany, where East German benefits were replaced by much higher West German benefits. (It is ironic that even some German experts—for example, Börsch-Supan (2001b)—are prone to overlook the depressive impact of German unification on the finances of the German pension system. The fast downsizing of East German employment raised the number of East German pensioners, and they were given sharply increased benefits.)

If we look back in time, it is rather difficult to question now the inevitability of the introduction of an unfunded system. Nevertheless, one may criticize the details of the process. Here we cite one critique, concentrating on the distributional side of the deal: "In the US there was the large plus that considerable benefits were given to poor cohorts, greatly alleviating poverty and saving the federal government revenues in its poverty alleviation programs. On the negative, the distribution of these transfers among members of the early cohorts went disproportionally to the well-off in those cohorts." (Diamond, 2002b, pp. 65–66.) Probably the defined benefit formula should have been drafted differently, preventing perverse redistribution to the early-retired rich.

The return from the unfunded to the funded system appears much more difficult, especially if the members of the first generations must pay the contributions to their parents' pensions as well as prefund their own pensions and cannot rely on the optimistic circumstances envisaged in Feldstein (1996). The revival is especially painful in a country where the unfunded system is comprehensive and ensures high average replacement rate.

Let us undertake the following thought experiment (Geanakoplos et al., 1998 but also Chapter 15 below). Assume that, at the introduction of the funded system, the government calculates individual pension entitlements and, by issuing recognition bonds, makes the corresponding *implicit* debt *explicit*. From that moment the unfunded system is closed down, and every participant either contributes to or uses up his pension fund, depending on his status (worker or pensioner). For the time being, *ignore* the following complications, real or imagined: (a) the operating costs of the funded system are much higher than those of the unfunded system; (b) the workers contribute much more extensively to the private pension system because they know that the individual accounts are theirs; (c) the efficiency of production, the growth rate of output and the rate of interest favorably depend on the capital/labor ratio; and (d) the explicit government debt is much more important than the implicit government debt of pension promises.

We shall prove

Theorem 9.1. *(Neutrality.) Under our assumptions, neglecting (a)–(d), the return from the unfunded system to the funded one is neutral: it does not change either pensions or the real burden of government debt.*

Sketch of a proof. The increased government debt does not cause any problem to the government since, from the date of the reform, the government ceases to pay any pensions. It is true that the additional debt is capitalized at the (higher) interest rate rather than at the (lower) internal rate of return. But funded pensions can be financed with much lower contributions than unfunded pensions, because the interest rate is higher than the internal rate of return, and this difference in contributions can be used for amortization of the increased debt. Nothing has changed. □

But what then is the meaning of a revival of the funded system? There is more than one answer to this question. (i) Certain dreamers forget about the burden of transition and concentrate only on the yields. (ii) Others (like Feldstein, 1996 and Kotlikoff, 1997) limit the increase in explicit debt, and advise society to accept the burden of transition, because they evaluate the yields very highly. Nevertheless, these two supporters of funding differ sharply on the method of distributing the burden: Kotlikoff would put the main burden on the shoulders of the old via introducing a value added tax, while Feldstein would make the young pay the bill through temporarily increased social security contributions.

I would like to cite Kotlikoff's following observation: "The weaker the marginal connection between the contributions and the benefits, the greater the probability that the privatization of social security enhances the efficiency of the system" (p. 9). It is worthwhile to compare this remark with the endeavor of the World Bank to weaken the connection between contributions and benefits, replacing earnings-related pensions with flat benefits in the public pillar (Chapter 5). This leads to a third answer-question: (iii) Is it not simpler to retain or even strengthen the link between contributions and the benefits in the public system and thus make privatization superfluous?

Building on earlier works of Breyer (1989) and Brunner (1996), Sinn (2000) gives an interesting summary of the pros and cons of prefunding. His main point is as follows: "The sum of the implicit and explicit tax burden that results from the need to respect the existing pension claims is the same under all systems and transition strategies. Nevertheless, a partial transition to a funded system may be a way to overcome the current demographic crisis because it replaces missing human capital with real capital and helps smooth tax and child rearing cost across the generations" (abstract). This verdict seems to be categorical, since it ignores the issue of bundling (various measures of rationalization may presuppose each other) but it correctly emphasizes that, at evaluating the cohorts' burden, the number of children should be taken into account (compare Example 7.6). van Groezen et al. (2003) correctly write about "pension and child allowances as Siamese twins" in their paper on social security and endogenous fertility.

Problem 9.1. Calculate the ratio of pension expectancy to the output in the simplest model. (In detail, see Chapter 15.) Everybody works for $T = 40$ years, everybody earns $w = 1$, and enjoys a pension benefit βw for $S = 20$ years. Assume that the aggregate wage accounts for $3/4$ of the GDP.

Since we have not reached the end of the story, we cannot give a definitive answer. We do not know how much the aging of society will affect the interest rate and according to Poterba (2001), the empirical evidence is weak. Among others, Brooks (2000) warned the public: the fabulous yields of the US pension funds may fall when the baby-boomers retire and withdraw their savings from the funds. Let us add that the recent (2000–2002) massive decline of share prices may be more than a temporary phenomenon, and even the prevention of a further decline requires a zero real interest rate.

We can, however, present two case-studies: one for a complete, and another for a partial transformation.

Chile: 1981–

It is well-known that a right-wing military dictatorship ruled Chile between 1973–1990, combining a lack of political freedom with an expansion of economic freedom. Since 1984, Chile has achieved impressive economic results; its GDP grew at an annual rate of 7% between 1983 and 1995. It should be added, however, that before 1984 Chile experienced dramatic economic crises and hardy grew at all between 1970 and 1983: Krugman–Obstfeld (2000) Table 22.2 puts the average growth rate between the long period of 1960 and 1992 at 1.6%. Furthermore, the Chilean miracle is associated with a most unequal distribution of incomes—Gini-coefficient of 54%, reminiscent of Brazil—which its defenders rarely if ever mention.

In Chapter 3 we referred to the microeconomic aspects of the system; here we turn to the macroeconomic problems. The Chilean revival of a fully funded system was helped by two factors: (i) the old unfunded system functioned rather poorly and few people missed it; and (ii) the Chilean military government did not encounter resistance while accumulating a budget surplus equal to 5% of GDP for years, making room for the transition. (It would be interesting to know if there was any connection between the creation of this surplus and the accentuation or preservation of sharp income inequalities.)

An outstanding result of the Chilean reform is that the new system has been able to protect itself from political influence. Nevertheless, we can add three more drawbacks to the two mentioned in Chapter 3 (compare, for example, Alier–Vittas, 2001; Callund, 1999, p. 531 and Hujo, 1999): 1. Only 56% of the working-age population contribute regularly to the system. 2. Under the influence of the strictly regulated and oligopolistic pension funds, one out of every two participants enters a new fund every year. This very expensive game absorbs about 20% of the contributions. 3. The Chilean funded pension system, functioning since 1981, collects contributions (3.3% of GDP vs. 0.5% under the old system) but as yet pays hardly any benefits (0.9% of GDP vs. 2.6% to the beneficiaries of the old system; Schmidt-Hebbel, 2001, p. 145).

Inspired by the actual and perceived results of the Chilean reform, a couple of countries in Latin America have followed its example; more and more countries are introducing mixed or funded pension systems. It will be a long time before these reforms can be evaluated (Hujo, 1999 and several papers in Feldstein, ed., 1998).

Hungary: 1998–

In a socialist (communist) economy, it was almost axiomatic that the pension system should be comprehensive and unfunded. During the years of economic transition, the heavy contraction of formal employment (Tables 8.2) and the steep fall in real earnings (Figure 4.1) have made it very difficult for the pension system in Hungary (and those in other ex-socialist countries) to function. Demographic problems must be added to these economic difficulties, threatening the long-run viability of the system (compare Figure 7.4). Notwithstanding these obstacles, several Hungarian experts (for example, Augusztinovics–Martos (1996) and Réti (1996)) maintain that a reformed unfunded system would have remained viable even in the long run.

Other economists (for example, Kornai (1992), (1999) and Csontos et al. (1998)) reject on principle the monopoly of the state social security system and the resulting vulnerability of the citizen. Experts at the World Bank (Palacios–Rocha, 1998) forecast deficits of the unreformed and the reformed purely public pension systems amounting to 7% and 4% of GDP by 2050, respectively. (Similar numbers were published by the Ministry of Finance–Ministry of Welfare (1997), sharply contradicting its own earlier forecasts of moderate tensions.) Following the Argentinean rather than the Chilean example (Müller, 1999), the Hungarian government of 1994–1998 accepted the proposals of its financial experts, decided on a piecemeal reform of the unfunded system, and immediately introduced a funded second pillar.

Retaining the dominance of the first pillar, the government largely disavowed the alleged superiority of the funded system; at the same time, it significantly reduced the further accumulation of visible government debt (compare with Theorem 9.1). From a macroeconomic point of view, this was a favorable variation to the Chilean solution; moreover, the whole process is delayed until the retirement of the corresponding cohorts. It is remarkable that the supporters of the reform hope that increased government debt will constrain the size of the welfare state. Here we refer to Ámon et al. (2002), which compares the original calculations with the experience of the first four years. The following idea is stressed: "The raising of normal retirement age makes room for the introduction of a funded pillar, because the raise creates surplus in those years (between 2003 and 2015) when the funded pillar is in the accumulation phase, drawing contributions from the public pillar without paying benefits to the

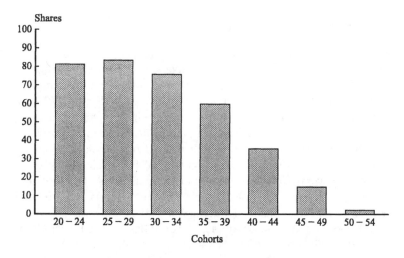

Figure 9.1. Age and the share of joiners

private beneficiaries" (p. 519). It is quite surprising that the alternative of creating a trust fund (as in the US) is not even mentioned in the text.

The pension reformers were very successful in popularizing the second pillar (or, more realistically, in undermining the credibility of the first pillar). By the original final transition deadline, August 31, 1999, about half the active contributors had opted for the mixed system, at least 30% more workers than originally forecast. (It is true that almost everybody could have returned to the pure unfunded system by December 31, 2000, and the gate was open until the end of 2002, but the number of returnees seems negligible.) As could be expected from the partial recognition of past contributions (Chapter 5), the share of entrants is decreasing with age (Figure 9.1). It is especially disturbing that a significant proportion of the new participants appear to be sure losers (compare with Table 5.2). Although the first three years (1998–2000) amount to too short a period to allow firm conclusions to be drawn, we mention that the average real net yield of the funded pillar was −3.7%, while that of the unfunded was around +3%.

Augusztinovics (1997a), (1999a), Ferge (1999), Müller (1999), Simonovits (1999) and Augusztinovics et al. (2002) have made numerous criticisms of the pension reforms. Here we list only the most important ones. (i) The reform of the first pillar (which is planned to remain dominant) is not fast enough: according to the proposals, the proportionality of the public pension subsystem will not be achieved until 2013. (ii) There remained a significant uncertainty in the rules of the private pillar, planned to be the strong point of the whole system. (iii) The private pillar is over-regulated; to go by all past experience, its operating costs will remain high; and the stock exchange seems to be unreliable. (iv) There is a danger that the increasing share of the private pillar will be financed by squeezing the public pillar (decreasing replacement rate, price indexation or *ad hoc* changes). The pretext of the radically restrained pension increase in 1999, mentioned in the Hungarian section of Chapter 4, was the pension budget deficit, increased by the introduction of the private pillar. (This is a good example of the central idea of the Generational Accounting: the budget deficit is not an entirely objective category.)

According to a few economists (for example, Müller, 1999), it is the very complexity of the reform that hides the real changes from the population. Some supporters of the reform also acknowledge that pensioners who pass through the long transition period will suffer losses. It is questionable whether the long-run results—if they are reached at all—justify the costs.

For the time being, there is no reliable scenario on the transition, which is a natural consequence of the permanent changes in government policy (see the end of Chapter 5).

Problem 9.2. Make the following calculation on the back of an envelope. In 2000 pension expenditure amounted to about 8% of GDP, about half the workers participated in the mandatory private pillar, and paid about 20% of their contributions to it in Hungary. (a) What is the share of the contributions to the second pillar in the GDP? (b) Assume that by introducing a flexible retirement age and combined indexation, public pension expenditure will be diminished to 6% of GDP, 80% of the workers will be members of pension funds, and they can pay about 25% of their contribution to the private pillar in 2013. What will be the GDP share of the contributions to the second pillar then?

It is an open question whether the increased obligation can be distributed in such a way that neither pensioners nor workers become overburdened: the increase in the personal income tax rates is not more popular than that of the social security contribution; moreover, the cost of servicing the increased government debt can destroy the advantages of rising private pensions.

Summary

The debate on the future of pension systems continues. The publication of the World Bank study (1994) mentioned above coincided with the start of a shift to multipillar systems in several countries in Latin America and in Eastern Europe. In the US, the debate is still continuing, but the latest plans (President's Commission, 2002) envisage a partially privatized and prefunded mandatory system. Few economists support the preservation of the pure unfunded system. (For a critique of the pension orthodoxy, see for example, Beattie–McGilliwray, 1995 and Barr, 2001). The strong reaction to the report of Joseph Stiglitz (Nobel-prize-winner in 2001, the former Chief Economist and Vice President of the World Bank), titled Ten Myths about the Social Security Systems (Orszag–Stiglitz, 2001), is symptomatic of the state of the debate on the topic.

Notwithstanding the spread of multipillar pension systems, there is some sobering evidence that the reforms have been less than perfect. Cooperating with officials in reforming countries, World Bank experts have had to deal with the difficulties caused by the reforms themselves (compare Rutkowski, 2000). Three remarks are in order here. (i) In several countries these advisers have had to abandon plans to significantly contract the first pillar and to replace the earnings-related component with a flat benefit. (ii) They have had to accept that the celebrated funded pillar plays a quantitatively subordinate role in many reform countries. (iii) It remains an open question whether the introduction of an even relatively modest second pillar can be coordinated with the normal functioning of the first pillar in the long run (Fultz, ed. 2002 for East-Central Europe). The experiences in the developed countries are not very bright (see Diamond–Orszag (2002) for the US).

Chapter 10

Distribution of pensions

We have already made several remarks on the distribution of pensions in discussing the flat (rate) benefit and the effect of the date of retirement (Chapter 4). But the discussion of *the* distribution of pensions has been left to this chapter.

Distribution of earnings

Since benefits frequently depend on earnings, we start by analyzing the distribution of earnings. There are various ways of depicting the distribution of incomes: for example, the histogram, dispersion, the Gini coefficient, and deciles (see Creedy, 1992 and Atkinson–Bourguignon, eds., 2000).

Table 10.1 shows a histogram of US earnings (OASDI is an abbreviation of Old-Aged, Survivor and Dependent Insurance).

This is the most unequal distribution of earnings in developed nations and it is changing over time. This distribution was similarly unequal in the 1930s; its dispersion diminished continuously until 1980, after which it began to increase again (Freeman–Katz, 1995). It is noteworthy that about two-thirds of workers earn less than the average. Of course, these numbers include widespread part-time earnings and refer to pre-tax earnings, and the progressive income tax and transfers diminish the inequalities. Nevertheless, final inequality remains quite high.

Table 10.1. Distribution of annual earnings
of workers covered by OASDI: US, 1993

Annual earnings category in thousands USD	Share in %
0.0– 8.5	33
8.5–13.2	12
13.2–18.0	11
18.0–22.8	10
22.8–27.6	8
27.6–32.4	6
32.4–37.2	5
37.2–42.0	4
42.0–46.8	3
46.8–51.6	2
51.6–57.6	2
from 57.6	5

Source: Diamond (1997, p. 48), Table 5.

Distribution of pensions

It is quite difficult to predict the distribution of pensions from the distribution of earnings in a given period, since the value of the future pension may deviate from the entry pension, which in turn depends on lifetime earnings rather than on final pay, and that dependence itself changes over time and space. (Chapters 16 and 17 present a complex and a simple model along these lines, respectively.)

Problem 10.1. In a system completely free from any redistribution, not only the benefits but also the contributions are flat (for example, the Japanese public system). Assume that there are three income classes: the poor earn 1 unit, the middle class 2 units, and the rich 4 units. The corresponding sizes of these classes are 4, 2, and 1, respectively. (a) Assuming that the length of the working period is equal to that of the retirement period, that there is no growth, and the poor want to consume the same amount when young as when old, compute the necessary contribution. (b) Compare this result with the usual (Dutch) one, when contributions are proportional to total earnings and benefits are flat (Problem 5.1a).

Problem 10.2. Problem 10.1 continued. Determine the distribution of benefits in an idealized Swiss system (of Problem 5.1b).

As I do not want to paint a full picture of any given country, I comment only briefly on the distribution of pensions in the US: the corresponding line in Table 8.1 represents only the average share of the three subsystems (as of 1985). In fact, the bulk of US pensioners mostly live on Social Security benefits, while the rich minority can rely on tax-subsidized mandatory and voluntary private pensions as well, not to mention capital income. To give a more precise picture, we cite footnote 12 of Diamond (1998, p. 4): "For the bottom quintile, 81% of income comes from Social Security, while only 6% comes from [private] pension plus income from assets. For the top quintile, 23% of income comes from Social Security, while 46% comes from [private] pensions plus income from assets."

At this point we must touch a basic critique of earnings-related pensions, formulated by the World Bank (1994, p. 11) Box 1: because the rich generally live longer than the poor, the proportional unfunded system achieves a perverse redistribution. This phenomenon is diminished or even offset by the progressivity of the pension system and other channels of social insurance like unemployment aid and disability pensions (compare Orszag–Stiglitz, 2001). Furthermore, the same critique applies to life annuities in mandatory private systems. This is illustrated by

Example 10.1. Everybody retires after R years of work. Workers with lifetime average wage w live another $S(w)$ years, an increasing function of w; the corresponding distribution function is $F(w)$. (a) There is a simple actuarially fair benefit rule, $b(w) = \tau w R / S(w)$, which is increasing but regressive if and only if $S(w)/w$ is a decreasing concave function. (b) If the benefit is proportional to the wage, then there is a perverse redistribution from the poor to the rich. □

Table 10.2 (adapted from Liebman, 2001) presents a calculation on the degree of redistribution in the current US Social Security system, using microsimulation for the 1925–1929 cohort. Note that the cohort internal rate was 1.3%. Recall from Chapter 4 that AIME is the average indexed monthly earning, here multiplied by 12 to get the annual equivalent.

Here the usual claim is clearly established: the poorer income groups obtain higher internal rates of return and average net transfers, while having lower lifetime net tax rates. However, if the impact

Table 10.2. Redistribution from Social Security
by income quintiles

	annual earnings 1000$	Average internal rate of return %	net transfer 1000$	Lifetime net tax rate %
All beneficiaries	34.0	1.5	0	0
Lowest AIME quintile	10.4	2.7	26.4	−6.0
Second AIME quintile	25.3	1.7	17.9	−1.7
Third AIME quintile	36.7	1.3	−2.0	0.2
Fourth AIME quintile	45.4	1.2	−10.2	0.7
Highest AIME quintile	52.9	0.9	−33.6	2.0

Source: Liebman (2001, p. 41) Table 2, Part 1

of other factors is also taken into account, then we obtain a more nuanced picture.

Table 10.3 reports a summary calculation, now extending the results for higher discount rates.

Table 10.3. Measuring aggregate income-related
redistribution from Social Security

Discount rate %	1.3		3		5	
	bn $	%	bn $	%	bn $	%
Total present value of benefits of birth years	460	100	396	100	342	100
Total transfers	60	13	99	25	192	56
Total income-related transfers based on AIME	23	5	65	17	143	42
Total income-related transfers based on total income	42	9	90	23	185	54

Source: Liebman (2001, p. 45) Table 5.

The first row shows the present value of benefits for the foregoing cohorts for three different discount rates: 1.3%, 3%, and 5%. (For latter comparison, each value is also represented as 100%.) The second row shows the total value of transfers (that is, redistribution). For the basic discount rate, the absolute number is about 60 bn dollars, in relative terms 13%. Separating income factors from the others, we receive 23 bn and 42 bn dollars or 5% and 9% for AIME and total income measures, respectively. Note that working with higher discount rates yields much higher redistribution.

We now turn to the distribution of pensions in Hungary. As already noted in Chapters 4–6, apart from certain years the *nominal* increase of any continuing pension could not be lower than a certain minimum (floor) and could not be higher than a certain maximum (ceiling). Such a practice is efficient in securing a reasonable minimum pension but is clearly inconsistent with the insurance principle. As Martos (1995, pp. 230–231) reports, in Hungary the inequality of pensions was much lower than that of net wages: "The decile ratio of closing wages of the new retirees amounted to 2.8 in 1992, that of their initial benefit to 2.48. In the same year, the inequality of all pensions... was not more than 1.8."

Table 10.4 is a relatively up-to-date (1998) report on the distribution of Hungarian pensions. Note that the value of 1 USD was about 200 HUFs in January 1998 and the average net monthly earning was about 45,000 HUFs.

Table 10.4. Distribution of own-right
monthly pensions: Hungary, 1998:01

Monthly earning category in thousands HUFs	Share in %
0–15	10.9
15–20	26.8
20–25	36.4
25–30	12.4
30–35	6.2
35–40	3.5
40–	3.8

Source: Hungarian Pension Fund (1998, p. 38).

So far we have mostly abstracted from the existence of family. But most people live(d) in families and this circumstance heavily influences our results. For example, in countries where a large share of women do not or did not belong to the labor force, non-contributory women may also receive pensions as wives. To understand the real situation of pensioners, one must examine the family structure (for example, Diamond, 2002b). But this is beyond the scope of our study.

Health expenditures and pension system

Since the elderly use many more health services and products than
others, we have to take into account free services and products in
calculating pensions (see Chapter 6 above). Fuchs (2000) gives the
following estimation for the US.

Table 10.5. The distribution of elderly's expenditures, US, 1997

| | Sources | | |
Use	Below 65	65 or older	Total
Health	27	8	35
Other	29	36	65
Total	56	44	100

Source: Fuchs (2000, p. 64) Table 1.

The total (imputed) income of a person at or above 65 is equal
to the sum of his monetary income and health expenditures financed
by the government; in 1997 it amounted to $28,800. Fuchs breaks it
down according to *sources*: in our Table 10.5, money coming from
people below 65 or at and above 65. For example, the aggregate
proportion is 56:44. Alternatively, total imputed income can be broken down into *use* for health and everything, for short, *other*. For
example, in total use, the former uses 35% and the latter uses 65%.

Table 10.6 gives an altogether different picture for the poorest
third of the population (this is why we report both tables here).

Table 10.6. The distribution of elderly's expenditures,
the poorest third, US, 1997

| | Sources | | |
Use	Below 65	65 or older	Total
Health	51	3	54
Other	41	5	46
Total	92	8	100

Source: Fuchs (2000, p. 65) Table 2.

In the lowest third, the per capita total imputed income was about
$14,250 in 1997. At the aggregate level the own share was only 8%,
while that of health was 54%.

Part III

Special topics

Part III is devoted to special problems that might have confused the reader if introduced at the beginning of the book: optimal consumption path, flexible retirement, overlapping cohorts, combined indexation, prefunding of pension systems, a dynamic model of the German pension reform, political models, and generational accounting for Hungary. Here the order of presentation is less important than in Parts I and II.

Chapter 11

Optimal consumption path

In this Chapter, we first derive the optimal path in a life-cycle model and then apply the result to ranking pension systems according to lifetime utility.

Optimal consumption path

In neoclassical economics, it is extremely important that individual decisions be derived from first principles, that is, from constrained optimization problems. In the case of a consumption path, a lifetime utility function should be maximized subject to the lifetime budget constraint.

We repeat an equation from Chapter 1. The individual's intertemporal budget constraint states that the present value of lifetime savings is zero:

$$\sum_{k=0}^{D}(w_k - c_k)r^{-k} = 0. \tag{11.1}$$

Let δ be a real number between 0 and 1, the so-called *discount factor* and $u(\cdot)$ a *per-period utility function*, which is a smooth and strictly concave function. We shall introduce an age-additive discounted lifetime utility function

$$U(c_0, \ldots, c_D) = \sum_{k=0}^{D} \delta^k u(c_k). \tag{11.2}$$

Moreover, the following regularity conditions hold:

$$u'(0) = \infty \quad \text{and} \quad u'(\infty) = 0.$$

For numerical calculations and analytic computations, it is often appropriate to consider a parametric utility function. Let σ be a (possibly) negative real number. We shall introduce the CRRA *utility function*, where CRRA stands for *constant relative risk aversion* and $1 - \sigma$ is the CRRA coefficient:

$$u(c) = \sigma^{-1} c^{\sigma} \quad \text{if} \quad \sigma \neq 0, \quad -\infty < \sigma < 1. \tag{11.3}$$

Inserting (11.3) into (11.2) yields

$$U(c_0, \ldots, c_D) = \sigma^{-1} \sum_{k=0}^{D} \delta^k c_k^{\sigma} \quad \text{if} \quad \sigma \neq 0, \quad -\infty < \sigma < 1. \tag{11.4}$$

It is to be underlined that we multiplied c_k^{σ} in (11.3) by σ^{-1} to obtain a per-period utility function which is an increasing function of consumption c_k even if $\sigma < 0$. (See (11.4b) for $\sigma = 0$.)

We need the following transformation of σ: $\omega = \sigma/(\sigma - 1)$, where $1 - \omega$ is the *elasticity of intertemporal substitution*. This explains another name for the utility function: *constant elasticity of substitution* (CES). Note that leisure is ignored except for Chapters 12, 15–16 and Appendix A.

Problem 11.1. Formulate (11.4) when per-period utility depends on relative rather than absolute consumption.

Although the relative formulation seems to be more realistic than the absolute one, for simplicity we shall follow the latter. Alternatively, we might think that c_k is itself relative rather than absolute consumption, etc.

It is useful to describe two special CRRA-utility functions. Leontief utility function ($\sigma = -\infty$, that is $\omega = 1$):

$$U(c_0, \ldots, c_D) = \min_{0 \leq k \leq D} c_k. \tag{11.4a}$$

Cobb–Douglas utility function ($\sigma = 0$, that is $\omega = 0$):

$$U(c_0, \ldots, c_D) = \sum_{k=0}^{D} \delta^k \log c_k. \qquad (11.4b)$$

We have

Theorem 11.1. *The optimal consumption path, maximizing the utility function (11.2) under the budget constraint (11.1), is determined by*

$$u'(c_k) = u'(c_0)(\delta r)^{-k}, \qquad k = 1, \ldots, D, \qquad (11.5)$$

where the initial consumption c_0 can be determined from (11.1).

Remark. Note that the optimal consumption path increases or decreases or is constant, depending on whether δr is greater than, less than, or equal to 1. This reinforces the common-sense observation that the high interest factor implies an increasing consumption path, while strong discounting implies a decreasing one.

Proof. Write down the Lagrange-function of the conditional maximization problem:

$$\mathcal{L}(c_0, \ldots, c_D, \mu) = \sum_{k=0}^{D} [\delta^k u(c_k) + \mu r^{-k}(w_k - c_k)].$$

Taking the partial derivative of $\mathcal{L}$ with respect to c_k and equating it to 0, yields $\delta^k u'(c_k) = \mu r^{-k}$, $k = 0, \ldots, D$. Rearranging it yields (11.5) with unknown c_0. Because the utility function is concave and the budget constraint is linear, the necessary conditions are also sufficient conditions. $\square$

Before stating Corollary 11.1, we introduce an important notation. The present value of lifetime earnings:

$$W(r) = \sum_{k=0}^{D} w_k r^{-k}.$$

Corollary 11.1. *For a CRRA utility function, the optimal consumption path is a geometric sequence whose quotient is determined* *exclusively by the discount factor (δ), the interest factor (r) and the elasticity of substitution (1 − ω):*

$$c_k = c_0(\delta r)^{(1-\omega)k}, \qquad k = 1, \ldots, D, \qquad (11.6)$$

where the initial consumption is given as

$$c_0 = \frac{W(r)}{I_D(\delta^{1-\omega}r^{-\omega})}. \qquad (11.7)$$

Proof. (11.5) reduces to $c_k^{\sigma-1} = c_0^{\sigma-1}(\delta r)^{-k}$, $k = 0, \ldots, D$. Rearranging it yields (11.6) with unknown c_0. Inserting (11.6) into (11.1) and using $W(r)$ results in the initial consumption in (11.7). $\qquad \square$

For greater clarity, we shall specify these formulas to the two simplest utility functions (compare Augusztinovics, 1992).

Example 11.1. Leontief utility function. For $\omega = 1$, the consumption path is flat:

$$c_k = c_0, \qquad k = 1, \ldots, D. \qquad (11.6a)$$

The initial consumption is given by

$$c_0 = \frac{W(r)}{I_D(1/r)}. \qquad (11.7a)$$

$\square$

Example 11.2. Cobb–Douglas utility function. For $\omega = 0$, the consumption entries discounted by the product of interest factor and the discount factor are independent of age:

$$c_k(\delta r)^{-k} = c_0, \qquad k = 1, \ldots, D. \qquad (11.6b)$$

The initial consumption is given by

$$c_0 = \frac{W(r)}{I_D(\delta)}. \qquad (11.7b)$$

$\square$

Following the 'bad' tradition of optimization-based macroeconomics, we describe the whole dynamics of the economy by a *representative agent*, reborn every period (compare Kirman, 1992). Our description would be much improved if we introduced different types of agents with different discount rates, elasticities of substitution and earning profiles. For simplicity, we forgo this generalization except in Chapters 12, 16 and 17.

Life-cycle theory has contributed to the development of modern macroeconomics with its interesting results, but has left many questions unanswered. Here we refer to only a few such questions. (For intermediate textbook discussion, see Mankiw (1997); for deeper insight, see Deaton (1992).) (i) Quite often, the consumer cannot obtain credit or the real interest rate for credit is unrealistically high, say 20% per year: *credit constraint*. (ii) A consumer may be very uncertain about his future earnings. If he is cautious enough, he will consume much less than suggested by the standard theory: *precautionary saving* (for example, Skinner, 1989). This is the opposite of the annuitization discussed in Chapter 2. (iii) If the per-period utility function depends on *habit formation*, then puzzling phenomena like faster growth leading to higher saving can also be explained (Carroll et al., 2000). At the same time, using endogenous labor supply, uncertain lifespan, and varying family size, Bütler (2001) was able to construct a traditional life-cycle model with a humped consumption path, where consumption and income move together.

Certain economists question whether the consumer maximizes a discounted additive utility function (for example, Laibson, 1997 and Frederick et al., 2002). The quasi-rational consumer of Thaler–Shefrin (1981) deviates even more from the standard description given here. These writers give weight to psychological factors, such as people saving much more from the salary of the thirteenth month than from ordinary monthly pay.

Problem 11.2. Determine the utility loss arising from the credit constraint (Problem 1.1) under the two special CRRA utility functions, (11.4a) and (11.4b).

In Chapter 2, we alluded to a useful application of the utility function: we can compare two consumption paths, arising (i) with or (ii) without life annuity according to their utilities. Moreover, to any consumption path $\{c_k\}_{k=0}^{D}$ we can assign a scalar $\bar{c}$, such that, if the consumer consumed that quantity in each period of his life, his lifetime utility would remain the same:

$$U(c_0, \ldots, c_D) = U(\bar{c}, \ldots, \bar{c}). \tag{11.8}$$

Let us call this quantity *iso-utility consumption* (see Nordhaus, 1973 and Creedy, 1992). For every CRRA utility function, this number can be expressed from

$$U(c_0, \ldots, c_D) = \sigma^{-1} \sum_{k=0}^{D} \delta^k \bar{c}^\sigma, \qquad (11.8')$$

that is,

$$\bar{c} = \left[\frac{\sigma U(c_0, \ldots, c_D)}{I_D(\delta)} \right]^{1/\sigma}. \qquad (11.8'')$$

It is easy to see that our iso-utility consumption can play the role of *money metric utility function* (compare Varian, 1992, Chapter 8).

Example 11.3. For the undiscounted Cobb–Douglas utility function, the iso-utility consumption is equal to the geometric mean of per-period consumption values:

$$\bar{c} = \sqrt[D+1]{c_0 \cdots c_D}.$$

For the Leontief utility function, the iso-utility consumption is equal to the minimum of per-period consumption values:

$$\bar{c} = \min_{0 \le k \le D} c_k. \qquad \square$$

Problem 11.3. Prove that for the undiscounted CRRA utility function of parameter σ, the iso-utility consumption is equal to the σ-order power-mean of per-period consumption values:

$$\bar{c} = \left[\frac{c_0^\sigma + \cdots + c_D^\sigma}{D+1} \right]^{1/\sigma}. \qquad (11.8^*)$$

Formula (11.8^*) yields the intuitive result: for a given consumption path, the higher the risk aversion $1 - \sigma$, the lower is the iso-utility consumption.

Ranking of pension systems

In Theorem 8.5 and the subsequent Remark, we referred to the problems arising from comparing unfunded and funded systems. Here we return to this issue (see Tobin (1967), Lee (1980), Augusztinovics (1992) and Simonovits (1995b)).

Recall from Theorem 8.4 that it was the growth factor of aggregate earnings (or output) which gave the internal return factor of the unfunded system. We shall refer to $r = \nu g$ as the *golden rule interest factor*. In fact, in this case not only the two optimal paths but also the budget sets coincide. For simplicity, we shall restrict our attention to the case $\nu = g = 1$ and normalize aggregate earnings and consumption to unity: $\sum_k w_k = 1$ and $\sum_k c_k = 1$.

Relying on the analogy with the mean age of a stable population (Chapter 7), we shall first define the *mean age of earning* as the average age of workers weighted by cohorts' shares and wages (t is dropped):

$$X_w = \frac{\sum_k n_k w_k k}{\sum_k n_k w_k}.$$

Next, define the *mean age of consuming* as the average age of consumers weighted by cohorts' shares and consumption

$$X_c = \frac{\sum_k n_k c_k k}{\sum_k n_k c_k}.$$

We shall classify consumption-earning paths as follows (Augusztinovics, 1992 and 2000b). Call a consumption-earning path *debtor* or *creditor*, or *symmetric* if the mean age of earning is higher or lower than or equal to the mean age of consuming, respectively:

$$\text{either} \quad X_w > X_c \quad \text{or} \quad X_w < X_c \quad \text{or} \quad X_w = X_c,$$

(compare Gale (1973)'s classical, Samuelson and coincidental cases, respectively).

As an illustration, we shall consider

Example 11.4. Consumption-earning paths are flat. Everybody lives until the maximum age. Evidently, $X_w = R/2 < X_c = D/2$, that is, a flat PAYG path is creditor. □

Problem 11.4. Discuss (a) how the concept of the mean age of consuming changes if L children cohorts are introduced into the model and (b) how the condition of maturity is modified.

Pareto-ranking of the two consumption vectors (corresponding to the two pension systems) is generally impossible. We have to resort to the *indirect utility function* $V(r)$—defined as the conditional maximum of the lifetime utility function $U(c)$ under the budget constraint belonging to interest factor r, (for example, Varian (1992) Chapter 7). We say that PAYG2 is better than the funded system with respect to the lifetime utility function U if $V(r) < V(1)$. (Note that in PAYG2 the structure of the consumption path is optimal, but no voluntary saving is allowed.)

Rather than checking this inequality directly, we shall rely on a generalization of the Aaron-theorem:

Theorem 11.2*. *(Compare Arthur and McNicoll, 1978.) Assume that the lifetime utility function U is differentiable, the optimum is an interior point and $r \approx 1$. (a) For creditor paths, PAYG2 is better than the funded system if and only if $r < 1$. (b) For debtor paths, PAYG2 is better than the funded system if and only if $r > 1$.*

Remarks. 1. For symmetric PAYG2 paths, there is no simple rule for comparing PAYG2 with the funded system. If $V(r)$ is strictly concave at 1, then PAYG2 is locally better than the funded system; if $V(r)$ is strictly convex at 1, then PAYG2 is locally worse than the funded system.

2. Samuelson (1975a) and (1975b) were the first papers to study this type of question. Unfortunately, Samuelson's necessary first-order conditions have often given the minimum rather than the maximum as the neglected second-order conditions testified (compare Deardorf, 1976 and Samuelson, 1976).

Proof. Denote the dependence of the optimal consumption at age k on the interest factor r as $c_k(r)$. Take the total derivative of the indirect utility function according to r:

$$V'(r) = \sum_k \frac{\partial U(c_0, \ldots, c_D)}{\partial c_k} c_k'(r).$$

Using the optimality conditions with the Lagrange-multiplier (in the proof of Theorem 11.1), we obtain

$$V'(r) = \sum_k \mu(r) r^{-k} c_k'(r).$$

Taking the derivative of the budget constraint (11.1) according to r, we obtain

$$\sum_k r^{-k}\{-kr^{-1}[c_k(r) - w_k] + c'_k(r)\} = 0.$$

Combining the last two formulas yields

$$V'(r) = \mu(r)r^{-1}\sum_k r^{-k}k[c_k(r) - w_k].$$

Taking into account that $\mu(1) > 0$ and $\sum_k c_k(1) = \sum_k w_k$, $V'(1) > 0$ holds if and only if $X_c > X_w$, etc. $\qquad\square$

Problem 11.5*. Prove the theorem with the help of the generalized envelope-theorem. (Sydsaeter–Hammond, 1995, formula (18.31) informs us that the partial derivative of a constrained maximum with respect to a parameter is equal to the corresponding partial derivative of the Lagrange-function.)

Chapter 12

Flexible retirement

Flexible retirement means that the age at which an employee retires is a choice variable for him. (For the much neglected case in which the employer chooses, see the survey by Spiezia (2002).) Anyone who wants to retire before normal retirement age may do so, but he will receive lower annual benefit since he contributes for a shorter period and draws the benefit for a longer expected period. Similarly, if somebody can (and is allowed to) work longer, he will receive higher annual benefit since he contributes for a longer period and obtains the benefit for a shorter expected period. It is obvious that an *actuarially fair solution* would be to reward work beyond normal retirement by the amount the Social Security saves by receiving the contributions for a longer period and paying benefits for a shorter period, and similarly to charge early retirees by as much as the Social Security loses by receiving contributions for a shorter period and paying benefits for a longer period (Sheshinski, 1978; Crawford–Lilien, 1981; Stock–Wise, 1990, Samwick, 1998; Gruber–Wise, eds. 1999 and Guegano, 2000).

There are two problems with this solution. (i) If the principle were applied dollar for dollar, then those retirees who retired early because of illness would be punished too severely (Diamond–Mirrlees, 1978). (ii) It is very probable that life expectancy at the minimum retirement age (used in the calculations) is much lower for early retirees than for late retirees (monotonicity), and individuals have much better information on their expected lifespans than does the government. Gruber–Orszag (1999) and Simonovits (1999) hinted at monotonicity; Waldron (2001) has documented it for the United States; and Fabel

(1994) and Simonovits (2001) have proved it analytically. A family of models is set up here, where the sharp dichotomy between working and retirement is assumed and the retirement age is derived from the simultaneous optimization of consumption and leisure, deliberately disregarding the effects of aging (Sheshinski, 1978; Simonovits, 2001). Appendix A (see also Fabel, 1994; Diamond, 2002a, Esö–Simonovits, 2002 and Simonovits 2002) will apply the theory of optimal linear mechanism design to our model to derive the optimal pension rules.

Optimal contribution and length of employment

In this section the simplest case is discussed, in which every individual is free to choose how much to save for his old age and how long to work: *autarky*.

For simplicity, we disregard issues of childhood, growth, inflation, and the existence of a real interest rate. Since time is *continuous* here, flows like benefits and contributions are intensities. We shall make the following assumptions.

A1. An individual starts to work at an age denoted by 0.

A2. An individual expects to live for D years, where D is a positive real number and its value is known to him in advance.

A3. Because of indivisibility, at every instant the individual chooses either *minimal leisure* l_m or *maximal leisure* l_M, $0 < l_m < l_M$. By normalization, the individual either *works* with intensity $l_M - l_m = 1$ or *retires* and has maximal leisure. The *length of employment*, being a positive real number, is denoted by R.

A4. Regardless of age, an individual has the same total wage rate (normalized to 1), consumes the same $a = 1 - \tau$ and the pensioner has a pension benefit b paid from the accumulated savings of the worker.

A5. Because of our wage concept and a zero interest rate, the lifetime budget constraint is given by the equality of expected lifetime consumption and expected lifetime earnings:

$$aR + b(D - R) = R \quad \text{or} \quad \tau R = b(D - R). \tag{12.1}$$

A6. The instantaneous utility functions of workers and pensioners are denoted by $u(\varepsilon, a)$ and $v(\varepsilon, b)$, respectively. Parameter ε, appearing in the utility functions, represents the fact that different people evaluate the utility of the combination of leisure and consumption differently. *Lifetime utility* is the linear combination of instantaneous utilities:

$$U = u(\varepsilon, 1 - \tau)R + v(\varepsilon, b)(D - R). \qquad (12.2)$$

The individual maximizes his lifetime utility function subject to his lifetime budget constraint.

We shall comment on some of the assumptions.

Ad 2. In our model, each individual knows his expected lifespan but not the exact value of his lifespan, $\tilde{D}$. Symbolically: $D = \mathbf{E}\tilde{D}$. Then an insurance system can be based on the following equality: the expected value of the lifetime consumption is equal to the lifetime consumption with the expected lifespan:

$$\mathbf{E}(\tilde{D}c) = (\mathbf{E}\tilde{D})c$$

and similarly for age-additive lifetime utility.

Ad 3. Note that in our model *part-time work*, that is, $l_\mathrm{m} < l(t) < l_\mathrm{M}$ is not feasible, although without this restriction genuine optimal leisure would be a constant $l(t) \equiv l$, fixed strictly between the two bounds throughout a lifetime. Of course, the practice of first working then retiring is strongly supported by biological factors (which could be expressed by l_M declining with age).

Ad 4. In general, earnings increase with age and calendar time. These important facts are also ignored here. For simplicity, we assume away personal income tax (health contributions may or may not be included).

Ad 5. Since here we skip the complexity of savings and credits, we ignore the changes within the working and retirement periods (for example, Wagener, 2001 and Diamond–Mirrlees, 2003). Furthermore, as a significant part of the population always spends all its current income, this assumption is valid for the members of this group. Note that we have excluded unemployment.

Example 12.1. A parametric utility function. In addition to l_m and l_M, here an individual objective function is characterized by two reals: (σ, ε), where $\sigma < 1$ and $0 < \varepsilon < 1$. $1/(1 - \sigma)$ is called the *intertemporal elasticity of substitution* and ε is called the *elasticity of utility with respect to consumption*. The instantaneous utility is a *Cobb–Douglas function*, that is, the product of consumption $c(t)$ to the power ε, and leisure $l(t)$ to the power $1 - \varepsilon$. Further, lifetime utility is a *CRRA-function* of instantaneous utility:

$$U = \sigma^{-1}[a^\varepsilon l_{\mathrm{m}}^{1-\varepsilon}]^\sigma R + \sigma^{-1}[b^\varepsilon l_{\mathrm{M}}^{1-\varepsilon}]^\sigma (D - R). \qquad \square$$

Example 12.2. Simplified CRRA utility function. At this point we introduce the *ratio of minimal and maximal leisure*: $\lambda = l_{\mathrm{m}}/l_{\mathrm{M}}$ and assume that it is the same for everybody. Of course, $0 < \lambda < 1$ and—apart from a scalar multiplier—(12.2) reduces to

$$U = \sigma^{-1}[\lambda^{(1-\varepsilon)\sigma}(1-\tau)^{\varepsilon\sigma}R + b^{\varepsilon\sigma}(D-R)]. \qquad (12.2')$$

$$\square$$

In the pension literature, τ and $\beta = b/a$ are called *contribution rate* and *net replacement rate*, respectively. We shall also need the following relations between certain variables:

$$b = \frac{\tau R}{D - R}, \qquad \beta = \frac{\tau R}{(D-R)(1-\tau)}, \qquad \tau = \frac{\beta(D-R)}{R + \beta(D-R)}. \quad (12.3)$$

Note that in the first equation of (12.3) the benefit is a strongly nonlinear function of retirement age, as emphasized by Diamond (2002a, Section 8.5).

We turn now to the characterization of the individually optimal contribution rate and length of employment.

Theorem 12.1. *For a well-behaved utility function U, the autarkic optimal contribution rate τ and benefit b are independent of the expected lifespan, and satisfy*

$$u(\varepsilon, 1 - \tau^\circ) - v(\varepsilon, b^\circ) + v_b'(\varepsilon, b^\circ)[\tau^\circ + b^\circ] = 0, \qquad (12.4)$$

$$u_a'(\varepsilon, 1 - \tau^\circ) - v_b'(\varepsilon, b^\circ) = 0. \qquad (12.5)$$

By (12.3), the optimal length of employment is proportional to expected lifespan:

$$R^\circ = \frac{b^\circ}{b^\circ + \tau^\circ}D. \qquad (12.6)$$

Remarks. 1. It is not difficult to recognize that (12.5) is the usual equality between the marginal utility of the worker's consumption and that of the pensioner's.

2. Since the pensioner has more leisure than the worker, it is reasonable to assume that $u'_a(\varepsilon, a) = v'_b(\varepsilon, b)$ implies $u(a, \varepsilon) < v(\varepsilon, b)$ (compare Diamond–Mirrlees, 1986). Then (12.4)–(12.5) may have a positive solution.

3. If $u'(\varepsilon, c) < v'(\varepsilon, c)$ for all the values of c, then $1 - \tau^\circ > b^\circ$.

Proof. Consider the Lagrange-function of the problem:

$$\mathcal{L}(\tau, b, R) = u(\varepsilon, 1 - \tau)R + v(\varepsilon, b)(D - R) + \mu\{\tau R - b(D - R)\}$$

and set its partial derivatives with respect to τ, b and R zero:

$$\mathcal{L}'_\tau = (-u'_a + \mu)R = 0, \quad \mathcal{L}'_b = (v'_b - \mu)(D - R) = 0,$$
$$\mathcal{L}'_R = u - v + (\tau + b)\mu = 0.$$

Eliminating μ, $\mathcal{L}'_\tau = \mathcal{L}'_b = 0$ yields (12.5). Substituting into $\mathcal{L}'_R = 0$, (12.4) obtains. $\qquad\qquad\Box$

Example 12.3. For given and known parameter values $(\sigma, \lambda, \varepsilon, D)$, maximizing (12.2′) under (12.1), the individual has an optimal replacement rate (the optimality index will be dropped)

$$\beta^\circ = \lambda^{(1-\varepsilon)\sigma/(\varepsilon\sigma - 1)} \qquad\qquad (12.5')$$

and his consumption at work is

$$a^\circ = \frac{\varepsilon}{(\varepsilon - \sigma^{-1})(1 - \beta^\circ)}, \qquad\qquad (12.4')$$

assuming that the solution is interior. $\qquad\qquad\Box$

Problem 12.1. Prove (12.4′)–(12.5′).

Remark. It is not so easy to see the stringency of interior optima: $a^\circ < 1$. If we obtain the result that it is optimal to work until death ($a^\circ \geq 1$), we should not forget our assumption that the state of the individual's health remains constant until death.

We shall portray Theorem 12.1 with a series of numerical examples in Table 12.1. Here we fix the adult expected lifespan: $D = 50$ years. In interpreting the results we should not forget that we measure age from 20.

Table 12.1. Autarkic optima

Consumption elasticity ε	length of employment [yr] R°	Optimal replacement ratio β°	contribution rate τ°	lifetime utility U°
0.32	28.1	0.468	0.267	−81.3
0.35	34.5	0.496	0.183	−79.9
0.38	41.9	0.524	0.092	−77.3

Note that, while the replacement rates are quite stable, both the length of employment and the contribution rate are very sensitive to the elasticity of consumption. Lifetime utilities are rather insensitive, making welfare comparisons difficult.

For future simulations, we shall also vary expected lifespans. To make comparison easy, we shall work with two symmetrical 3-element distributions: $\varepsilon = 0.35 \pm 0.03$; and $D = 50 \pm 5$, and assume that the marginal distributions are independent. We present the aggregate indicators of the 9-type simulation. Aggregate earning is $W^\circ = 313.5$ units, while the *utilitarian social welfare function* being the sum of individual utility maxima (compare also Varian (1999) Chapter 31), is $V^\circ = -715.8$.

We formulate a simple consequence of Theorem 12.1:

Corollary 12.1. *If the individual can choose only his optimal length of employment R, but the contribution rate is determined by the government, then (12.4) and (12.6) hold but (12.5) does not.*

Given contribution rate and benefit function, and the optimal length of employment

In this section we shall move to a more realistic model in which the government sets the mandatory contribution rate but individuals can still determine how long they work: *constrained choice.*

Obviously, to have a relevant model, we must assume that the government and individuals have different parameter values for ε and D.

We list the modified assumptions.

A1.* Every individual starts to work at the same age denoted by 0.

A2.* Every worker has an unbiased expectation D of his lifespan $\tilde{D}$.

A3.* Minimal leisure l_m and maximal leisure l_M and their ratio λ may vary with individuals but the normalization $l_\mathrm{M} - l_\mathrm{m} = 1$ should hold.

A4.* Regardless of age, every worker has the same total wage rate (normalized to 1) and contributes a constant share τ to social security.

A5.* The government announces that anyone who works R years will obtain a lifetime per-period retirement benefit $b(R)$ following his retirement.

A6.* Individuals maximize their own utility functions.

We shall again comment on our (modified) assumptions.

Ad A1.* Since individuals participate in learning and child care to different degrees, their periods of employment differ, even if they retire at the same age. This important fact is ignored here.

Ad 2.* Assume that an individual *expects* to live for $D = \mathbf{E}\tilde{D}$ years. The government takes the average of individual expectations: D^*; this is also unbiased but at an aggregate level. The difference between expectations leads to *asymmetric information*.

In the bulk of the literature, it is assumed that individuals and government have the same unbiased expectations: $D = D^*$ or, more generally, there is no statistical correlation between the age of retirement and the expected age of death. As already emphasized, these assumptions are replaced here. In the simplest case, individuals know their lifespans $\tilde{D} = D$, which vary from individual to individual.

Ad A3.* If individuals differed only in expected lifespans and the government knew the common values of the utility parameters, then in principle the government would be able to infer individual expected lifespans from individual optima. We exclude, however, the government using this information later on. Since expected lifespans as well as elasticities are dispersed, the government cannot infer from the length of employment the true value of the expected lifespan.

Ad A4.* It would be interesting to consider the heterogeneity of earnings, because most pension formulas are not strictly earnings-related. Moreover, there is a strong correlation between lifetime earnings and expected lifespans (Example 10.1). However, we omit these complications.

Ad A5.* A short comparison with Chapter 4 underlines our simplifications concerning entry pension versus continued pensions, disability and survivor's pensions, and male versus female life expectancies.

Ad A6.* If the individual parameter values ε were too low, then employment periods could be very short.

We can now formulate

Theorem 12.2. *For a well-behaved lifetime utility function* U, *benefit function* $b(R)$ *and contribution rate* τ, *the optimal length of employment* $R(D, \varepsilon)$ *satisfies*

$$u(\varepsilon, 1 - \tau) - v(\varepsilon, b) + v_b'(\varepsilon, b)b'(R)(D - R) = 0. \tag{12.7}$$

(b) In addition to (12.7), a sufficient condition of the optimum is

$$U_{RR}'' = (v_{bb}''b'^2 + v_b'b'')(D - R) - 2v_b'b' < 0, \tag{12.8}$$

implying $R(D, \varepsilon)$ *is an increasing function of expected lifespan* D.

Remarks. 1. For a well-behaved utility function, the optimum is interior: $0 < \hat{R} < D$.

2. Since neither the contribution rate nor the benefit is optimal to the individual, the optimal length of employment is not proportional to the expected lifespan, either. Understandably, incentive compatibility (for example, Varian, 1999, Chapter 36) here is equivalent to $R(D, \varepsilon)$ being an increasing function of D. Condition (12.8) holds in both special cases to be discussed below.

Proof. (a) Having inserted $b(R)$, take the derivative of U in (12.2) with respect to R and equate it to zero.

(b) The second-order sufficiency condition gives (12.8). Applying the implicit function theorem to $U_R'(D, \varepsilon, \tau, R) = 0$ [(12.7)], we obtain

$$R_D'(D, \varepsilon) = -\frac{U_{RD}''}{U_{RR}''} = \frac{v_b'b'}{2v_b'b' - (v_{bb}''b'^2 + v_b'b'')(D - R)}. \tag{12.9}$$

Taking into account that $v_b' > 0 > v_{bb}''$, $b' > 0$, our condition implies $R_D'(D, \varepsilon) > 0$. □

To evaluate actuarial fairness, we need the concept of *lifetime individual (expected) net contribution*: $z = \tau R - b(R)(D - R)$.

It will be a central observation of our study that, for a broad range of situations, individual lifetime net contributions differ from zero; moreover, they decrease with expected lifespan.

Corollary 12.2. *If $b > \tau$ and $b'' \leq b'^2(-v_{bb}''/v_b')$ hold, then individual lifetime net contribution is a decreasing function of expected lifespan:*

$$\frac{dz}{dD}(D, \tau, b(R(D, \varepsilon)), R(D, \varepsilon)) < 0.$$

Remark. The conditions in Corollary 12.2 are practically quite general. The first condition is empirically obvious. We note that, if b is concave (including linear), then $b'' \leq 0$, implying the second condition. If b is convex (as in the case of naive benefits), then the second condition simplifies to $b'' \leq b'^2 \zeta$, where $\zeta = -v_{bb}''/v_b'$ is the absolute risk aversion coefficient of the pensioner's utility function. Moreover, the second condition implies (12.8).

Proof. Take the total derivative of $z(D, \cdot)$ with respect to D:

$$\frac{dz}{dD}(D, \tau, b(R(D, \varepsilon)), R(D, \varepsilon)) =$$
$$= [\tau + b(R)]R_D'(D, \varepsilon) - b'(R)(D - R) - b(R).$$

Using (12.9), the second condition implies $R_D'(D, \varepsilon) < 1/2$. Due to the first condition, $1/2 < b(R)/[\tau + b(R)]$. Since $b'(R) > 0$, $dz(D, \tau, b(R(D, \varepsilon)), R(D, \varepsilon))/dD < 0$ holds. □

In the remaining part, we shall consider naive and dampened incentives, respectively.

Naive incentives

Assumption A5* is usually specified as follows (for example, Börsch–Supan, 1998).

A5̃. The government announces that anyone who works R years will obtain a lifetime annuity

$$\tilde{b}(R) = \frac{\tau R}{D^* - R}, \qquad 0 < R < D^*; \qquad (12.\tilde{1}0)$$

derived from constraint (12.1) with the average lifespan D^*. We speak of *naive incentives* in this case but they are described as *actuarially fair* in the literature. It is important to notice that τ can be derived from government optimization with D^* and ε^*.

We also emphasize an artificial limitation: nobody can retire after passing the average lifespan D^* because he would get negative benefit by (12.1̃0).

Taking into account (12.1̃0), we obtain

$$\tilde{b}'(R) = \frac{\tau D^*}{(D^* - R)^2} = \tilde{b}(R)\frac{D^*}{(D^* - R)R}.$$

This formula provides the percentage change in the 'fair' benefit: for example, with $R = 35$ year, $\tilde{b}'(R)/\tilde{b}(R) = 50/(15 \cdot 35) = 0.095$/year is quite close to the US reward, 7%/year.

We separately formulate

Corollary 12.3. *(a) For a well-behaving utility function, a naive incentive system* (12.1̃0), *and a given contribution rate τ, the optimal length of employment satisfies*

$$u(\varepsilon, 1 - \tau) - v(\varepsilon, \tilde{b}(R)) + v_b'(\varepsilon, \tilde{b}(R))\tau \frac{D^*}{(D^* - R)^2}(D - R) = 0. \quad (12.\tilde{7})$$

(b) The individual lifetime balance is equal to the product of the benefit and the difference between average and individual expected lifespans:

$$\tilde{z} = \tilde{b}(R)(D^* - D).$$

Proof. (a) (12.7̃) follows from (12.7). (b) Substituting the benefit rule into the definition of lifetime balance yields

$$\tilde{z} = \tau R - \tau R\frac{D - R}{D^* - R} = \tau R\frac{D^* - D}{D^* - R} = \tilde{b}(R)(D^* - D). \quad \square$$

Example 12.4. For the CRRA and Cobb–Douglas specification, (12.7̃) simplifies to

$$\tilde{p}(R) = \sigma^{-1}\lambda^{(1-\varepsilon)\sigma}(1-\tau)^{\varepsilon\sigma} + \left[\varepsilon\frac{(D-R)D^*}{(D^* - R)R} - \sigma^{-1}\right]\left(\frac{\tau R}{D^* - R}\right)^{\varepsilon\sigma} = 0,$$

assuming that the root is less than D (and D^*).

Computer simulation is by now inevitable. For illustration, we choose $\lambda^* = 0.4$; $\varepsilon^* = 0.35$; $D^* = 50$ year for the government's parameters, yielding the 'optimal' $\tau^* = 0.183$ (σ remains -2). The individual values of the parameters ε and D are dispersed around these values shown in Table 12.2.

Table 12.2. Optima at naive incentives

Individual expected lifespan	Consumption elasticity	Optimal length of employment	replacement rate	lifetime net contribution	utility
D (years)	ε	$\tilde{R}$ (years)	$\tilde{\beta}$	$\tilde{z}$	$\tilde{V}$
45	0.32	30.6	0.351	1.4	-76.5
	0.35	32.5	0.413	1.7	-74.9
	0.38	34.0	0.476	1.9	-73.0
50	0.32	32.5	0.416	0	-81.8
	0.35	34.5	0.496	0	-79.9
	0.38	36.1	0.579	0	-77.8
55	0.32	34.5	0.499	-2.0	-86.5
	0.35	36.5	0.605	-2.5	-84.3
	0.38	38.1	0.717	-2.9	-81.9

The aggregate data are as follows: aggregate earnings $\tilde{W} = 309.3$, aggregate contribution $\tilde{T} = 56.5$. In terms of aggregate contribution, the net deficit is not that big but is not negligible: $-\tilde{Z} = 2.4$. Social welfare is only slightly lower than that of autarky: $\tilde{V} = -716.6$.

It is evident that the optimal length of employment is very sensitive to individual expected lifespan and elasticity. For example, if the expected lifespan increases by 5 years, then the optimal length of employment increases by about 2 years (compare Remark to Corollary 12.2). If elasticity increases by 0.03, then the corresponding value jumps by about 2 years. We stress that, except for the middle third, where individual and government expectations of lifespans are the same, lifetime net contributions $\tilde{z}$ are not zero: in harmony with Corollary 12.2, people with shorter (longer) than average expected lifespans contribute more (less) than needed (see the first and third parts of Table 12.2, respectively). The absolute value of deviation increases in both directions with the increase in elasticities. Note also that, in contrast to (12.6), the optimal length of employment is not proportional to expected lifespan: $32.5/45 = 0.722 \neq 34.5/50 = 0.79$.

Table 12.2 even demonstrates that, in the improbable case that a society consists of individuals with short expected lifespans and high consumption elasticity (row 3) and those with long expected lifespans and low consumption elasticity (row 7), then the macrobalance is -0.1, that is, almost zero. The reason is that here the ex-ante short-lived individual hardly works less than the ex-ante long-lived one (34 vs. 34.5 years), almost turning the sign of the balance into negative. In the sequel we search for assumptions which eliminate such a case. □

First, consider the following simple situation. Let there be $K > 1$ types, $k = 1, \ldots, K$ and let p_k be the share, R_k the length of employment, D_k the expected lifespan and by (12.1̃0),

$$\tilde{b}_k = \tau \frac{R_k}{D^* - R_k}$$

the fair benefit of type k; furthermore, lifetime balance is $\tilde{z}_k = \tilde{b}_k(D^* - D_k)$. Assume *monotonicity*, that is, that those people who expect to live longer also work longer. By proper indexation of the types:

$$D_1 < D_2 < \cdots < D_{K-1} < D_K \text{ and } R_1 < R_2 < \cdots < R_{K-1} < R_K.$$

Theorem 12.3. *Under the monotonicity assumption, the macrobalance is negative:*

$$\tilde{Z} = \sum_k p_k \tilde{z}_k < 0.$$

Remark. If the monotonicity assumption is replaced by $R_1 = R_2 = \cdots = R_K$, then the macrobalance holds: $\tilde{Z} = 0$.

Proof. Due to monotonicity, $\tilde{b}_k$ is increasing and $D^* - D_k$ is decreasing. Let k^* be the largest integer for which $D^* - D_k \geq 0$. Then $\tilde{b}_k \leq \tilde{b}_k^*$ for $k \leq k^*$ and $\tilde{b}_k > \tilde{b}_k^*$ for $k > k^*$. By monotonicity, we have $\tilde{b}_k \cdot (D^* - D_k) \leq \tilde{b}_{k^*} \cdot (D^* - D_k)$ in both cases, yielding

$$Z < \tilde{b}_k^* \sum_k p_k(D^* - D_k) = 0. \qquad \square$$

Problem 12.2. (a) Calculate 'fair' benefits in a two-class model when the government knows and does not know individual lifespans.

(b) Compute the numerical values for $L = 0$, $p_1 = 3/4$, $R_1 = 41$, $R_2 = 45$, $D_1 = 53$, $D_2 = 57$ and $\tau = 0.2$.

Note, however, that in the three blocks of Table 12.2 different periods of employment correspond to given expected lifespans. What can we say in such a case? Assume that for any given expected lifespan D_k, there are J types of individuals with different periods of employment $R_{k,j}$ (possibly corresponding to different consumption elasticities) and indexed by $j = 1, \dots, J$: their population share is $r_{k,j}$. Assume *generalized monotonicity*: for any type j, individuals with higher expected lifespans with a given type work longer. With suitable indexation,

$$D_k < D_{k+1} \quad \text{and} \quad R_{k,j} < R_{k+1,j}, \quad k = 1, \dots, K-1, \quad j = 1, \dots, J.$$

We shall also need the *stochastic independence* of expected lifespans and periods of employment (or elasticities): there exist marginal distributions $\{p_k\}_{k=1}^K$ and $\{q_j\}_{j=1}^J$, such that

$$r_{k,j} \equiv p_k q_j.$$

Corollary 12.4. *Under generalized monotonicity and independence assumptions, the macrobalance of naive incentives is negative:*
$\tilde{Z} = \sum_k \sum_j p_k q_j \tilde{z}_{k,j} < 0.$

Problem 12.3. Prove Corollary 12.4.

Dampened incentives

We have seen in the previous section that the so-called actuarially fair system (12.10) is far from fair. As is known from the economics of information (for example, Varian, 1992, Chapter 25), in order to find a compromise between efficiency and insurance the government must dampen incentives.

In practice, the government does dampen incentives. Of course, the weaker the incentives, the stronger is the insurance. Similar results can be obtained from the analysis of a *progressive* US or Hungarian formula, where higher earnings and longer employment yield marginally less benefit (Chapter 4).

We speak now of *absolutely or relatively dampened incentives* if 1) the benefit is an increasing function of the length of employment and 2) the derivative or the logarithmic derivative is lower than that of the so-called actuarially fair benefit function:

$$b'(R) < \tilde{b}'(R) \quad \text{or} \quad \frac{b'(R)}{b(R)} < \frac{\tilde{b}'(R)}{\tilde{b}(R)},$$

at least between the minimal and the maximal periods of employment: $0 < R_m \leq R \leq R_M < D^*$.

We shall modify our assumption A5* as follows.

A$\hat{5}$. The government uses a dampened incentive system with a benefit function $b(R)$.

Problem 12.4. Study the *logarithmically dampened benefit function* with weight α, $0 < \alpha < 1$, where the modified benefit is the product of two powers: the government optimum $b^* = \tilde{b}(R^*)$ to the power $1 - \alpha$ and the 'fair' benefit taken to power α. In formula:

$$b(R) = b^{*\,1-\alpha} \left(\frac{\tau R}{D^* - R} \right)^{\alpha}.$$

Choosing α well, the conflict between incentives and insurance can be weakened. Prove that this system is relatively dampened.

We turn now to another dampened incentive system which is quite widespread in practice: a *linear benefit function*

$$b(R) = \gamma + \alpha R, \tag{12.$\hat{1}$0}$$

where $\alpha > 0$ is the *absolute accrual rate* and $\gamma + \alpha R_m$ is the minimal benefit.

Note that with $\gamma < 0$, a sufficiently low R may imply negative benefits, calling for a lower bound on length of employment. For illustration, it will be helpful to display a linear dampened incentive system together with the naive one in Figure 12.1.

We have

Corollary 12.5. *If the government uses a linear benefit function $b(R)$ [(12.$\hat{1}$0)] and contribution rate τ, then the optimal length of employment ($\hat{R}$) of an individual satisfies*

$$u(\varepsilon, 1 - \tau) - v(\varepsilon, \gamma + \alpha R) + v_b'(\varepsilon, \gamma + \alpha R)\alpha(D - R) = 0. \tag{12.$\hat{7}$}$$

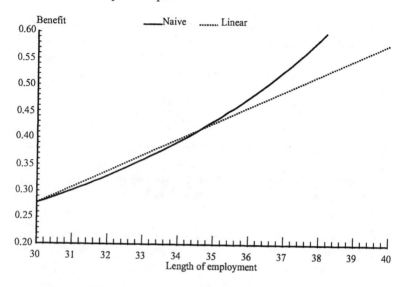

Figure 12.1. Naive and linear incentives

Example 12.5. We shall present only a series of runs in Table 12.3 with the data of Example 12.4. As will be shown in Appendix A, $\hat{\alpha} = 0.03$ and the corresponding $\hat{\gamma} = -0.622$ are the two parameters of the *socially optimal* linear benefit function (defined there) and $\hat{\tau} = 0.191$ is the corresponding contribution rate. We shall work with them and the corresponding benefit $b^* = 0.405$ and replacement rate is $\beta^* = b^*/(1 - \hat{\tau}) = 0.405/0.809 = 0.5$.

The aggregate data are as follows. $\hat{Z} = 0.3$ (round-off error), $\hat{V} = 719.4$ and aggregate earnings: $\hat{V} = 299.5$. We stress only one change: in the case of a hard-working and long-lived person, because of dampening the optimal employment period drops from 38.1 to 35.7 years, and the replacement rate from 71.7% to 55.4%. Small wonder that the resulting lifetime net contribution increases from -2.9 to -1.9 units. (Note also that in the last two rows higher elasticity does not imply lower net lifetime contribution.)

It is to be underlined that *relative* rather than absolute accrual rates are used in practice: $\kappa = b'/b = \hat{\alpha}/[(1 - \hat{\tau})\beta] = 0.0794$ is quite close to the US value. It should be taken into account, however, that in the United States employment beyond 35 years does not contribute

Table 12.3. Optima at a linear benefit function

Individual expected lifespan	Consumption elasticity	Optimal			
				Lifetime	
		length of employment	replacement rate	net contribution	utility
D (years)	ε	$\hat{R}$ (years)	$\hat{\beta}$	$\hat{z}$	$\hat{U}$
45	0.32	31.0	0.381	1.6	−76.6
	0.35	32.1	0.422	1.7	−75.0
	0.38	33.2	0.460	1.9	−73.2
50	0.32	32.1	0.423	0.0	−81.7
	0.35	33.3	0.467	0.0	−80.1
	0.38	34.5	0.509	0.2	−78.3
55	0.32	33.2	0.462	−1.8	−86.6
	0.35	34.5	0.509	−1.9	−84.9
	0.38	35.7	0.554	−1.9	−83.1

to the benefit. Our social optimum apparently is much higher than the German or the Hungarian value: 3.6%. If we take into account, however, that in both countries each year of employment contributes to the benefit, then the value 3.6% should be increased. For example, in the German example, $R^* = 45$ year, $b^* = 0.7 \cdot 0.8 = 0.56$; that is, $\kappa = b'/b = 0.5724 \cdot 1.036/0.56 - 1 = 0.059$. $\qquad\Box$

Finally, we present a summary Table 12.4.

Table 12.4. Comparison of three systems

Incentive system	Aggregate total wage	Absolute accrual rate	Net contribution rate	Aggregate net contribution	Social welfare
	W	α	τ	Z	V
Autarky	313.5	0.04	—	0	−715.5
Naive (fair)	309.3	0.04	0.183	−2.4	−716.6
Second-best	299.5	0.03	0.191	0	−719.4

The following picture emerges. Autarky achieves maximal social welfare, but asymmetric information prevents its application. Under the naive benefit rule, the maximal social welfare is quite closely approximated but its use demands unacceptable redistribution from the short-lived to the long-lived and produces substantial aggregate loss. The linear second-best solution simultaneously reduces work incentives and redistribution, but achieves acceptable redistribution and financial balance.

Before closing the analysis, we present a simple *adjustment* of the naive benefit rule (suggested by P. Diamond) which eliminates the imbalance. In (12.10) the contribution rate τ is replaced by an adjusted rate $\bar{\tau}$. An easy computer simulation yields that $\bar{\tau} = 0.175$ eliminates the imbalance, moreover, together with $\tau = 0.183$ it is the second best naive pair. Note that due to the adjustment, people work longer, even the average-aged person's net contribution is positive. Turning to the macroindices: the total earnings is $\bar{W} = 312.6$; and the social welfare is equal to $\bar{V} = -720.4$, definitely lower than with the naive rule.

Further analysis is needed to clarify the sensitivity of the results to the assumptions employed. It seems probable that technical assumptions (for example, age- and time-independent earnings, zero real interest rate) do not really influence the conclusions.

Diamond (2002a, pp. 128–129) strongly criticizes the use of linear formulas. "As workers age, mortality probabilities rise. Therefore, to offset a delay of benefits, it is necessary to give larger increases in benefits the older the worker who is delaying the start of benefits. In contrast, a linear formula gives a decreasing percentage increase in benefits as a worker ages." Although the present model does not work with a smooth mortality curve (see, however, Chapter 2), our results demonstrate that an appropriate linear formula can well approximate optimally designed rule (see also Eső–Simonovits, 2002).

Note also that the present Chapter examines an *adverse selection* problem (for example, Arrow, 1963), where people with above-average expected lifespans participate in the scheme disproportionately. Philipson–Becker (1998) addresses a related question: what happens if higher life annuity (including health care) implies higher expected lifespan?

Chapter 13

A closed model of overlapping cohorts

Until now the interest rate has been taken as a constant and as exogenously given. This assumption is acceptable in a small open economy but is unacceptable in a large closed economy. We shall now study what happens if interest rates change endogenously over time.

Samuelson (1958), Diamond (1965), Gale (1973, Part I), and, among others, Blanchard–Fischer (1989), Simonovits (2000a, Appendix B) have studied *overlapping generations* models, where only two generations interact in each period: the young and the old. The young generation is just born, the old is to die at the end of period. These elementary models yield elegant insights into the possible dynamics of pension systems (see Appendix B for details).

Recently, *overlapping cohorts models* have come to the fore, where the number of interacting cohorts is arbitrary. Among others, Aaron (1966), Tobin (1967), Gale (1973, Part II), Kim (1983), Auguszti-novics (1989), (1992) (2000b), Auerbach–Kotlikoff (1987), Deaton (1992), Molnár–Simonovits (1998), Simonovits (1996), (2000a, Appendix C) and (2000b) have tried to go deeper.

Here we confine ourselves to a very simplified presentation of the rather complicated results by Molnár–Simonovits (1998). We use several technical assumptions: no population or productivity growth: $\nu = g = 1$ and no death risk: $l_k \equiv 1$, unit cohort size: $n_{k,t} \equiv 1$.

Feasible steady states

We assume that consumers have a common CRRA utility function
(11.4). Let $s_k(r)$ be the optimal saving of a k-aged person or cohort,
and $S(r)$ the aggregate saving of the society, both taken at a time-
invariant (steady state) interest factor r:

$$S(r) = \sum_{k=0}^{D} s_k(r). \qquad (13.1)$$

Assume that the society is unable to accumulate a surplus, so aggregate saving is zero:

$$S(r) = 0.$$

Then we speak of a *feasible* interest factor, notation: r_F, $S(r_\mathrm{F}) = 0$.
Question: are there any feasible interest factors, and, if so, how
many? To provide an answer, we have to introduce several definitions.

Let a_i be the *stock of closing assets* of an i-aged consumer. By
definition, this stock is equal to the previous stock plus interest plus
current saving: $a_i = r a_{i-1} + s_i$. Let A be the society's aggregate
assets, being the total of individual stocks:

$$A = \sum_{i=0}^{D} a_i.$$

By definition, $A_\mathrm{F} = r_\mathrm{F} A_\mathrm{F}$. Therefore, either $r_\mathrm{F} = 1$ or $A_\mathrm{F} = 0$.
As in Chapter 11, in the first case we speak of a *golden rule state* and
use the notations $r_\mathrm{G} = 1$ and A_G. In the second case, we speak of a
balanced state and denote its characteristics by r_B and $A_\mathrm{B} = 0$. We
shall also need to distinguish *debtor*, *creditor* and *symmetric* golden
rule states. In the first case, $A_\mathrm{G} < 0$; in the second, $A_\mathrm{G} > 0$; and in
the third, $A_\mathrm{G} = 0$. Observe that by (13.1), for $r = 1$, the budget constraint (11.1) is identical to the feasibility condition $S(1) = 0$, yielding
a higher optimum. (In fact, the optimum value of a constrained maximization problem is at least as high with one constraint as with two
constraints.)

We shall introduce an assumption of *regularity of earnings*, following Kim (1983): the worker enters the labor force before the last
period $[t = D]$ and retires after the first period $[t = 0]$. In formula:

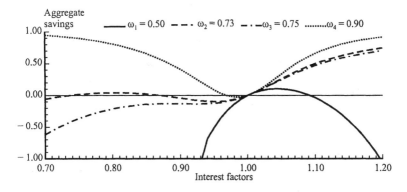

Figure 13.1. Interest factor and saving

$L < D$ and $R > 0$. We shall soon need a distinction between the two critical parameter values, also following Kim:

$$\omega_1 = \min\left(\frac{R}{D}, 1 - \frac{L}{D}\right) \qquad \text{and} \qquad \omega_2 = \max\left(\frac{R}{D}, 1 - \frac{L}{D}\right).$$

We present the theorem on balanced steady state interest factors.

Theorem 13.1. *(Kim, 1983 and Simonovits, 1995b.) Let the earnings path be regular.*

(a) If $0 \leq \omega < \omega_1$, then there exists at least one balanced interest factor: $r_B > 1$ for the debtor case, $r_B < 1$ for the creditor case and $r_B = 1$ for the symmetric case.

(b) If $\omega_2 < \omega < 1$, then there exists at least one balanced interest factor: $r_B < 1$ for the debtor case, $r_B > 1$ for the creditor case and $r_B = 1$ for the symmetric case.

(c) If $\omega_1 < \omega < \omega_2$ (window), then either there is no balanced interest factor or there is more than one.

For illustration, we present function $S(r)$ for four qualitatively different values of ω. At annual calculation, we shall work with $D = 71$ years. Figure 13.1 displays a run with $L = 20$ years, $R = 57$ years and $\delta = 0.99$.

Remarks. 1. Observe that, in the definition of window, the minimum and the maximum of the following two quantities appear:

(childhood + working period)/lifespan and (working period + retirement period)/lifespan. Kim emphasized that the earlier literature confined its attention to case (a), where the creditor state is not
Pareto-optimal. Case (b) is also important; here it is the debtor state
that is not Pareto-optimal.

2. It is easy to verify that the golden rule state corresponds to the
unfunded system, while the balanced state corresponds to the funded
system (Theorem 8.1).

Sketch of the proof. The basic idea is as follows: consider the
signs of $S(0)$ and $S(\infty)$. If the two signs are identical, then Bolzano's
theorem and $S(1) = 0$ imply the existence of a balanced root to the
left or to the right of 1.   □

For illustration, we again specify our theorem for the two extreme
cases discussed in (11.4a) and (11.4b).

Example 13.1. (Augusztinovics, 1992, Section 5.) Assume that
the consumer optimizes a Leontief utility function: $\omega = 1$. Assume
that the human life path consists of three stages: in the first and the
third stages earnings are lower than the lifetime average, while in the
second they are higher. In formula: there exist integers L^* and R^*
$(1 \leq L^* < R^* \leq R)$, such that

$$w_i < \frac{1}{D+1}, \qquad (0 \leq i \leq L^* - 1, \quad R^* + 1 \leq i \leq D);$$

$$w_i > \frac{1}{D+1} \qquad (L^* \leq i \leq R^*).$$

Then there is exactly one balanced interest factor.   □

Example 13.2. (Gale, 1973, p. 35.) For a Cobb–Douglas utility
function ($\omega = 0$), there exists a unique balanced state.   □

We shall divide the *dynamic analysis* into two parts: rational expectations and naive expectations.

Rational expectations

According to the assumption of the deterministic version of *rational
expectation*—perfect foresight— we shall assume that the path of the
interest factors is known: $\{r_t\}$.

Then the budget constraint of the individual born in year t is

$$\sum_{i=0}^{D}(r_{t+1}\cdots r_{t+i})^{-1}s_{i,t+i} = 0. \tag{13.2}$$

The optimum condition of Theorem 11.1, generalized to time-dependent interest factors, yields the conditional optimum consumption functions: $c_{i,t+i} = c_i(r_t,\ldots,r_{t+D})$. As a short-cut used by Gale (1973), suppose that the optimal policy is time-invariant: $c_{i,t} = c_i(r_{t-i},\ldots,r_{t+D-i})$. Having substituted these functions into the feasibility condition (13.1), a $(2D-1)$-order difference equation is obtained:

$$S(r_{t-D+1},\ldots,r_{t-1},r_t,\ldots,r_{t+D}) = 0. \tag{13.3}$$

Note that the new feasibility condition (13.3) concerning date t determines the interest factor of date $t+D$. If we calculated with only two generations (Appendix B), and cavalierly called the period of 36 years starting in 36 years 'tomorrow', then this delay would not cause any headache. Working with realistically calibrated annual models, it is crystal clear that in our model the macrobalance condition of this year determines the interest factor in 71 years. Is it a reasonable description? No.

What can be said of the path determined by the difference equation (13.3)? Its steady states are determined in Theorem 13.1. It is not certain, however, whether the difference equation has a solution at all, or, if it has, whether it is unique. There is an additional problem: starting the system at date $t = 0$, only the historical initial conditions $r_{-D+1},\ldots,r_{-1}$ are given and nothing is known of the non-historical initial conditions $r_0,\ldots,r_{D-1}$. According to the orthodox approach (Laitner, 1984), in a 'lucky case' the number of locally unstable directions at *saddle-point instability* around a steady state is equal to that of the undetermined initial conditions, namely, $D-1$. Then one can choose the latter so as to eliminate the former. Even if the condition fails to hold, there is no problem unless the number of unstable directions is lower than the number of undetermined constants, leading to *indeterminacy*. Except for this case, believing in the omnipotence of optimization we can stretch the model to the point where it always yields a stable and determinate path.

In my opinion, however, the situation is not so simple. Who will solve the saddle-point problem? Friedman's billiard player? This

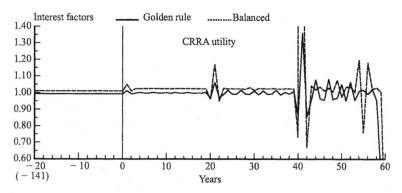

Figure 13.2. Instability under rational expectations

game is not as simple as billiards! If both steady states of the difference equation are as unstable as in Molnár–Simonovits (1998), reproduced in Figure 13.2, then serious problems arise even with the checking of the steady states. At the solution of the Auerbach–Kotlikoff (1987) model, time is reversed to eliminate the above problems; but this method assumes that everything is known in advance.

We summarize our findings in

Theorem 13.2. *(a) For rational expectations, there are two steady states: the golden rule and balanced interest factors. (b) In general, both steady states are so very unstable that for certain initial states, quite close to the steady states, the path of difference equation (13.3) is not defined at all.*

We modify the data of Figure 13.1: $\omega = 0.5$; $\delta = 0.99$; $R = 51$ years: $r_B = 1.024094$. Figure 13.2, constructed by computer simulation, displays the destabilization of both paths starting from the golden rule or the balanced state: $r_{-141} = \cdots = r_{-1} = r_F$ and $r_F = r_G$ or r_B. For better visual demonstration, only 20 of 141 initial conditions are represented.

Naive expectations

Generalizing an idea of Gale (1974), we shall define *naive expectations* for overlapping cohorts. It is assumed that agents always believe naively that the current interest factor, to be determined from the balance equation, remains constant for ever. (In practice, bankers lending with variable interest rates do the same.) Then (13.2) is replaced by a new budget constraint with varying and shortening horizons:

$$a_{i-1,t-1} + \sum_{i=0}^{D-i} r_t^{-i} s_{i,t+i} = 0, \qquad i = 0, 1, \ldots, D.$$

Similarly, inserting the current values rather than the future values into (13.3), a $(D-1)$-order difference equation obtains:

$$S(r_{t-D+1}, \ldots, r_{t-1}, r_t, \ldots, r_t) = 0. \tag{13.4}$$

Nowadays, the application of naive expectations seems to be out-dated. It is true that this assumption is not as consistent in itself as the application of rational expectations, but it has a number of advantages. For example, there is no problem with initial conditions and stability.

Theorem 13.3. *(a) The dynamic system (13.4), based on naive expectations, has the same steady states as that based on rational expectations. (b) In general (but not always) the steady state with the lower interest factor is locally stable and its domain of attraction is quite large.*

We continue the simulation started at Figure 13.2, now with naive expectations. For initial conditions $r = 0.99$; 1.02 and 1.025, there are two stable paths and one unstable path, respectively. At the comparison with Figure 13.2, note that Figure 13.3 displays a much smaller part than before, and out of 71 initial conditions only 10 are represented.

We emphasize here only that, at the formulation of Theorems 13.2 and 13.3, we considered realistically calibrated multicohort models. Somewhat surprisingly, the special 2-cohort models behave *atypically*: for example, for CRRA utility functions, the stability conditions of the steady states are the same under rational expectations and naive expectations (Simonovits, 2000a, Appendix B). One important difference between the two formulations is that, in the multicohort models, the first and the last earnings are zero, while in the two-generations models both earnings are positive.

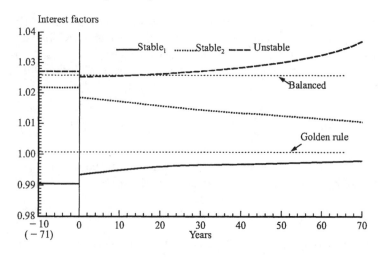

Figure 13.3. (In)stability under naive expectations

Problem 13.1. Specify the most important formulas (13.1)–(13.4) for the case of overlapping generations ($R = 0$, $D = 1$) and deduce the stability conditions.

Dynasties

People have finite lives but this does not imply that they consider only their own life paths in optimization. In modern economics, it was Barro (1974) who first studied such an OLG model, where the individual's utility function depends on young-age consumption, old-age consumption, and his heir's utility (compare Blanchard–Fischer, 1989, Chapter 3). Of course, the parent can leave a bequest to his child, but that can be only a non-negative number. Assume that the optimal bequest is positive. Then the introduction of a sufficiently small unfunded pension benefit is ineffective because the parent increases his bequest by the value of the benefit in order to counterbalance the increase in the child's tax burden due to the benefit: thus government intervention is neutralized. Since the publication of Barro's paper there has been a heated discussion over whether or not neutrality applies.

Chapter 14

Macroeffects of combined indexation

The indexation of benefits to wages has attractive features (see Chapter 4 above). There is an international trend, however, to replace wage indexation with price indexation or, as a compromise, with combined wage and price indexation (compare the Hungarian pension reform in Chapters 4, 9 and 18). In this Chapter, we shall show that this change yields only a *temporary slow-down* in the growth of total pension expenditures, and results in a step-by-step *permanent* relative deprivation of the older cohorts vis-a-vis workers. (János Réti called my attention to this apparently overlooked phenomenon and I express my gratitude to him here.)

We shall use the following simplifying assumptions.

1. The growth factor of the number of births drops from 1 to $\nu < 1$ in year 0. The size of every cohort is equal to 1 for $t < 0$ and then is equal to ν^{t+1} for $t \geq 0$. The survival probabilities $\{l_k\}$ are time-invariant.

2. The age of entering and leaving the labor force and the age at death are time-invariant and are the same for everyone: $0 < R < D$.

3. For any given age, age-specific earnings grow according to a time-invariant growth factor: $g > 1$: $w_i = w_0 g^i$, $i = 1, \ldots, R$.

According to Assumptions 1–3, in year t average earnings $\mathbf{w}_t$ also grow with factor g: $\mathbf{w}_t = \mathbf{w}_0 g^t$.

4. The wages taken into account at calculating the entry pension also grow at factor g and the delay in valorization has a fixed effect, and so can be ignored.

5. The entry pension is proportional to previous average earnings: $b_{R+1,t} = \hat{\beta}_{\mathbf{w}}\mathbf{w}_t$. (Note that this replacement rate differs from those discussed in Chapters 3–4.)

6. In year 0, the average benefit of j-aged was $b_{j,0}$, $j = R+1, \ldots$ $\ldots, D$. (If wage indexation was correct from the beginning until year 0, then $b_{j,0} = \hat{\beta}_{\mathbf{w}}\mathbf{w}_0$, $j = R+1, \ldots, D$.) From the next year a *combined wage-price indexation* with *weight* θ, $0 \le \theta \le 1$, is introduced, that is, $b_{j,t} = g^{\theta}b_{j-1,t-1}$, that is, in year t age-dependent benefits are as follows:

$$b_{j,t} = \begin{cases} g^{\theta(j-R-1)}\hat{\beta}_{\mathbf{w}}\mathbf{w}_0 g^{R+t+1-j}, & j = R+1, \ldots, R+t; \\ g^{\theta t}b_{j-t,0}(= g^{\theta t}\hat{\beta}_{\mathbf{w}}\mathbf{w}_0), & j = R+t+1, \ldots, D. \end{cases}$$

In fact, the official combined indexation rule chooses the simpler arithmetic average $(1 - \theta + \theta g)$ rather than the logical geometric average g^{θ}. If there is no great change in real earnings, then the difference between the two methods is negligible.

We turn now to the macroanalysis. The size of the k-aged cohort in year t is equal to

$$n_{k,t} = \begin{cases} \nu^{t-k+1}l_k, & \text{if} \quad t > k, \\ l_k, & \text{if} \quad t \le k. \end{cases}$$

Therefore the aggregate benefit of j-aged in year t is equal to $n_{j,t}b_{j,t}$, the aggregate benefit of the whole population is given by $B_t = \sum_{j=R+1}^{D} n_{j,t}b_{j,t}$. The aggregate wage is $W_t = \sum_{i=0}^{R} n_{i,t}w_{i,t}$. The contribution rate is equal to the ratio of aggregate benefits to aggregate earnings: $\tau_{w,t} = B_t/W_t$.

We shall separate the analysis into three parts: (i) Only the indexation rule changes but the number of births is constant: $\nu = 1$. (ii) Only the number of births changes but the indexation rule is constant: $\theta = 1$. (iii) Both the indexation rule and the number of births change. We formulate the corresponding three theorems accordingly.

Theorem 14.1. *(New indexation, old demography.) During the transition period of indexation, $t = 0, \ldots, D-R$, (a) the contribution rate $\tau_{w,t}$ decreases more and more slowly and (b) the simultaneous ratio of the final benefit to the entry benefit $b_{D,t}/b_{R+1,t}$ decreases. When the transition is over, both the contribution rate and the final/entry benefit ratio are stabilized at a lower value, but aggregate benefits grow again parallel to average real earnings.*

Theorem 14.2. *(New demography, old indexation.)* During the demographic transition period, $t = 0, \ldots, D$, the contribution rate $\tau_{w,t}$ increases more and more slowly. When the demographic transition is over, the contribution rate is stabilized at a higher value, and aggregate benefits grow again along with average real earnings.

Theorem 14.3. *(New indexation, new demography.)* (a) During the transitional period of indexation, contribution rates are lower than they would be with wage indexation, while the simultaneous ratio of final benefit to the entry benefit $b_{D,t}/b_{R+1,t}$ decreases. (b) During the demographic transition, contribution rates are higher than they would be in an unchanged world. (c) During the demographic transition period, contribution rates do not drop fast enough.

It is assumed that there was correct wage indexation prior to the reform. To simplify the formulas, we express the volumes in terms of the current wage level and assume that everybody lives until the maximum: $l_k \equiv 1$. Notations $q = g^{\theta-1}$ and $S = D - R$ will be used.

We shall describe the third, general story in a scheme. Each year has three rows: the first row contains the calendar time/age, the second row contains the sizes of the corresponding cohorts, and the third row depicts benefits per earnings.

$t\backslash k$	0	1	$\ldots$	R	$R+1$	$R+2$	$\ldots$	D
-1								
$n_{k,t}$	1	1	$\ldots$	1	1	1	$\ldots$	1
$b_{k,t}$					1	1	$\ldots$	1
	$\ldots$	$\ldots$	$\ldots$					
$0 \le t \le S-1$								
$n_{k,t}$	ν^{t+1}	ν^t	$\ldots$	1	1	1	$\ldots$	1
$b_{k,t}$					1	q	$\ldots$	q^t
	$\ldots$	$\ldots$	$\ldots$					
$S \le t \le R$								
$n_{k,t}$	ν^{t+1}	ν^t	$\ldots$	1	1	1	$\ldots$	1
$b_{k,t}$					1	q	$\ldots$	q^S
	$\ldots$	$\ldots$	$\ldots$					
$R+1 \le t \le D$								
$n_{k,t}$	ν^{t+1}	ν^t	$\ldots$	ν^{t-R+2}	ν^{t-R+1}	ν^{t-R}	$\ldots$	1
$b_{k,t}$					1	q	$\ldots$	q^S

Along the scheme we can describe the macro-equations:

$$0 \leq t \leq S - 1: \quad M_t = \nu \frac{\nu^{t+1} - 1}{\nu - 1} + R - t,$$

$$P_t = S, \quad B_t = b \frac{q^{t+1} - 1}{q - 1} + bq^{t+1}(S - t - 1),$$

$$S \leq t \leq R: \quad M_t = \nu \frac{\nu^{t+1} - 1}{\nu - 1} + R - t,$$

$$P_t = S, \quad B_t = b \frac{q^S - 1}{q - 1},$$

$$R + 1 \leq t \leq D: (j = t - R) \quad M_t = \nu^j M_R,$$

$$P_t = \frac{\nu^{j+1} - 1}{\nu - 1} + S - j - 1, \quad B_t = b \frac{q^{t+1} - \nu^{t+1}}{q - \nu} + b \frac{q^S - q^{j+1}}{q - 1}.$$

We turn to numerical analysis.

Example 14.1. Average real earnings growth factor: $g = 1.03$, the share of the earnings index: $\theta = 1, 1/2, 0$, respectively. The age at entering the labor force: $L = 0$ years, the age at retirement: $R + 1 = 40$ years, the age at death: $D = 59$ years. The first curve depicts the steady increase of the dependency ratio from 0.5 to 0.9 during 60 years. The three types of the contribution rate paths are shown by the three other curves.

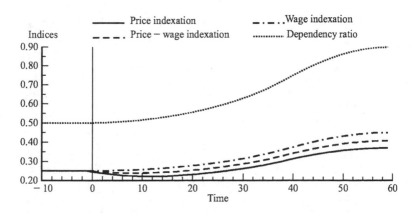

Figure 14.1. Contribution rate under three types of indexation

The highest contribution curve shows the effects of the wage indexation of pensions. Then, the contribution rate grows in parallel with the dependency ratio: from 0.25 to 0.45. The lowest curve shows the work of price indexation. During the first 15 years the contribution rate can be diminished rather than increased. It is true that after 27 years the contribution rate returns to its initial value, and after 59 years it rises to 0.37. Of course, there is a heavy price to pay: the simultaneous ratio of final to entry pension drops from 1 to 0.675. The middle curve shows a compromise between the two extremes. □

One of the objectives of any pension system is to offer protection against the longevity risk. If one calculates correspondingly with death risks, then the simultaneous final/entry pension ratio becomes even lower.

Problem 14.1. Recalculate Example 14.1 with the survival function of Example 7.4.

On the basis of the German example, I still hope that wage indexation of pensions can be preserved, even at the price of reducing the entry replacement rate.

An important qualification must be made. Until now we have ignored the specifics of old-age consumption. It is quite obvious that older people, especially very old people, have different needs from young people; in particular they need much more health care. If health care is financed from public sources (compare Tables 10.5 and 10.6), then milder indexation can be accepted.

Chapter 15

Prefunding the unfunded system

We have presented Theorem 9.1 (neutrality) in Chapter 9 in its most concise form, which shows that under certain ideal conditions there is a scenario (*no pain–no gain*), where prefunding an unfunded system can be costless but such a transition is superfluous. This description may not convince everyone because it does not spell out the details and ignores other scenarios. In this Chapter I try to fill these gaps. Presentation of mathematical details will be followed by two other scenarios, *double burden* and *voluntary joining*. The three scenarios are analyzed from the cost–benefit viewpoint. We shall use the following three *ideal conditions*: (a) the operating costs and (b) the participation rates of the working age population are the same in both systems; (c) the efficiency of production, the growth rate of output, and the rate of interest are independent of the capital/labor ratio. The assumption of dynamic efficiency $r > \nu g$ is accepted here.

Two pure and mature systems

First we shall model pure and mature funded and unfunded systems. (A system is *mature* if the complexities with its introduction has already disappeared.) To keep the notations and formulas simple, we ignore inflation, changes in population size, and the level of productivity. It is assumed that the size of each cohort is equal to 1.

We start the discussion with the *mature unfunded pension system.* Let us assume that the individual enters the labor force at the beginning of year 0, retires at the end of year R, and dies at the end of year D, $0 \leq R < D$. The worker's earnings are equal to 1 during all his career, and he contributes τ_U to the unfunded pension system, $0 < \tau_U < 1$ (U stands for unfunded). Let the pensioner's benefit also be time-invariant: b. Since every individual contributes τ_U for $R + 1$ years to the Social Security and draws benefit b for $D - R$ years, we have the following equality (compare Chapters 8 and 12):

$$(R + 1)\tau_U = (D - R)b. \tag{15.1}$$

We shall need the following notations: let e_k be the *pension expectancy* of a k-aged at the beginning of the year, the sum of the accumulated (remaining) pension promises (Augusztinovics, 1992). (Many authors discount expectancy by the interest factor but at the end of this section we shall see the advantages of no discounting or, more precisely, hidden discounting with the wage growth coefficient g.) The sum of expectancies is called *aggregate pension expectations*:

$$E = \sum_{k=0}^{D} e_k.$$

The expectancies are given by

$$e_i = \tau_U i, \qquad i = 0, \ldots, R;$$
$$e_j = b(D - j + 1), \qquad j = R + 1, \ldots, D;$$
$$E = \frac{\tau_U R(R + 1)}{2} + \frac{b(D - R)(D - R + 1)}{2} = \frac{b}{2}(D - R)(D + 1).$$

In fact, an i-aged worker paid contribution τ_U for i years and a j-aged pensioner will receive benefit b for $D - j + 1$ more years. It should be stressed that in deriving the second form of E we have applied (15.1).

It is now time to discuss the mature *funded system* (Chapter 3). To do so we must calculate the contribution rate in a funded system, τ_F (F stands for funded) which ensures the same benefit as the unfunded system. Let r be the *interest factor*, which is assumed to be larger than 1: $r > 1$. (If growth is to be taken into account, then we have to use a relative rather than an absolute interest factor, where the former is the ratio of the latter to the growth factor, see also Theorem 8.5.) Assuming that all payments occur at the beginning of every year, we set out from the equality of the present values of the contributions and the benefits:

$$\tau_F \sum_{i=0}^{R} r^{-i} = b \sum_{j=R+1}^{D} r^{-j}, \quad \text{that is,}$$

$$\tau_F \left(r^{-(R+1)} - 1 \right) = b \left(r^{-(D+1)} - r^{-(R+1)} \right).$$

$$(15.2)$$

We shall need the following notations: let a_k be the *pension capital* of a k-aged at the beginning of the year, the sum of the accumulated (remaining) pension contributions. The sum of capital is called *aggregate pension capital*:

$$A = \sum_{k=0}^{D} a_k.$$

The assets are determined by the following equations:

$$a_i = \tau_F \sum_{h=0}^{i-1} r^h = \tau_F I_{i-1}(r), \qquad i = 0, \ldots, R;$$

$$a_j = b \sum_{h=0}^{D-j} r^{-h} = b I_{D-j}(1/r), \qquad j = R+1, \ldots, D;$$

where an empty sum naturally equals zero. In fact, an i-aged worker accumulated contribution τ_F for i years on his own account, and a j-aged pensioner's remaining pension capital a_j should ensure (at its present value) benefit b for $D - j + 1$ years. Of course, no one has any pension expectancy. Hence

$$A = \frac{\tau_F}{r-1}[I_{R-1}(r) - R] + \frac{b}{r^{-1}-1}[r^{-1}I_{D-R-1}(1/r) - (D - R)].$$

Comparing (15.1) and (15.2), and using Problem 4.1, we can easily see that, under the condition of dynamic efficiency, in a mature funded system a lower contribution rate is needed for the same benefit than in a mature unfunded system: $\tau_F < \tau_U$.

No gain–no pain

It is time to turn to modeling the transition. In scenario 1 (Geanako-plos et al. 1998) it is assumed that, in prefunding the system in year $t = 0$, the government calculates and aggregates individual pension expectancies, and the corresponding *implicit debt* is transformed into an *explicit debt*. From that moment the public pension system is closed down and everyone saves into or dissaves from his own pension account. The transition is over in year D.

For the time being, a fourth assumption is introduced: (d) although explicit government debt has increased tremendously, this does not affect the creditworthiness of the country. Then there exists a *cost-free transition* but—taking everything into account—the efficiency of the new system is the same as that of the old. This scenario is therefore called *no pain–no gain* and we refer to this proposition as the 'indifference proposition'.

We shall need the following notations: let $e_{k,t}$ be the *pension expectancy* of a k-aged at the beginning of year t. Similarly, let $a_{k,t}$ be the *pension capital* of a k-aged at the beginning of year t, $k = 0, \ldots, D$. In a given year, we have two $(D + 1)$-vectors, and the sums of their entries are *aggregate pension expectations* and *aggregate pension assets*, respectively:

$$E_t = \sum_{k=0}^{D} e_{k,t} \quad \text{and} \quad A_t = \sum_{k=0}^{D} a_{k,t}.$$

In what follows, we shall analyze the dynamics of these quantities.

The simplest approach is to look after those already retired at the start of the reform. For them,

$$e_{j,t} = e_j, \qquad a_{j,t} = 0, \qquad j = R + 1 + t, \ldots, D.$$

Analyzing the paths of those participating in both systems, we have to distinguish between the accumulation and the drawing down stages. Let us start with the first stage. Concentrate on that person who was just k-aged at the beginning of year 0, $k = 1, \ldots, R$: he contributed to his pension account for $R - k + 1$ years. Thus

$$a_{k+t,t} = a_t, \qquad t = 0, \ldots, R - k + 1,$$

and then he received a partially funded benefit b_k such as is ensured by the maximum of his capital. We shall also need the ratio of the truncated maximum and the mature maximum:

$$\alpha_k = \frac{a_{R+1-k}}{a_{R+1}} \quad \text{and} \quad b_k = \alpha_k b, \qquad k = 1, \ldots, R.$$

According to this equation, the time path of his pension capital is proportional to the age-dynamics of the mature system:

$$a_{j,t} = \alpha_{j-t} a_j, \qquad j = R+1, \ldots, D, \qquad j > t.$$

Since the missing proportion $b - b_k$ is financed by the Social Security, his pension expectancy diminishes proportionally at his retirement and then evaporates step-by-step:

$$e_{j,t} = (1 - \alpha_{j-t}) e_j, \qquad j = R+1, \ldots, D, \qquad j > t.$$

With the help of these formulas, the aggregate indexes can also be calculated.

What is the source of pension capital? The transformation of an implicit government debt into explicit debt. Let us introduce the *government debt* G_t at the beginning of year t and the *primary budgetary deficit* F_t in year t which is the difference between aggregate public benefits B_t to be paid in year t and the transition tax T. By definition,

$$G_{t+1} = r(G_t + F_t), \quad \text{where} \quad F_t = B_t - T. \qquad (15.3)$$

Every worker has to pay a transition tax $\tau_U - \tau_F$, so the aggregate tax—not only for the years of transition but for ever after—is equal to $T = (R+1)(\tau_U - \tau_F)$. In addition, the government sells the necessary amount of bonds to just cover the cost of the temporary increase in debt. It is from these two sources that the government finances the decreasing amount of unfunded pensions and the increasing government debt. The implicit debt becomes explicit debt step-by-step and this is compensated by the emerging pension capital:

$$A_t = G_t, \qquad t = 0, \ldots, D.$$

The determination of the new steady state government debt is very simple:

$$G_D = r(G_D - T), \quad \text{that is,} \quad G_D = \frac{(\tau_U - \tau_F)(R+1)r}{r-1}. \qquad (15.3')$$

Summing up: The neutrality theorem is true, the transition is costless and pointless.

As an illustration and a check, we present

Problem 15.1. Work out the details for the case of two working generations and one retired: $R = 1$ and $D = 2$.

We also present a much more realistic, *annual-based* simulation.

Example 15.1. $R = 39$ years, $D = 59$ years, $r = 1.02/$year and $b = 0.5$. Then $\tau_U = 0.25$ and $\tau_F = 0.135$; indeed, there is a huge gap between the two contribution rates.

Let us start the presentation with the characteristics of the two mature systems: $E_0 = 300$. If capital income is ignored (about 30% of the GDP), then the value of the annual (restricted) output is equal to $R + 1 = 40$: that is, the ratio of aggregate pension expectancy to output is alarmingly high, 7.5. In reality, this ratio is much lower, about 1–3 (column 1 in Table 15.1 below).

The final value of aggregate pension capital is about $A_D = 234$, the capitalized present value of the original aggregate pension expectancy at interest factor $r = 1.02$. This number is also quite high.

What happens during the transition? Figure 15.1 displays the dynamics of our macrovariables, debt is depicted as negative.

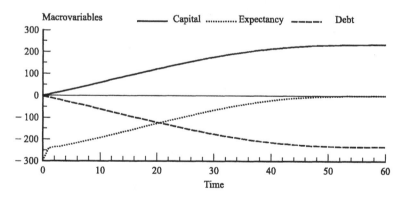

Figure 15.1. Expectancy and capital macrodynamics

Due to our somewhat arbitrary solution, in the first year aggregate pension expectancy drops dramatically, by about 20%, although the capital accumulation and the concomitant explicit debt accumulation have only just started. Observe that the aggregate capital is identical to government debt, showing that the transition is costless but also pointless.

Figure 15.2 presents four snapshots of the age distribution of capital and expectancy: at 0, $D - R$, $R + 1$ and D. (For enhanced transparency, the expectancies are depicted as negative numbers.) The step-by-step transformation is clearly visible. It is at this point that we can explain why expectancy was not discounted: with discounting, we could not have derived our simple relations.   □

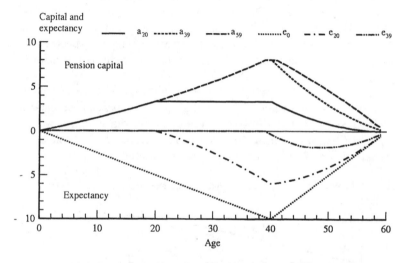

Figure 15.2. Snapshots on profiles

Of course, the assumptions of the indifference theorem are strongly debatable and are indeed debated. Perhaps the strongest counterargument is that the business world does not accept the transformation of implicit debt into explicit debt. This is clearly the case with the Maastricht Treaty criterion. For me it is somewhat mysterious that the internal debt of Belgium, Italy and Japan—surpassing their annual GDPs—attracts much stronger criticism than the ever-growing external debt of the United States (compare, for example, McKinnon, 2001). We turn now to the other two scenarios.

Double burden

The second scenario, articulated for example by Feldstein–Samwick (1998), would introduce the mandatory funded private pillar in addition to the existing mandatory unfunded public pillar and eliminate the latter only by a long process. Here many cohorts pay twice: first for their parents' unfunded benefits and second for their own pension funds. The additional burden becomes acceptable only under Feldstein–Samwick's (1998) unrealistic parameter values: with 5–9% real interest rate. With a replacement rate of 40%, 40 years of work, and 20 years of retirement, the necessary contribution rate is only about 3–4% (compare Chapter 3). The transition appears particularly easy if (a*) the operating costs do not significantly surpass those of the public system and (b*), because of the reform, workers work much more and much longer than they did in the public system. We list the following debatable assumptions: (d*) The transitional extra saving does not induce a similar contraction in voluntary savings and (e*) it does not place an unbearable burden on the shoulders of those persons who had no voluntary savings before the reform.

In this model, we calculate with a much more modest interest rate, only 2% in excess of the growth rate of output.

As in Scenario 1, the Social Security must pay the pension benefits of those who were already retired and the partial pension benefits of those who had already acquired pension rights at the start of the reform. The additional private pensions of those who continue to work after the start and the full pensions of those who enter the labor force after the start are paid from pension funds. We have to complete the notation introduced for Scenario 1: the time-dependent contribution rate of the unfunded system (to be phased-out) is denoted by $\tau_{\mathrm{U},t}$. (15.1) is now replaced by a branching formula. Let B_t be the unfunded pension expenditure in year t, that is, $\tau_{\mathrm{U},t} = B_t/(R+1)$, then with initial condition $B_{-1} = (D-R)b$ dynamic relations can be derived. To figure them out, it is worthwhile to describe unfunded pension benefits in a matrix form, where the column j of row t shows the public benefit of a person of age j in year t.

time\ age $t\backslash j$	$R+1$	$R+2$	...	D
-1	b	b	...	b
0	$b - b_R$	b	...	b
1	$b - b_{R-1}$	$b - b_R$	...	b
	$\vdots$	$\vdots$	$\vdots$	$\vdots$
$D-R-1$	$b - b_{2R-D+1}$	$b - b_{2R-D+2}$	...	$b - b_R$
$D-R$	$b - b_{2R-D}$	$b - b_{2R-D+1}$	...	$b - b_{R-1}$
	$\vdots$	$\vdots$	$\vdots$	$\vdots$
$R-1$	$b - b_1$	$b - b_2$	...	$b - b_{2R-D}$
R	0	$b - b_1$	...	$b - b_{2R-D-1}$
	$\vdots$	$\vdots$	$\vdots$	$\vdots$
$D-1$	0	0	...	$b - b_1$

Hence it is easy to deduce the recursions

$$
B_t = \begin{cases}
B_{t-1} - b_{R-t} & \text{if } t = 0, \ldots, D-R-1; \\
B_{t-1} - b_{R-t} + b_{D-t} & \text{if } t = D-R, \ldots, R-1; \\
B_{t-1} - b_{D-t} & \text{if } t = R, \ldots, D-1.
\end{cases}
$$

In the spirit of assumption (b), it is assumed that the temporarily increasing total contribution rate does not influence the participation rate but only diminishes workers' consumption: $c_{i,t} = 1 - \tau_{U,t} - \tau_F$, $i = 0, \ldots, R$. It would be difficult to compare the consumption paths of the cohorts participating in the transition. For that reason, it is useful to evaluate the (consumption, leisure) paths with a suitable CRRA utility function (the discretized version of Chapter 12):

$$
U(c_0, l_0, \ldots, c_D, l_D) = \sigma^{-1} \sum_{k=0}^{D} l_k^{(1-\varepsilon)\sigma} c_k^{\varepsilon\sigma},
$$

where l_k is relative leisure at age k (not to be confused with survival probability in other chapters); the real number $\sigma < 1$ is the elasticity of lifetime utility with respect to annual utility; there is no discounting and ε is a real between 0 and 1, representing the utility weight of consumption.

It is well-known that, in a time-invariant setting with zero discount and interest rate, age-independent optimal worker and pensioner consumption paths are obtained, where

$$l_k = \begin{cases} \lambda < 1 & \text{if } k = 0, \ldots, R; \\ 1 & \text{if } k = R+1, \ldots, D. \end{cases} \qquad (15.4)$$

The *optimal replacement rate* $\beta^o = b/(1 - \tau_U)$ is provided by (12.5'). To ensure that the worker's consumption is larger than the pensioner's consumption, we have to assume $\sigma < 0$.

Then under (15.4), $U_t = \bar{U}(c_{0,t}, \ldots, c_{D,t+D})$ denotes the lifetime utility of a person born in year t which is—because of lack of voluntary savings—generally not maximal. This time-dependent utility function shows the cost of transition in terms of lifetime utility.

As is well-known, it is quite difficult to interpret the numerical value of a utility function. Relying on the notion of iso-utility consumption of (11.8), we can assign to every consumption path an equivalent flat path. However, taking into account the role of leisure in lifetime utility, we define the equivalence as follows:

$$U(c_0, l_0 \ldots, c_D, l_D) = \sigma^{-1}[\lambda^{(1-\varepsilon)\sigma}(R+1)\bar{c}^\sigma + (D-R)(\beta\bar{c})^\sigma],$$

that is,

$$\bar{c} = \left[\frac{\sigma U}{\lambda^{(1-\varepsilon)\sigma}(R+1) + \beta^\sigma(D-R)} \right]^{1/\sigma}.$$

Since $\bar{c}$ is changing in time, it will be more convenient to study its *relative deviation* from the initial value: $\Delta_t = (\bar{c}_t - \bar{c}_0)/\bar{c}_0$.

We choose again realistic parameter values.

Example 15.2. For $\sigma = -2$, $\varepsilon = 0.3$: data from Chapter 12 imply that it is $\lambda = 0.6291$ which yields $b = 0.5$ as an optimum.

Using our formulas, we can determine the time path of the transition tax and lifetime utility. To save space, we date lifetime utility by the time of retirement rather than birth (or entering the workforce): $U_t = \bar{U}(c_{0,t-R}, \ldots, c_{D,t-R+D})$.

To obtain a full picture of the effects of the reform of Scenario 2, in Figure 15.3 we start the description 10 years before the reform begins and close it down $D + R + 2 = 80$ years after. It is remarkable that it takes 32 years for the total contribution rate to drop below the initial rate, and another 54 years are needed to reach the funded

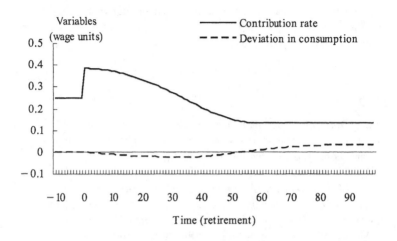

Figure 15.3. Double burden

contribution rate. The dynamics of lifetime utility and of the relative deviation are similar: they deteriorate for 32 years and improve only rather slowly, exceeding the initial value only 54 years after the reform. □

As already mentioned, Feldstein–Samwick (1998) have painted a much more favorable picture. In addition to their assumption of a much more efficient and attractive private system than ours, they assume a very slow and protracted phasing-in of the private pillar. It seems to be very questionable whether such a slow process is at all feasible.

Voluntary joining of the funded pillar

In Scenario 3 it is assumed that joining the funded system is *voluntary*, but the newcomer loses the rights he obtained in the unfunded system (compare the Hungarian pension reform in 1998, Chapters 5 and 9). The contribution rate of the joiners does not change (though their benefits may increase) and everyone—worker and pensioner alike—has to pay a time-variant transition tax ι_t proportional to his net of contribution income.

Let k^* be the index of that cohort whose members enter the funded system in year 0 while those of cohort $k^* + 1$ do not. Younger workers save for their own funded (partial or full) pensions. Since the entrants still pay the old contribution, but now to their own accounts, on the basis of (15.2) the partly funded pension $\tilde{b}_k$ of k-aged is determined by

$$\tau_U \left(r^{-(R+1-k)} - 1 \right) = \tilde{b}_k \left(r^{-(D+1-k)} - r^{-(R+1-k)} \right). \qquad (15.\tilde{2})$$

By assumption, a k-aged enters the funded system if and only if his new benefit is larger than the old one: $\tilde{b}_{k^*} > b \geq \tilde{b}_{k^*+1}$

Workers remaining in the unfunded system also pay contributions at rate τ_U and receive unfunded pension b after retirement. Until year $R - k^*$ the number of cohorts receiving unfunded pensions is constant: $D - R$, then each year it diminishes by one until it reaches zero. Accordingly, we have a branching equation for the two stages:

$$\iota_t = \frac{(R - k^* - t)\tau_U + [(R+1)(1 - \tau_U) + (D - R)b]}{(D - R)b},$$

$$t = 0, \ldots, R - k^*$$

and

$$\iota_t = \frac{(R+1)(1 - \tau_U) + (D - k^* - t)b + \sum_{j=R-t}^{k^*} \tilde{b}_j}{(D - k^* - t)b},$$

$$t = R - k^* + 1, \ldots, D - k^*.$$

Note that $\tilde{b}_k = \tilde{b}_0$ if $k < 0$.

The consumption of an i-aged worker, who was k-year-old at the start, is as follows:

$$c_{i,i-k} = 1 - \iota_{i-k} - \tau_U \quad \text{if} \quad i = 0, \ \ldots, \ R.$$

The description of the pensioners' consumption has to be divided into two: that under the new system and that under the old. The consumption of a j-aged pensioner, who was k-year-old at the start $(j = R + 1, \ \ldots, \ D)$, is as follows:

$$c_{j,j-k} = \begin{cases} \tilde{b}_k(1 - \iota_{j-k}) & \text{if} \quad k = 0, \ldots, k^*; \\ b(1 - \iota_{j-k}) & \text{if} \quad k = k^* + 1, \ldots, D. \end{cases}$$

Of course, for every negative t, $\iota_t = 0$.

In our new scenario, lifetime utilities U_t and corresponding iso-utility consumptions or relative deviations can also be calculated.

We shall continue our illustrations started in Examples 15.1 and 15.2.

Example 15.3. For our parameter values, $k^* = 14$, that is, those people who worked fewer than 15 years before the reform enter the funded system and the others remain in the unfunded one.

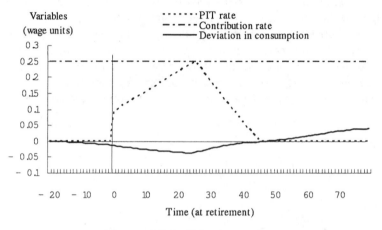

Figure 15.4. Voluntary entry

To obtain a full picture on the effects of the reform, in Figure 15.4 we begin the description 20 years before the reform starts and close it down $D + R + 2 = 80$ years after. Since current pensioners now also share the burdens of the transition, those who retired later than year $R - D = -20$ have to pay the transition tax until death. In contrast to Scenario 2, we cannot now speak of a total contribution rate because the personal income tax (PIT) and the pension contribution have different bases. We can say only that the personal income tax rate increased to 25% in 25 years (during that period the number of old contributors has continuously diminished and that of the beneficiaries has remained constant; during the next period the old contributors die out and the number of beneficiaries of the unfunded system is decreasing.) Here, in comparing the welfare of different cohorts, we have no option but to use lifetime utility or relative deviations of the iso-utility consumption. Those indexes decrease from year −20 to year 24, then start to improve (exceeding the initial level only in year 36) and stop improving in year 80. □

At the end of the Section we mention a similar study by Kotlikoff et al. (1998), which considered a voluntary prefunding of the US Social Security system by using a much more sophisticated Computable General Equilibrium model, taking into account income differentials. The main conclusion of that study was the following: "Adverse selection is a key reason why many economists oppose opting out and why, for example, numerous proposals to privatize the social security system of the US and other countries mandate participation. The paper, however, shows that this wisdom to be wide of the mark.... [The] results suggest that giving people freedom of choice might actually generate more favorable outcomes than mandates" (Abstract).

Discussion

After completing the mathematical deductions and illustrations, we shall verbally discuss the limits of our models.

1. In this chapter, our main aim was to present in detail three possible scenarios of prefunding an unfunded pension system. For the sake of clarity, we have ignored several complications: the step-by-step aging of the population and the differences between the participation and cost processes in the two systems.

2. In reality, different scenarios occur in different combinations. It appears that the Hungarian pension reform of 1998 was a special combination: (a) The government has to transform the pension system so that the explicit government debt to GDP ratio must remain largely constant. (b) The government prefunds only a part of the pension system and voluntary entrants partially lose their pension expectancies (see Chapter 5 above). (c) The benefits of the remaining public pillar are diminished relative to earlier promises: for example, wage-indexation is replaced by wage-price-indexation (Chapter 14). (d) The government may cut other budgetary expenditures (for example, health care or education), and may open the source of deficit financing to prefunding. The only question to be answered is as follows: is it really necessary to prefund and privatize the pension system to solve its problems, or is it enough if the government debt is cut? We call attention to Elmendorf–Liebman (2001), which an-

alyzes the interaction between social security reform and budgetary policy in the United States under various assumptions.

Facts

Finally we refer to two surveys—Holzmann's (1998) and Holzmann et al. (2001)—and cite a table from the former:

Table 15.1. Implicit and explicit debt in several OECD countries, GDP %

Country	Gross pension debt	Pension expenditure	Virtual repayment time (years)	Government debt	Consolidated debt
	(1)	(2)	(3)=(1)/(2)	(4)	(5)
Germany	216	9.0	24.0	40	256
Italy	242	10.6	24.4	101	343
Great Britain	139	6.6	21.1	35	174
US	112	5.1	22.0	55	167

Source: Holzmann (1998, p. 5) Table 2.

Column 1 reveals the dispersion of the ratio of gross pension debt to GDP in four important countries between 110% and 240%. (Net debt is lower than the gross debt only in the United States, but there the difference is important: 89% versus 112%.) Column 2 displays annual public pension expenditures in terms of GDP (see Chapter 8 above). Note the huge differences between the continental West European countries and the Anglo-Saxon countries: 10% versus 5%. The stability of the ratio of pension debt to pension expenditure (column 3) is noteworthy: 21–25. This index could be called *virtual repayment time* because, if no new promises were made, it would show the number of years needed to make good the old promises. In analyzing public finances, the ratio of government debt to GDP (column 4) is a very important index and it fluctuates a lot across countries: from the British 35% to the Italian 101%. Finally, adding up implicit and explicit debts, in column 5 we obtain the *consolidated gross debt*. Here the Anglo-Saxon countries fare well while the Continental ones do not.

Chapter 16

A dynamic model of the German pension reform

The German pension system has already played an important role in the discussion as a well-designed proportional unfunded system (see especially Chapter 4). We have already mentioned that this system also needs reform, above all for demographic reasons. This chapter will survey a dynamic model of German pension reform by Fehr (2000), with a particular emphasis on taxation and income distribution. Due to its complexities, we cannot reproduce the details.

A simulation model

The simulation model is based on the Auerbach–Kotlikoff (1987) model (compare Chapter 13). It works with households rather than individuals, which are distinguished by the age and productivity of the head of household. The model abstracts from childhood as well as from the uncertainty of the lifespan. However, it takes into account the future increase in life expectancy: the adult lifespan increases from 58 (read: 78 years) in 1998 to 64 (84) years by 2060. The population is divided into five earning-groups of equal size. Consequently, each year 290–320 types of family populate the model.

The individuals' utility function corresponds to that of Chapters 11–13; moreover, annual utility function is a general CRRA rather than Cobb–Douglas-type but it is also independent of income position. The households' budget constraints are obvious.

The production possibilities are also described by CES functions, with convex investment costs (Blanchard–Fischer, 1989, Section 2.4). The government sector is characterized by two budget constraints: (i) Taxes finance exogenous public consumption plus the given share of aggregate pension expenditures. (ii) In the current pure unfunded pension system, benefits are financed from contributions plus the government subsidy. It is assumed that everyone retires at the same age.

Even in the analysis of the almost proportional German system, the subsidization of low earners and the existence of an earnings ceiling (Chapter 4) cause some headache. At the same time, Fehr considers the distortion arising from the difference between the interest rate and the GDP growth rate (Chapter 8), which exists even in a proportional system but which converges to zero as the worker approaches retirement age.

For given parameter values, the dynamic model can be solved numerically. A new complication arises: contrary to the Auerbach–Kotlikoff (1987) assumption, even the initial state is not a steady state. This demographic complication is described in Table 16.1.

Table 16.1. Official and simulated population dynamics, Germany

Year	1998	2000	2010	2020	2030	2040	2050	2100
Life exp., year	78	78	78	79	80	80	82	84
Population, million								
Model	83.1	82.7	80.1	77.1	74.5	70.9	67.4	62.3
Official	82.8*	82.2	81.0	78.4	74.3	68.8		
Cohorts, %								
1–20	19.5	19.0	18.6	19.2	19.9	20.9	22.0	23.8
21–40	31.2	30.8	24.9	20.4	19.9	20.9	22.0	23.8
41–60	26.9	26.9	31.0	33.1	26.8	22.0	22.0	23.8
61–84	22.4	23.2	25.5	27.3	33.4	36.0	33.9	28.6
Old-age dependency ratio %								
Model	38.5	40.1	45.6	51.0	71.4	83.5	77.1	60.0
Official	37.0*	40.8	44.8	53.1	73.2	76.4	80.2	

Source: Fehr (2000, p. 427) Table 1.

Note that the official data* of 1998 refer to 1996. The divergence between the model and the official dependency ratios for 2040–2050 is also remarkable.

Table 16.2 compares the initial values of the German economy and of the model.

Table 16.2. Equilibrium: model and reality, Germany

	Model	Germany, 1998
Expenditures with respect to GDP %		
Private consumption	63.7	57.5
Government consumption	21.0	18.9
Gross fixed investment	15.3	21.9
Export–import	0.0	1.7
Fiscal indicators %		
Pension expenditures/GDP	13.3	11.5
Pension contribution rate		
average	18.8	20.3
marginal	10.2	
Tax revenues/GDP	21.0	22.9
Labor income tax	9.1	7.7
Capital income tax	1.4	1.8
Consumer tax rate	10.5	9.0
Interest rate %	4.1	5.6
Capital/Output	2.5	2.9

Source: Fehr (2000, p. 429) Table 2.

In the *base run*, Fehr calculates with a net replacement rate of 70% and zero government subsidy. He takes into account that the internal rate of return of the unfunded system decreases over time (but he ignores a similar decrease in the interest rate: compare Brooks, 2000).

The model deliberately ignores the openness of the economy, the existence of government debt, and other important details. Notwithstanding these omissions, the model appears to be acceptable.

To continue our survey, in Table 16.3 we present the dynamic characteristics of the base run, taking snapshots every tenth year, and relate the variables to the initial values in percent terms except for percentage indicators like the interest rate and the contribution rate.

In the short run, (b)-type variables grow fast, since the denominator decreases. In the long run, employment drops by 7%. It is

Table 16.3. Baseline path of the economy[a], Germany

Year	2000	2010	2020	2030	2040	2050	2060
Employment[b]	6.5	33.7	32.5	16.5	3.1	−2.0	−6.7
Capital stock[b]	5.1	26.6	40.0	43.9	28.3	8.6	1.7
Consumption[b]	5.4	27.6	27.5	18.5	6.5	−0.7	−9.1
Earning	−0.3	−1.6	1.6	6.5	6.7	3.1	2.6
Interest rate	2.4	3.8	3.3	0.8	2.5	5.3	3.1
Consumption tax	18.5	15.5	13.2	13.1	14.4	14.4	16.0
Aver. earning tax	12.5	13.9	15.3	17.2	17.4	16.3	15.1
Aver. contr. rate	19.4	21.0	22.6	28.8	31.7	30.0	25.7

[a] All the variables are related to the initial values in percent terms except for percentage indicators like the interest rate and the contribution rate.
[b] These variables refer to the per-capita values of the cohort just starting work.
Source: Fehr (2000, p. 431) Table 3.

to be underlined that, during the demographic transition, increasing consumption reduces the equilibrating consumption tax (from 18.5% to 13.1%) without restoring it later on. At the same time, the rates of wage (income) tax and pension contribution steeply increase: the latter by more 63%, from 19.4% in 2000 to 31.7% in 2040.

Modeling reforms

In further analysis, we shall consider three moderate and two radical reform packages.

Starting with the moderate reforms: 1. Raising of the retirement age: $R + 1$ increases to 62 in 1999 and to 63 in 2009. 2. Reduction in the replacement rate: β drops to 68% in 2008, 66% in 2018, and 64% in 2028. 3. In addition to packages 1 and 2, the government subsidy is gradually increased. Under the radical reforms, in addition to the rising retirement age the replacement rate diminishes four times faster than in package 2 and the second, funded pillar is introduced. Within it: 4. the low earners' subsidy is eliminated and 5. flat benefit is introduced.

We have no space to discuss all the relevant results but we outline some of them; numbers refer to the serial number of the reform.

Table 16.4. Macroeconomic effects of pension reforms, Germany

| Variable | Moderate (pure unfunded) | | | Radical (mixed) | |
	1 Increase in retire. age	2 Replace- ment reduction	3 Increase in govt. grant	4 Variable pension	5 Flat pension
Employment					
2020	0.5	0.8	0.5	2.4	−1.9
long run	0.4	0.5	0.2	2.1	−0.6
Capital					
2020	1.1	2.4	3.3	4.9	3.5
long-run	1.1	5.7	8.0	30.6	23.7
Earning					
2020	0.1	0.4	0.8	0.7	1.6
long-run	0.2	1.4	2.2	7.5	6.7
Interest rate					
2020	−0.1	−0.2	−0.3	−0.2	−0.4
long-run	−0.1	−0.4	−0.6	−1.9	−1.7
Consumer tax rate					
2020	0.9	0.6	5.7	−0.2	1.1
long-run	0.9	0.3	6.1	−2.6	−1.5
Contribution rate					
2020	−2.2	−3.1	−6.3	−3.4	−3.0
long-run	−1.4	−3.0	−6.5	−10.4	−9.1

[a] All the variables are related to the baseline values in percent terms except for percentage indicators like the interest rate and the contribution rate.

[b] These variables refer to the per-capita values of the cohort just starting work.

Source: Fehr (2000, p. 434) Table 4.

1. The effect of raising retirement age is evident and it shows up most strongly in the contribution rate, which drops by 2–3% points.

2. If, in addition to raising the retirement age, the government moderately reduces the replacement rate, then the capital stock significantly increases (in the long run by 5.7%) and the contribution rate decreases gradually: the steepest drop of 4.5% occurs in 2030 (not shown in the table) and the long-run drop is 3% points.

3. The most interesting effect of the gradual increase in the government subsidy is the following: for the richest households, the increase in the consumption tax replaces the zero marginal contribution rate. The acceleration of capital accumulation is impressive.

4. Since the changes are pre-announced and the participants are able to adapt to them, the initial changes are modest, even under the radical reforms. The medium- to long-term results, however, are really important, especially for retaining the proportional benefit. Then long-run employment rises by 2%, the capital stock by an unbelievable 30.6%, earnings by 7.5%, while consumer tax rate and the pension contribution rates drop by 2.6% and 10.4% points, respectively.

5. What is wrong with the introduction of the popular flat benefit? In this case, the rise in employment lags behind even that of the base run, and the increase in capital is 7% lower than in package 4. Otherwise, they behave similarly.

What are the efficiency and the welfare effects of the reforms? Table 16.5 presents the answers at an aggregate level.

Table 16.5. The aggregate efficiency effects of the pension reforms, Germany

	Moderate (pure unfunded)			Radical (mixed)	
			reforms		
	1	2	3	4	5
Variable	Increase in retire. age	Replace-ment reduction	Increase in govt. grant	Variable pension	Flat pension
In terms of base run %	1.03	1.64	1.58	6.08	−4.03

Source: Fehr (2000, p. 436) Table 5.

The aggregate welfare effects are favorable but modest with moderate reforms. They are significant with radical reforms; however, they are favorable only with the proportional benefit and so unfavorable with the flat benefit.

The emerging picture is much more complex if the analysis is broken down into income groups. For conciseness, we ignore moderate reforms (see Fehr, 2000, p. 437, Table 6) and summarize the effects of radical reforms in Table 16.6.

Table 16.6. The welfare effects of radical pension reforms,
Germany

	Birth years*	Proportional	Flat
		benefit	
Lowest quintile			
	1930	0.33	0.15
	1950	−1.32	−1.43
	1970	−1.71	−0.27
	1990	−1.14	2.04
	2010	1.62	4.43
	2030	2.90	5.60
	long-run	3.53	6.59
Middle quintile			
	1930	0.31	0.15
	1950	−0.75	−1.43
	1970	−0.62	−0.79
	1990	0.12	0.88
	2010	2.15	2.56
	2030	3.47	3.54
	long-run	3.83	3.91
Highest quintile			
	1930	0.20	0.08
	1950	−0.51	−1.77
	1970	−0.55	−2.31
	1990	0.57	−0.83
	2010	3.02	0.86
	2030	3.86	1.20
	long-run	4.22	1.34
Average			
	1930	0.24	0.11
	1950	−0.70	−1.60
	1970	−0.77	−1.54
	1990	0.22	0.13
	2010	2.55	2.01
	2030	3.56	2.64
	long-run	4.01	3.02

* The changes are expressed as the percentages of the present values of the
remaining life paths.
Source: Fehr (2000, p. 438) Table 7.

At the introduction of proportional benefits everybody gains but poorer households gain less than the others because they lose their favored tax status as a result of increased earnings.

It is much more interesting and much more surprising to analyze the introduction of flat benefits. Because of the elimination of the connection between contributions and benefits, the cohorts born around 1970 experience a steep rise in their marginal contribution rates, and they are not compensated by the eventual income tax reduction (especially the rich, who lose 2.3%). That observation is similar to Kotlikoff's (1997) remark, cited in our Chapter 9 above.

To sum up: it is impossible to properly evaluate a pension system without considering the income tax system. It is not sufficient to characterize a reform by the degree of the reduction of the replacement rate: from this point of view, packages 4 and 5 are quite similar but the resulting intragenerational redistribution is diametrically different. It is not enough to consider intergenerational redistribution; intragenerational redistribution also needs attention.

Chapter 17

Political models

So far, we have not modeled the political issues raised by pension systems. (Chapter 12 was only a naive attempt at modeling the interaction between government and the individual, while Appendix A is normative rather than descriptive.) There are plenty of papers on the political issues raised by pension systems and especially by pension reforms. Müller (1999) and Orenstein (2000) provide a rich qualitative analysis in the context of pension reforms in ex-socialist countries. In this chapter we shall sketch a model by Casamatta et al. (2000) on the relationship between democracy and pension systems, but first we outline the median voter model (for a simple introduction, see Stiglitz, 1988, Chapter 6).

The median voter

Models of democratic voting procedures go back to Hotelling (1929). Hotelling set up an extremely simple model, where the preference of a voter is represented by a scalar τ: for example, the rate of the current or permanent pension contribution. Staying with our example, assume that there are two parties: the Left (L) and the Right (R). The Left proposes a higher contribution rate, the Right proposes a lower one: $0 \leq \tau_R \leq \tau_L$. Voter τ votes for that party whose proposal is closer to his preferred value: single-peaked preferences. Thus voter τ votes for the Left if and only if $|\tau - \tau_L| < |\tau - \tau_R|$. Denoting the distribution function of the voters' characteristics by

$G(\cdot)$, which is assumed to be a continuous and increasing function, for a given pair of proposals (τ_L, τ_R) the Right gets the share $p_R = G((\tau_L + \tau_R)/2)$ of the votes. The Right wins the election if it gets more than half the votes: $p_R > 1/2$. (Because of continuity, the case of equal numbers of votes is in principle irrelevant, although the US Presidential election in 2000 demonstrates the limits of our ideal model.)

The question is the following: what should opportunistic parties propose? The answer relies on the concept of Nash-equilibrium (compare Varian, 1992, Chapter 15). In the case of two parties, the *Nash-equilibrium* is a pair of proposals such that, if one party deviates from it unilaterally, then that party receives fewer votes than at equilibrium.

Theorem 17.1. *(Hotelling, 1929.) In a voting equilibrium, both parties propose the preferred rate of the median voter:*

$$\tau_L^o = \tau_R^o = \tau^o, \qquad where \quad G(\tau^o) = 1/2.$$

Remarks. 1. Our result is a paradox: both parties make the same proposal at equilibrium. In fact, in many two-party democracies the differences between the actual policies of the two parties are quite small.

2. Of course, this description is too simplistic. Neither in politics in general nor in pension politics in particular is it true that the voters follow only their selfish interests. But even if they do, those interests cannot be expressed with a scalar. Thus the model to be presented should not be accepted at face value.

Outline of the proof. Assume the contrary: if $\tau_L^o > \tau^o$, then the Right can win the election by proposing $(\tau_L^o + \tau^o)/2$. Contradiction.
□

Most researchers of pension voting concentrate on age difference (starting from Browning (1975), see also Verbon's (1988) monograph). The starting point is that, the older the voter, the higher is his preferred contribution (replacement) rate. (In fact, if he is retired, he only receives a pension and pays no contribution. If he is close to retirement, he will pay contributions only for a short period but will receive large benefits quite soon and for a long time.) As a result, in aging societies, the median voter prefers a higher to a lower rate.

Problem 17.1. Determine the median age of an adult population and examine its dependence on the population growth coefficient in a stable population.

A pension voting model

The model to be presented is from Casamatta et al. (2000). It takes into account the age and the (past or present) earnings of the voter. While the description of distribution of earnings is quite general, the modeling of age is at its most rudimentary: there are only two generations, the young and the old (for overlapping generations, see Appendix B).

We consider a macromodel of a small open economy where a unit of time is equal to the span of a generation. The interest factor is equal to r, the population growth factor is ν. As is usual, it is assumed that $r \geq \nu > 1$. If the number of pensioners is denoted by P, then that of workers is equal to $P\nu$. It is assumed that average productivity is constant and the individual's total earnings are given by w. We shall use the following notations for earnings; minimal: w_m, maximal: w_M, average: $\mathbf{w}$, median: w_o, where $w_\mathrm{o} < \mathbf{w}$ as is in reality. Finally, the distribution of earnings is denoted as $F(w) = \mathbf{P}(w' < w)$, $F(w_\mathrm{o}) = 1/2$.

We represent various earnings-related rules with a simple one; it is assumed that the proportional part of the pension has weight α, while the flat part has weight $1 - \alpha$:

$$b_{t+1}(w) = \nu \tau_{t+1}[\alpha w + (1 - \alpha)\mathbf{w}], \qquad 0 \leq \alpha \leq 1. \qquad (17.1)$$

First we shall determine the optimal saving s_t of a worker maximizing his lifetime utility function U:

$$U(c_{0,t}, c_{1,t+1}) = u(c_{0,t}) + \delta u(c_{1,t+1}) \to \max, \qquad (17.2)$$

subject to

$$c_{0,t} = w(1 - \tau_t) - s_t \qquad \text{and} \qquad c_{1,t+1} = rs_t + b_{t+1}(w). \qquad (17.3)$$

The necessary condition for a local maximum is

$$u'(c_{0,t}) = \delta r u'(c_{1,t+1}). \qquad (17.4)$$

Let the worker believe that the contribution rate is constant during his life: $\tau_t = \tau_{t+1} = \tau$. Let $s_t \geq 0$ be optimal saving, and then—dropping the time index—an individual with earnings w has the *indirect utility function*

$$V(\tau, w) = u(w(1-\tau) - s) + \delta u(rs + b(w)).$$

First we determine the contribution rates 'voted' by workers and pensioners, respectively. The pensioners trivially vote for $\tau^{\mathrm{P}} = 1$. The workers's choices depend on the yield of the pension system. In a pure proportional system, the yield is ν (Theorem 8.5), in a pure flat benefit it is given by $\nu\mathbf{w}/w$, their weighted average is $[\alpha + (1 - \alpha)\mathbf{w}/w]\nu$. Denote $\hat{w}$ the earnings of that worker who is indifferent between contributing to a pension and to saving: $r = [\alpha + (1 - \alpha)\mathbf{w}/\hat{w}]\nu$, that is,

$$\hat{w} = \frac{1-\alpha}{r/\nu - \alpha}\mathbf{w}. \tag{17.5}$$

Let us observe that in the distinguished golden-rule case, when $r = \nu$, $\hat{w} = \mathbf{w}$ holds.

Assuming that the intertemporal elasticity of substitution is constant and less than 1, ($\sigma < 0$ in Chapter 11), we have

Theorem 17.2. *(Casamatta et al., 2000, Proposition 1.) For a worker with earning w, the optimal contribution rate is equal to zero if $w > \hat{w}$ and it is an increasing function of w, always lower than 1, otherwise.*

We now turn to the outcome of majority voting.

In the following theorem we need to distinguish two cases, where the border depends on

$$\varepsilon = \frac{\nu - 1}{2\nu} > 0.$$

Theorem 17.3. *(Casamatta et al., 2000, Proposition 2.) (a) If $F(\hat{w}) < \varepsilon$, then the majority votes for the preferred contribution rate $\tau^* = 0$. (b) In the opposite case, the vote is for the contribution rate of that worker whose earnings $\tilde{w}$ satisfy equation*

$$F(\hat{w}) - F(\tilde{w}) = \varepsilon. \tag{17.6}$$

Proof. (a) Who wants a positive contribution rate? P pensioners and those among $P\nu$ workers whose earnings are lower than $\hat{w}$, in sum $P + P\nu F(\hat{w})$. This group forms a minority if and only if $P + P\nu F(\hat{w}) < (P + P\nu)/2$. After rearrangement $F(\hat{w}) < \varepsilon$ obtained, where the critical value ε is determined as above.

(b) In turn, if $F(\hat{w}) \geq \varepsilon$ holds, then a majority of the population wants a positive contribution rate. Because of the optimal tax rate is an increasing function of the earning in the interval $0 \leq w \leq \hat{w}$ (Theorem 17.2), then the result is a contribution rate belonging to earnings $\tilde{w}$ and the number of workers between $\tilde{w}$ and $\hat{w}$ plus all the pensioners are just equal to half the population: $P + \nu P[F(\hat{w}) - F(\tilde{w})] = (P + P\nu)/2$, that is, (17.6). □

We can analyze the tendency depicted in Table 4.6: the more proportional the system—that is, the larger the α—the higher are the contribution rate and the replacement rate. (Note, however, that the United Kingdom and especially the Czech Republic are outliers.)

Since we lack the space to present all the interesting details, we concentrate on the choice between unfunded and funded systems.

Assume that we must choose between two mature systems. (Note that around 1945 the real question was different: what to do with a bankrupt funded system?) To assure the fairness of comparison, we assume that the average yields of the two systems are the same: $\nu = r$, and the benefit rules are also equal.

We shall demonstrate

Theorem 17.4. *(Casamatta et al., 2000, Proposition 3.) With majority voting and common average yield, the mature funded system is smaller than the unfunded one:* $\tau_\mathrm{F} < \tau_\mathrm{U}$.

Remark. Note the difference from Example 15.1, where identical benefits and different yields implied different contribution rates.

Proof. The main difference between the two systems is as follows: in the funded system pensioners are already indifferent to voting, while in the unfunded one they are maximally interested. Therefore, following the argumentation of the previous theorem, the earnings of the critical worker, $\tilde{w}$ satisfy equation $F(\mathbf{w}) - F(\tilde{w}) = 1/2$. (Since we assumed that the median is smaller than the average, there exists such a critical earning $\tilde{w}$.) And the critical earning is the average earning in the unfunded system. □

We shall sketch the results on the distortionary effect of the redistributive system. For a quadratic loss function, the benefit is given by

$$b(w) = \nu\tau[\alpha w + (1 - \phi\tau)(1 - \alpha)\mathbf{w}], \qquad (17.1')$$

where $\phi > 0$ is the coefficient of distortion.

Now the pensioners may not vote for the maximal contribution rate, because they must take into account the distortionary effect. The new optimum is

$$\tau^{\mathrm{P}} = \min\left[\frac{1}{2\phi}\left(1 + \frac{\alpha}{1-\alpha}\frac{w}{\mathbf{w}}\right), 1\right].$$

Because of the distortion, it may now happen that some workers want unfunded benefits: $\tau^{\mathrm{W}}(w)$ and private saving: $s^{\mathrm{W}}(w)$, where (17.3) is replaced by

$$c_0 = w(1-\tau) - s \quad \text{and} \quad c_1 = rs + \nu\tau[\alpha w + (1-\phi\tau)(1-\alpha)\mathbf{w}]. \ (17.3')$$

To formulate our next theorem, we need a new notation: w^* is that earning whose owner wants the same contribution rate as the worker on the minimum wage: $\tau^{\mathrm{W}}(w^*) = \tau^{\mathrm{W}}(w_{\mathrm{m}})$ and $w^* > w_{\mathrm{m}}$.

Theorem 17.5. *(Casamatta et al., 2000, Proposition 5.) If the distortion arising from the flat benefit is described by (17.1'), then three cases must be distinguished.*

(a) If $F(\hat{w}) < \varepsilon$, then $\tau^* = 0$.

(b) If $F(w^*) \leq \varepsilon \leq F(\mathbf{w})$, then the decisive player is that worker whose earning $\breve{w}$ satisfies $F(\breve{w}) = \varepsilon$.

(c) If $F(w^*) > \varepsilon$, then the two decisive players are with earnings w_1 and w_2, satisfying $F(w_2) - F(w_1) = \varepsilon$ and $\tau^{\mathrm{W}}(w_2) = \tau^{\mathrm{W}}(w_1)$.

Outline of proof. It is easy to show that $\max \tau^{\mathrm{W}}(w) < \min \tau^{\mathrm{P}}(w)$. It can be demonstrated that $\tau^{\mathrm{W}}(w)$ first increases then decreases and becomes zero just at $\hat{w}$. To complete the proof, we must follow the argumentation in the proof of Theorem 17.3. $\square$

Breyer–Stolte (2001) present an alternative model, where the current pensioners choose the contribution rate and it is a repeated process and the disincentives created by high contribution rates are taken into account by the elderly. Of course, this model leads to different results: an increasing dependency ratio may imply lower rather than higher contribution rates.

Razin et al. (2002) also reached this surprising result in a model similar to Casamatta et al. (2000). Furthermore, they claimed they econometrically verified this relationship for 13 OECD countries in the period 1965 and 1992. Unfortunately, they have used counterfactual assumptions as (i) that the workers receive the same benefits as the old and (ii) have static expectations on future tax rates and benefits. Replacing their assumption (i) by a more general and realistic one (workers receive proportionally to the old's benefit) and (ii) replacing the static expectations by naive ones, the paradox still survives. Note, however, that the implied credits for poor workers may be quite high and never found in reality. The econometric estimation is unreliable and is based on wrong data: the children have not been removed from dependents and the degree of proportionality has been left out from the explanatory variables.

Problem 17.2. Specify the theorems for Leontief-utility functions.

Chapter 18

Generational pension accounting for Hungary

First of all, recall our outline of the method of *Generational Accounting* at the end of Chapter 8. In the present chapter we depict the corresponding calculations of R. I. Gál, A. Simonovits and G. Tarcali concerning the Hungarian pension system (Gál et al., 2001). We emphasize the following specifics of our work.

Generational accounting does not give a forecast but computes the long-run consequences of the maintenance of present trends. It gives forecasts only for the demographic processes which are more or less independent of the economy. (Note, however, that Philipson–Becker (1998) argue that a higher annual pension benefit yields a higher life expectancy.) There is no alternative, since according to conventional wisdom it is aging which is mainly to blame for intercohort tensions.

Another general feature is that generational accounting usually covers the whole public sphere: it is not confined to the pension system. We only refer to full generational accounting, where all Hungarian public expenditures were broken down by cohorts (Gál et al., 2000).

In contrast, the investigation to be presented here is restricted to the pension system and it places a particular emphasis on the gradual transformation of the Hungarian pension system started in 1997. To recapitulate material in Chapters 4, 5, and 9: the normal retirement age is increasing from 55 and 60 years to a uniform 62 years between

1996 and 2009; continued pensions are set by combined price-wage indexation from 2001, regression is gradually phased out by 2009, the pension scale becomes linear from 2013, pensions will be taxable from 2013, and, last but not least, the second pillar was introduced in 1998.

Without going into the details of the foregoing study, we mention only that we used an anonymized data-set provided by the Hungarian Tax and Finance Control Office (the Hungarian equivalent of the Internal Revenue Service).

In the base runs, we calculated with the internationally used parameter values—annual growth rate of productivity 1.5%, discount rate 5%, real interest rate 4%— but we also made sensitivity calculations.

It will be sufficient to present the summary table of Gál et al. (2001), where the reform steps are evaluated separately and in sum. We shall compress and round off the figures in Table 18.1.

Table 18.1. Hungarian pension accounts, thousand dollars, 2000

Type in 2000	Base run	Com-bined index	Ret. age raise cont.	Phase-out of deg-ression	Linear pension scale	Partial pre-funding	Com-plete re-form
Future	19.0	11.1	14.3	20.2	17.1	15.6	5.5
Newborn	1.1	3.3	1.8	0.9	1.5	1.1	3.3

Source: Gál et al. (2001), Table 1.

We omitted the older cohorts; since their accounts do not contain the net contributions already paid, they are of limited use.

We shall evaluate our results in words, too. In *our base run*, we considered the situation prevailing at the beginning of 1998 except for the increase in the normal retirement age, where we took into account the situation at 2000. In this scenario, a newborn must contribute $1,100 while a typical member of a future cohort is to contribute about $19,000.

The first step is the introduction of *combined price-wage indexation*. This measure triples the burden of a newborn but reduces that of future cohorts by 40%.

The second step is the *completion of the increase in the normal retirement age*. This measure increases the burden of the newborn by 60% while reducing that of future cohorts by 25%.

The *phasing out of regression* is a step in the opposite direction but its quantitative impact is insignificant. Nevertheless, it is important because it simplifies the pension formula and makes the whole system more attractive.

The introduction of a *linear pension scale* has a similarly small macro impact. Nevertheless, this step is important, as the following remark shows: if someone works in two countries with similar pension systems, then it is desirable that his total pension be the same as if he worked exclusively in one or the other country throughout his working life.

We have arrived at the measure considered as *the reform* by many experts and non-experts: *the partial prefunding and privatization* of the pension system. In itself, this measure has a quantitatively similar effect to the completion of the increase in the normal retirement age, and its impact is definitely much more modest than that of combined indexation: the newborn hardly notice any change while the burden on future generations is eased by 20%.

Finally let us consider the *full impact of the reform*. The burden of the newborn is tripled while that of the future cohorts drops to 25% of the original.

Of course, these are only tentative numbers. The proponents of prefunding and privatization may argue that, without such prefunding and privatization, the population would not have accepted the 'rationalization' of the public system, that is, the introduction of combined indexation and the raising of the normal retirement age. We have already discussed these questions in Chapters 9 and 14 and we can only repeat our doubts here.

Chapter 19

Closing remarks

On the basis of the book, we have reached the following six conclusions (compare Augusztinovics, 1999a and Orszag–Stiglitz, 2001):

1) Pension systems are very complex, as is well demonstrated by the coexistence of very different systems in space and time (compare Chapters 3–5).

2) Even for a single person, since the process of paying pension contributions and receiving pension benefits comprises several decades, its regulation requires special attention.

3) Since relatively important sums are mandatorily collected by the government, one needs a simple and logical system which most participants understand and accept.

4) Governments should not use temporary budget deficits or surpluses to punish or reward pensioners, especially those retiring at the moment, because the cumulative processes may preserve these temporary changes.

5) Governments should not cling to *ab ovo* ill-conceived systems, nor to originally appropriate systems which have become outdated.

6) Pension models should simplify reality to be manageable; but, in applying them, the user should always remember that the models are simplifications.

Approaching the end of the study, one may also ask: what have we learned from the discussion of general and specific problems? On the one hand, we have seen that the simplifications applied in Parts I and II are frequently acceptable: for example, we are able to work without deriving the consumption paths with constrained optimization, simply assuming constant growth rates. We have also witnessed that the relationships of a transition to a funded system can be spelled out, generational accounts can be filled in, and the cost and benefits of transition can be determined.

At the same time, the detailed analyses of Part III have frequently painted a more reliable picture. To give only two examples: (i) It turned out that it is *not* irrelevant whether we calculate with rational or with naive expectations (Chapter 13). (ii) We may realize that the study of intergenerational redistribution must be complemented with an analysis of intragenerational redistribution (Chapter 16).

The assumption of stationarity or time-invariant structures permeates the whole literature, including the present study. As Auguszti-novics (2000b) forcefully argues, this weakens if it does not undermine the applicability of much of the theory.

We have concentrated throughout on the developed world. It is evident, however, that the pension systems of the developing world cannot be neglected. For a detailed analysis, see World Bank (1994) and Charlton–McKinnon (2001).

Only new, sophisticated, and more disaggregate analyses can throw light on whether or not our old, naive, and aggregate investigations were acceptable.

Appendix A

Designing optimal linear benefit rules

In Section 12 we studied the issue of flexible (variable) retirement with *ad hoc* contribution rates and benefit functions. The incentive problem was caused by the *asymmetry of information*: while individuals know their own lifespans and elasticities for leisure, the government knows only their distribution. Although existing governments also enact quite arbitrary (for example, frequently changing) benefit rules, in modern economics a normative approach cannot be avoided.

It was Mirrlees (1971) who first set and solved an optimal incentive problem, namely, that of *optimal income taxation*. Since the general solution was quite difficult (for example, Myles, 1995), a linear suboptimum by Sheshinski (1972) was welcome (compare Atkinson and Stiglitz, 1980, Chapter 13).

In the pension literature, it was Diamond–Mirrlees (1978) and (1986) who first studied optimal mechanism design problems, concerning disability benefits. Independently of the forgotten book of Fabel (1994), Diamond (2002a, Chapters 6 and 7) and Eső–Simonovits (2002) have applied the foregoing method to find an optimal benefit function (and contribution rate) for flexible retirement. Both studies restrict the distribution of the pair lifespan and labor disutility to one dimension. In contrast, the present Appendix (Simonovits, 2002) considers arbitrary *two-dimensional* distributions but restricts the analysis to *linear* benefit functions.

The model of pension design

In this Appendix we recapitulate the model of flexible (variable) retirement (Chapter 12) and develop it into an optimal mechanism design problem.

Time is continuous; wages, contributions, and benefits are flows. It is assumed that everybody earns a unit total wage while working and receives a life annuity after retirement. Individuals are characterized by possibly heterogeneous characteristics: $D =$ (expected adult) lifespan, $R =$ length of employment, $\tau =$ pension contribution rate, $b =$ pension benefit in annuitized form, possibly an increasing function of the length of employment. It is assumed that workers have minimal *leisure*, while pensioners have maximum leisure, yielding instantaneous utility functions $u(a), v(b)$, depending exclusively on consumption $a = 1 - \tau > 0$ and $b > 0$, respectively. It will be suitable to introduce a parameter ε to represent the heterogeneity in individuals' utility derived from consumption: $u(\varepsilon, \cdot)$ and $v(\varepsilon, \cdot)$; higher ε implies higher u, v. The ratio of pension benefit to net earnings is called the *replacement rate*: $\beta = b/(1 - \tau)$. Saving and income taxation are excluded. To model the difference between the utility functions of workers and pensioners, in addition to the usual concavity assumptions, it is assumed that $u'(\varepsilon, c) < v'(\varepsilon, c)$ for all values of c, generally leading to lower consumption during retirement than during work: $b < a$ (compare Theorem 12.1).

Each individual has a *lifetime utility function* and an *individual lifetime net contribution*, respectively:

$$U(D, \varepsilon, \tau, b, R) = u(\varepsilon, 1 - \tau)R + v(\varepsilon, b)(D - R) \quad \text{and}$$
$$z(D, \tau, b, R) = \tau R - b(D - R).$$

The individual optimum is determined by Theorem 12.2a.

We shall develop this model as follows: Let $F(D, \varepsilon)$ be the distribution function of the number of people with individual lifespan D and consumption parameter ε. (We shall not normalize it.) Then the aggregate net contribution (dependent on scalar τ and function $b(\cdot)$) is

$$\begin{aligned}
Z[\tau, b] &= \int z[D, \tau, b, R(D, \varepsilon)] \, dF \\
&= \int \{\tau R(D, \varepsilon) - b(R(D, \varepsilon))[D - R(D, \varepsilon)]\} \, dF.
\end{aligned} \tag{A.1}$$

where [·] refers to a functional rather than a function. We speak of equilibrium if the macrobalance holds:

$$Z[\tau, b] = 0. \tag{A.2}$$

Let $U^*[D, \varepsilon, \tau, b]$ be the maximum of individual utility of type (D, ε), given the benefit rule b and the contribution rate τ. We shall define the simplest *social welfare function* as the aggregate of individual maximal utilities:

$$V[\tau, b] = \int U^*[D, \varepsilon, \tau, b]\, dF. \tag{A.3'}$$

Considering a general case, before aggregation, the individual maximum should be transformed by an increasing scalar-scalar concave function ψ:

$$V[\tau, b] = \int \psi(U^*[D, \varepsilon, \tau, b])\, dF. \tag{A.3}$$

In the literature (for example, Atkinson–Stiglitz, 1980 and Varian, 1999, Chapter 31), three important cases are distinguished: (i) *utilitarianism*: $\psi' = 1$, (ii) Cobb–Douglas-function: $\psi(U^*) = \log U^*$, assuming $U^* > 0$ and (iii) Rawls-function: the minimum of the individual maxima, $V[\tau, b] = \min_{(D,\varepsilon)} U^*[D, \varepsilon, \tau, b]$. A joint generalization of these cases is the family of functions $\psi(U^*) = \phi^{-1} U^{*\phi}$, assuming $U^* > 0$ and $\phi \leq 1$. (At first sight, in case (iii), there is no function ψ. However, taking $\phi \to -\infty$, the limit is the Rawls-function.)

We must answer the following question: How should the government choose the contribution rate τ and the benefit function $b(R)$ so as to maximize the social welfare function (A.3) subject to the macrobalance (A.1)–(A.2) and the incentive-compatibility conditions? That solution is called the *second-best* optimum.

I cannot yet solve the general problem and must be satisfied with an important special case of the *linear* benefit function:

$$b(R) = \gamma + \alpha R, \tag{A.4}$$

where γ is the intercept of the benefit function and α is its slope, the *absolute accrual rate*. Here we reproduce Corollary 12.4 as

Theorem A.1. *For a well-behaved utility function U and a linear benefit function (A.4) with given contribution rate τ, the constrained*

optimal length of employment $\hat{R}$ of an individual of type (D, ε) satisfies

$$u(\varepsilon, 1 - \tau) - v(\varepsilon, \gamma + \alpha R) + v_b'(\varepsilon, \gamma + \alpha R)\alpha(D - R) = 0. \quad \text{(A.5)}$$

The second-order sufficient condition for optimum holds.

It is obvious that, in a heterogeneous population, for most people the individual lifetime net contribution is different from zero (see Corollary 12.2).

An abstract problem

The solution is more transparent if we first solve an abstract problem and then apply it to our pension problem.

Assume that there is a set of individuals, each person is characterized by an m_P-dimensional individual parameter vector p, distributed according to a distribution function $F(p)$. The government announces an m_G-dimensional *government parameter vector* q and the individual chooses an n-dimensional *decision vector* e. The *individual utility* $U(p, q, e)$ depends on the pair of individual and government parameter vectors (p, q) and the decision vector e in a smooth way. It is assumed that the individually optimal decision $\hat{e} = e(p, q)$ exists for every (p, q) and satisfies the stationary condition $U_e'(p, q, e) = 0$. Here every type is interested to reveal his true type and his participation is ensured by the mandatory character of the system.

Let us denote the maximal individual utility as

$$U^*(p, q) = U(p, q, \hat{e}) \quad \text{(A.6)}$$

and measure *social welfare* as the aggregate ψ-transform of individual maxima:

$$V(q) = \int \psi(U^*(p, q)) \, dF(p), \quad \text{(A.7)}$$

where ψ is an increasing concave function. As we have already seen, in some problems there is a *social constraint*, where the aggregate value of a function g (depending on the individual and government parameter vectors p, q and the individual decision vector $\hat{e}$) is zero:

$$G(q) = \int g(p, q, \hat{e}) \, dF(p) = 0. \quad \text{(A.8)}$$

Apart from the problem of individual rationality, we have

Theorem A.2. *If the government maximizes social welfare $V(q)$ in (A.7) under constraint (A.8), then there exists a scalar μ such that*

$$\int \{\psi'(U^*(p,q))U_q'(p,q,\hat{e}) + \mu g_q'(p,q,\hat{e})$$
$$- \mu g_e'(p,q,\hat{e})U_{ee}''(p,q,\hat{e})^{-1}U_{eq}''(p,q,\hat{e})\}\, dF = 0,$$

where U_{eq}'' and U_{ee}'' are $n \times m_P$ and $n \times n$ matrices, respectively; and the power -1 refers to an inverse matrix.

Remarks. 1. Theorem A.2 has $m_G + 1$ unknowns and $m_G + 1$ equations, the latter typically determine the former.
2. The sufficiency of the condition is not considered here.

Proof. Consider the following Lagrange-function with an unknown vector q and Lagrange-multiplier μ, corresponding to constraint (A.8):

$$\mathcal{L}(q) = \int \{\psi(U^*(p,q)) + \mu g(p,q,\hat{e})\}\, dF(p).$$

Taking the partial derivatives according to vector q and using the formula for the total derivative of g with respect to q:

$$\mathcal{L}_q'(q) =$$
$$\int \{\psi'(U^*(p,q))U_q^{*'}(p,q) + \mu g_q'(p,q,\hat{e}) + \mu g_e'(p,q,\hat{e})\hat{e}_q'(p,q)\}\, dF(p).$$

Because of the envelope theorem, $U_q^{*'} = U_q'$. Substituting the theorem on implicit function concerning $U_e'(p,q,e) = 0$ (for $\hat{e}_q'(p,q)$) into the necessary condition for the constrained maximum of V, $\mathcal{L}_q'(q) = 0$, yields the result. $\qquad\square$

Optimal contribution and linear benefit function

Having solved the abstract problem, we can much more easily tackle the special problem of the optimal contribution rate and the optimal linear benefit function. We now have the following translation:

$p = (D, \varepsilon)$, $q = (\tau, \alpha, \gamma)$ and $e = R$, that is, $m_P = 2$, $m_G = 3$ and $n = 1$. Moreover, $g = z = \tau R - (\gamma + \alpha R)(D - R)$.

Returning to the linear benefit function (A.4), we have

$$U^*(D, \varepsilon, \tau, \alpha, \gamma) = \max_R U(D, \varepsilon, \tau, \alpha, \gamma, R)$$

and functional $V[\tau, b]$ simplifies to a 'simple' 3-variable function

$$V(\tau, \alpha, \gamma) = \int \psi(U^*(D, \varepsilon, \tau, \alpha, \gamma)) \, dF$$

to be maximized under a single constraint (A.1)–(A.2).

Theorem A.2 implies

Theorem A.3. *A necessary condition for the contribution rate τ and the linear benefit function (A.4) to be the second-best optimal is that scalars τ, α, γ and μ satisfy the balance condition (A.1)–(A.2) and the following equations:*

$$\int \{-\psi' u'_a R + \mu R + \mu \varphi u'_a / Q\} \, dF = 0,$$

$$\int \{[\psi' v'_b - \mu - \mu \varphi \alpha v''_{bb}] R(D - R) - \mu \varphi v'_b (D - 2R)/Q\} \, dF = 0,$$

$$\int \{\psi' v'_b (D - R) - \mu(D - R) - \mu \varphi [\alpha v''_{bb}(D - R) - v'_b]/Q\} \, dF = 0,$$

where

$$\varphi = \tau - \alpha D + 2\alpha R + \gamma, \qquad Q = \alpha^2 v''_{bb}(D - R) - 2\alpha v'_b$$

and $R(D, \varepsilon, \tau, \alpha, \gamma)$ satisfies the individual optimality condition (A.5), and μ, τ, α, $\gamma + \alpha R_m$ are positive, where R_m is the minimal length of employment.

Remark. As is usual, we have the same number of unknowns as equations. In a well-chosen case, there is at least one solution to this system of equations. However, if there is only a single (representative) agent, then the equations are not independent, and the problem reduces to Theorem A.1.

Proof. We must calculate the quantities appearing in the proof of Theorem A.2: for example, $g'_R = \varphi$. Furthermore,

$$U'_\tau = -u'_a R, \qquad g'_\tau = R,$$

$$R'_\tau = -\frac{U''_{R\tau}}{U''_{RR}} = \frac{u'_a}{Q};$$

$$U'_\alpha = v'_b R(D - R), \qquad g'_\alpha = -R(D - R),$$

$$R'_\alpha = -\frac{U''_{R\alpha}}{U''_{RR}} = -\frac{\alpha v''_b R(D-R) + v'_b(D - 2R)}{Q};$$

$$U'_\gamma = v'_b(D - R), \qquad g'_\gamma = -D + R,$$

$$R'_\gamma = -\frac{U''_{R\gamma}}{U''_{RR}} = \frac{-\alpha v''_{bb}(D - R) + v'_b}{Q}.$$

Substitution of the formulas into Theorem A.2 yields Theorem A.3.

□

On the basis of experience with optimal mechanism design, we risk

Conjecture A.1. *The slope of the optimal linear benefit function is lower and the corresponding contribution rate is higher than the corresponding values in the naive incentive at the government optimum.*

Conclusions

In this Appendix we have applied the method of optimal mechanism design to formulate and determine the socially optimal pension rule when the government does not know the individual values of lifespans and elasticities for consumption. My model is a very simple one, which deliberately ignores many important features of pension systems (see the comments in Chapter 12). For example, we have neglected the heterogeneity in earnings and in the age of starting to work, and, most importantly, the complexity of tax rules (Gruber–Wise, eds. 1999). Even within this very simple framework, we were able to determine only the *linear* optimal benefit function. Further work is needed to clarify the effects of these and other omissions. What is already clearly established, however, is that the traditional rule is not actuarially fair.

Appendix B

Overlapping generations

Chapter 13 outlined the Overlapping Cohorts Models from a bird's-eye view. In this Appendix, we shall examine the simplest special case, *Overlapping Generations (OLG) Models*, in more detail. This family of models considers the interaction between the young and the old. First we shall discuss the exchange between them; we then introduce production with capital; and finally we apply the basic theorems to the pension systems.

In this Appendix, we do not model the increase in endowments (increase in productivity) and assume the economy is closed. In each time-period, every (unisex) old person born in the previous time-period gives birth to ν young. (Of course, in OLG models *the population growth factor ν* can be any positive real number. In reality, the number of children of each couple is an integer (what about divorces?) and only the combination of families with different sizes can produce a noninteger 2ν.)

Exchange OLG economy

This section is a simplified and revised version of Gale (1973, Part I) and Simonovits (2000a, Appendix B). Here the production process is ignored, current incomes (endowments) are taken as given exogenously in each time-period: *exchange economy*. The (time-invariant) current incomes of the young and of the old are w_0 and w_1, respectively. Similarly, at time-period t the consumption of the young and that of the old are $c_{0,t}$ and $c_{1,t}$, respectively. The consumption path of a person born at date t is $c_{0,t}, c_{1,t+1}$. The series $\{c_{0,t}, c_{1,t+1}\}$ is called *consumption program*. It will be useful to introduce the *per-period savings*: $s_{i,t} = w_i - c_{i,t}$.

Another feature of the exchange economy is that, since output is not storable, aggregate income and aggregate consumption are equal, and so aggregate saving is equal to zero. Since ν young persons correspond to a single old one, in view of the zero-saving assumption a saving profile $\{s_{0,t}, s_{1,t}\}$ is called *feasible* if

$$\nu s_{0,t} + s_{1,t} = 0, \quad t = 0, 1, \ldots. \tag{B.1}$$

Using the standard method of neoclassical economics, we will derive consumption paths from the maximization of a well-behaved utility function. For the sake of simplicity, let the utility function be additive in time:

$$U(c_{0,t}, c_{1,t+1}) = u(c_{0,t}) + v(c_{1,t+1}). \tag{B.2}$$

It is quite customary to assume, especially for the case of many cohorts, that per-period utility functions differ only in a scalar, called *discount factor*: δ. In our 2-period case:

$$v(c) = \delta u(c), \qquad 0 < \delta \leq 1.$$

In Chapters 11–13 we discussed CRRA utility functions in detail. Here we have $u(c) = \sigma^{-1} c^\sigma$, $\sigma \neq 0$ or $u(c) = \log c$ ($\sigma = 0$) *Cobb–Douglas utility function*. It is very simple and often realistic to work with *Leontief utility function*: $U(c_{0,t}, c_{1,t+1}) = \min\{c_{0,t}, c_{1,t+1}\}$. In the Leontief case, the conditional optimum is given by $c_{0,t} = c_{1,t+1}$. Of course, this utility function is not additive but it can be approximated by the transformations of CRRA utility functions at $\sigma \to -\infty$.

For the time being, the *interest factor* (=1+interest rate) of time-period t is taken as given and is denoted by r_t. It is assumed that the bequest at the corresponding interest factor is zero at any time-period:

$$r_{t+1} s_{0,t} + s_{1,t+1} = 0. \tag{B.3}$$

A program is called *competitive* if it is optimal with respect to the given interest factor series. Feasible competitive programs are called *equilibrium programs*.

How does the model work? Express $s_{1,t+1}$ from (B.3) and, after adding the endowments, substitute the resulting consumption vector into (B.2). Except for the Leontief case, the local maximum can be determined from the following first-order condition:

$$u'(c_{0,t}) = r_{t+1}v'(c_{1,t+1}). \tag{B.4}$$

Then we express $s_{0,t}$ and $s_{1,t+1}$ as functions of r_{t+1}: $s_{0,t} = s(r_{t+1})$ and by (B.3), $s_{1,t+1} = -r_{t+1}s(r_{t+1})$, these are the *conditional saving functions*. Using Gale's short-cut, it is assumed that the policy functions are time-invariant, namely, $s_{1,t} = -r_t s(r_t)$. Inserting them into the feasibility condition (B.1) yields the implicit equation

$$S(r_t, r_{t+1}) = \nu s(r_{t+1}) - r_t s(r_t) = 0. \tag{B.5}$$

It is not certain whether for an initial value r_{-1} the implicit difference equation has a solution or, if it has, whether it is unique.

We shall occasionally interrupt the flow of general concepts and theorems and discuss several concrete examples.

Example B.1. In the Cobb–Douglas case, the young's conditional consumption and saving functions are respectively

$$c_0(r) = \frac{w_0 + w_1 r^{-1}}{1 + \delta} \quad \text{and} \quad s(r) = \frac{w_0 \delta - w_1 r^{-1}}{1 + \delta}. \qquad \square$$

Problem B.1. Demonstrate that, in the Leontief case, the conditional consumption functions are

$$c_0(r) = \frac{r w_0 + w_1}{1 + r} = c_1(r).$$

Example B.2. For Cobb–Douglas utility function ($\sigma = 0$), $S(r_t, r_{t+1}) = 0$ leads to the difference equation

$$r_{t+1} = \frac{\nu w_1}{w_1 + \nu \delta w_0 - \delta w_0 r_t}. \qquad \square$$

As is the case in all dynamic models, in this model a special role is played by *steady states*, where the subsequent generations' savings paths are identical to each other. Subindex F refers to a *feasible* steady state:

$$s_{0,t} = s_{0,F} \quad \text{and} \quad s_{1,t+1} = s_{1,F}.$$

With substitution,

$$\nu s_{0,F} + s_{1,F} = 0, \tag{B.1°}$$

$$r_F s_{0,F} + s_{1,F} = 0, \tag{B.3°}$$

whence $(\nu - r_F)s_{0,F} = 0$. This equation suggests the following definitions: The steady state in which there is no trade is called *autarky*. In Chapter 13, this concept was generalized to the *balanced steady state* and subindex B is retained here:

$$s_{0,B} = 0 \quad \text{and} \quad s_{1,B} = 0.$$

In turn, we shall call the other steady state the *golden rule* and refer to it by subindex G.

Using the terms introduced above, we arrived at

Theorem B.1. *(Gale, 1973, Theorem 1.) In the OLG exchange economy there exist two steady states; (i) the golden rule and (ii) autarky:*

$$either \quad r_G = \nu \quad or \quad s_{0,B} = 0, \quad where \quad r_B = \frac{u'(w_0)}{v'(w_1)}.$$

Remark. Note that, for $r_G = \nu$, the budget constraint (B.3°) coincides with the feasibility condition (B.1°). Therefore one constraint, rather than two, is to be taken into account, making the golden rule steady state optimal.

We shall use the following distinction. The golden rule program of an OLG exchange economy is called *debtor* or *creditor* or *symmetric* if at the golden rule the young dissave or save or are just in equilibrium:

$$either \quad s_{0,G} < 0 \quad or \quad s_{0,G} > 0 \quad or \quad s_{0,G} = 0.$$

Gale (1973) spoke of *classical, Samuelson* and *coincidental* golden rule. We prefer the figurative terms of Augusztinovics (1992). (Alternatively, some other authors speak of a 'monetary' steady state if the golden rule is debtor and of a 'nonmonetary' steady state in the case of autarky or, more generally, in the case of a balanced steady state.)

Example B.3. For a discounted Cobb–Douglas utility function, the golden rule consumption pair are equal to

$$c_{0,G} = \frac{w_0 + w_1 \nu^{-1}}{1 + \delta}, \quad c_{1,G} = \delta \frac{\nu w_0 + w_1}{1 + \delta}$$

and the autarkic interest factor is given by

$$r_B = \frac{w_1}{\delta w_0}. \qquad \square$$

The type of the golden rule depends on the relationship between the autarkic interest factor and the population growth factor.

Theorem B.2. *(Gale, 1973, Theorem 2.) The golden rule of the OLG exchange economy is creditor (or debtor) if and only if the autarkic interest factor is less (or greater) than the population growth factor:*

$$r_B < \nu \quad (or \quad r_B > \nu). \qquad (B.6)$$

Proof. Since $r_B \neq \nu$, c_G does not satisfy the individual budget constraint (B.3°), it costs more than is feasible: $r_B s_{0,G} + s_{1,G} < 0$. By (B.1°), $\nu s_{0,G} + s_{1,G} = 0$. By deduction, $(r_B - \nu) s_{0,G} < 0$, and together with the definitions of the types of steady states, this implies (B.6). $\qquad \square$

We shall present the following Example.

Example B.4. Cobb–Douglas illustration. With the comparison of Examples B.1 and B.3, it is easily checked that Theorem B.2 holds. Indeed, $s_0(\nu) = (w_0 \delta - w_1 \nu^{-1})/(1 + \delta) > 0$ and $r_B = w_1/(\delta w_0) < \nu$ are equivalent. $\qquad \square$

Finally, one can formulate

Theorem B.3. *(Gale, 1973, Theorem 3.) In the OLG exchange economy, autarky is Pareto-optimal if and only if the golden rule is debtor, that is, when the autarkic interest factor is larger than the population growth factor:* $r_B > \nu$.

Proof. Assume the contrary.

(a) If the golden rule is creditor, then by definition $s_{0,G} > 0$. Therefore the autarkic program $\{w_0, w_1\}$ can be improved, since we can turn to program $\{c_{0,G}, c_{1,G}\}$.

(b) If the golden rule is debtor, then consider a program $\{c_{0,t}, c_{1,t+1}\}$ which is as good as the Pareto-optimal, autarkic $\{w_0, w_1\}$. Then, using the principle applied in the proof of Theorem B.2, $r_B s_{0,t} + s_{1,t+1} < 0$. Inserting condition (B.1) for $t+1$, $\nu s_{0,t+1} + s_{1,t+1} = 0$, after rearrangement we obtain $0 < (r_B/\nu) s_{0,t} < s_{0,t+1}$. Taking the products of the left and right-hand sides of these inequalities for $t = 0, 1, 2, \ldots, T-1$ respectively, yields $(r_B/\nu)^T s_{0,0} < s_{0,T} < w_0$. By (B.6), $r_B > \nu$, and $s_{0,0} > 0$, hence for $T \to \infty$ we obtain a contradiction. $\square$

We remind the reader that, in the traditional general equilibrium models (for example, Arrow and Debreu, 1954), the equilibrium is generally Pareto-optimal. In contrast, here this is not usually the case. The most plausible explanation for this anomaly may be that there exists an infinite number of consumers and goods. If we go deeper, however, it turns out that the real problem is different, namely, that certain *markets are missing*.

Note that the optimal path with a given initial condition is not necessarily stable (Problem 13.1).

Productive OLG economy

Having surveyed the most important theorems on the exchange economy, we turn now to the case of the productive economy, first studied by Diamond (1965). Following Section 3.1 of Blanchard–Fischer (1989), we shall examine the decentralized equilibrium first and then compare it with the centralized equilibrium. The sphere of consumption is the same as before, but earnings are deduced from production. It is assumed that the young work and save, while the old are retired and use up their savings. The golden rule is creditor, and $w_{0,t} = w_t$ and $w_{1,t} = 0$.

A *decentralized market economy* consists of consumers and firms. Let r_t be the interest factor of time-period t. The consumer born in time-period t has the following budget constraint:

$$c_{0,t} = w_t - s_t \quad \text{and} \quad c_{1,t+1} = r_{t+1} s_t.$$

For the sake of simplicity, let us assume that the utility functions of different periods differ only because of discounting:

$$U(c_{0,t}, c_{1,t+1}) = u(c_{0,t}) + \delta u(c_{1,t+1}), \quad \text{where} \quad 0 \leq \delta \leq 1. \quad \text{(B.2')}$$

The optimum conditions now are

$$u'(c_{0,t}) = r_{t+1} \delta u'(c_{1,t+1}). \quad \text{(B.4')}$$

That condition provides the optimal consumption.

The saving of the young of time-period t is $s_t = w_t - c_{0,t}$. With substitution, the *saving function* can be derived: $s_t = s(w_t, r_{t+1})$, where $0 \leq s'_w \leq 1$, s'_w is the partial derivative of function s with respect to w.

Assume also that the traditional production function is homogeneous of first degree with the usual concavity conditions. Let k be per capita capital and $f(k)$ per capita output, $f'' < 0 < f'$. Technological progress is ignored, and it is assumed that capital evaporates in a period. The behavior of firms, notably wage $w(k_t)$ and interest factor $r(k_{t+1})$, is determined by the usual profit maximization condition:

$$f(k_t) - k_t f'(k_t) = w_t, \quad \text{(B.7)}$$
$$f'(k_t) = r_t - 1. \quad \text{(B.8)}$$

Since for an increasing population per capita capital is derived from net saving, the equilibrium condition on the capital market is

$$k_{t+1} = \frac{s(w_t, r_{t+1})}{\nu}. \quad \text{(B.9)}$$

Without assuming the evaporation of capital, we would use equation $\nu k_{t+1} = (1 - \psi)k_t + s_t$, where ψ is the amortization coefficient during a period. This strange assumption ($\psi = 1$) would only serve simplification.

From (B.7)–(B.9) we can now derive the dynamics of the model:

$$k_{t+1} = \frac{s[w(k_t), r(k_{t+1})]}{\nu},$$

that is,

$$k_{t+1} = \frac{s[f(k_t) - k_t\{f'(k_t) + 1\}, f'(k_{t+1}) + 1]}{\nu}.$$

According to the theorem on implicit function, k_{t+1} can be expressed as a function of k_t: $k_{t+1} = \phi(k_t)$. According to that theorem,

$$\frac{dk_{t+1}}{dk_t} = \frac{-s'_w(k_t)k_t f''(k_t)}{\nu - s'_r(k_t)f''(k_t)}, \tag{B.10}$$

where s'_r is the partial derivative of function s with respect to r. Because of $f'' < 0$, the numerator is positive. If $s'_r \geq 0$, then the denominator is also positive, that is, $dk_{t+1}/dk_t > 0$, thus ϕ is increasing. We speak of a *steady state* if $k_{t+1} = k_t = \cdots = k^\circ$. Then $c_{t+1} = c_t = \cdots = c^\circ$.

To summarize, we have

Theorem B.4. *The dynamics of a productive OLG economy is given by equation (B.9). In that model there can exist one steady state, or more than one steady state, or no steady state.*

For the sake of simplicity, let us assume that there is a unique steady state. The issue of stability is quite delicate even in this case. We shall again illustrate our findings:

Problem B.2. Let $f(k) = Ak^\alpha$, $0 < \alpha < 1$. Prove that $w_t = A(1 - \alpha)k_t^\alpha$ and $r_t - 1 = A\alpha k_t^{\alpha-1}$, moreover,

$$k_{t+1} = \frac{\delta A(1 - \alpha)}{(1 + \delta)\nu}k_t^\alpha = \kappa k_t^\alpha,$$

that is, the steady state is $k^\circ = \kappa^{1/(1-\alpha)}$.

According to the basic idea of general equilibrium theory, even if we neglect incentive and informational problems, a *centralized economy* cannot yield more than a decentralized one. Let us discuss the issue in our case. Before turning to the issue of a centralized optimum, we touch the golden rule known from growth theory and discussed in the previous section. At a steady state, $c = f(k) - (\nu - 1)k$, hence

$$0 = \frac{dc}{dk} = f'(k) - \nu + 1. \tag{B.11}$$

It is known that steady state consumption is maximal if $r^\circ - 1 = f'(k^\circ) = \nu - 1$: the interest rate is equal to the population growth rate. Similarly, $dc/dk > 0$ if $f'(k) > \nu - 1$, that is, if there is saturation, capital decumulation increases consumption.

How does it look like the centralized optimum for T subsequent pairs of overlapping generations? Let V be a social welfare function:

$$V = \delta u(c_{1,0}) + \sum_{t=0}^{T-1} \delta^{*t+1} U(c_{0,t}, c_{1,t+1}),$$

where δ^* is a social discount factor. If the central planner discounts the future to the present, then $\delta^* < 1$. If he appreciates all periods alike, then $\delta^* = 1$. Finally, if he also considers the size of the generations, then $\delta^* = \nu$. The new, intergenerational balance equation is

$$k_t + f(k_t) = \nu k_{t+1} + c_{0,t} + \nu^{-1} c_{1,t}.$$

Expressing and substituting $c_{0,t}$, yields the first-order condition for the centralized optimum:

$$c_{1,t}: \qquad \delta u'(c_{1,t}) - \delta^* \nu^{-1} u'(c_{0,t}) = 0, \qquad (\text{B.12})$$

$$k_t: \qquad -\nu u'(c_{0,t-1}) + \delta^*[1 + f'(k_t)]u'(c_{0,t}) = 0. \qquad (\text{B.13})$$

Combining the two equations,

$$u'(c_{0,t-1}) = [1 + f'(k_t)]\delta u'(c_{1,t}). \qquad (\text{B.14})$$

Comparing the consequence (B.14) of the centralized optimum with the condition (B.4′) of the decentralized one yields the well-known relation, that is, the two optima are the same if the interest rate is equal to the marginal productivity of capital at each time period: (B.8).

Let us consider the optimal steady state, where c^o and k^o are the corresponding values. Substituting into (B.12)–(B.13):

$$\delta u(c_1^o) = \delta^* \nu^{-1} u'(c_0^o), \qquad (\text{B.12}^o)$$

$$1 + f'(k^o) = \nu/\delta^*. \qquad (\text{B.13}^o)$$

(B.13°) and (B.8) together yield the following observation.

Theorem B.5. *(Modified golden rule.) At a centralized optimum, the interest factor is equal to the ratio of the population growth factor to the discount factor:*

$$r^o = \nu/\delta^*.$$

Before announcing our next theorem, consider the following situation. Suppose that towns A and B lie far enough from each other but close enough to a motorway (turnpike). The fastest way to travel from A to B is to reach the motorway as soon as possible and to proceed along it as far as possible. We can now present the result:

Theorem B.6. *(Turnpike theorem.) Given the initial state k_0 and the terminal state k_T and a long enough time horizon T. Then the OLG optimal path $\{k_t\}$ stays close to the steady state k^o for most of the time.*

We have already mentioned that in certain cases *dynamic inefficiency* may arise in an OLG economy, that is, at least one generation's welfare can be increased without diminishing the others' (Theorem B.3).

Let $c_t = c_{0,t} + \nu^{-1} c_{1,t}$ be the consumption for a daughter and a mother and let c^o be the steady state value. Then we reduced the issue to the classical problem discussed in (B.11) and proved the productive economy's counterpart of exchange economy's Theorem B.3.

Theorem B.7. *Dynamic inefficiency. The steady state consumption of a productive OLG economy can be increased by dissaving if the steady state value of the capital stock is higher than its golden rule value: $k^o > k_G$.*

Considering practice, one should not forget the steady increase in labor productivity, either. Blanchard–Fischer (1989) cites evidence that such over-accumulation is not possible in practice.

Pension system and over-accumulation of capital

In this section we shall consider pension issues with the help of a productive OLG model (see also Chapter 17). This application of OLG is a very frequent one in macroeconomics. Blanchard–Fischer (1989, Section 3.2) serves as a basis for our presentation.

We shall need a new form of the optimum condition (B.4$'$), obtained with substitution of savings:

$$u'(w_t - s_t) = r_{t+1} \delta u'(r_{t+1} s_t). \tag{B.15}$$

We shall introduce the following new notations for period t: the social security contribution of the young: τw_t and a pension benefit of the old: b_t.

We recall the basic concepts of funded and unfunded pension systems. In the former, the young save in advance for their old age: $b_t = r_t \tau w_{t-1}$; in the latter, the government finances the current benefits of the old from the taxation of the young: $b_t = \nu \tau w_t$. The optimality conditions of the funded system are as follows:

$$u'((1 - \tau)w_t - s_t) = r_{t+1}\delta u'(r_{t+1}(s_t + \tau w_t)), \qquad (\text{B.16})$$

$$s_t + \tau w_t = \nu k_{t+1}. \qquad (\text{B.17})$$

Comparing (B.16)–(B.17) with (B.15)–(B.8) yields

Theorem B.8. *If the social security contribution does not exceed the savings of an economy without social security ($\tau w_t \leq \nu k_{t+1}$), then by introducing a funded system the capital stock k_t remains invariant, and so that pension benefit does not influence capital accumulation.*

The optimality conditions of the unfunded system are as follows:

$$u'((1 - \tau)w_t - s_t) = r_{t+1}\delta u'(r_{t+1}s_t + \nu \tau w_t), \qquad (\text{B.18})$$

$$s_t = \nu k_{t+1}.$$

From the point of view of the individual, the yield of an unfunded system is $\nu - 1$, in contrast with that of funded one: $r_t - 1$. In our toy model, the unfunded system is superior to the funded one if and only if the growth rate of population is higher than the real interest rate (Aaron-theorem, Theorem 8.5).

There is a further question: how does the introduction of an unfunded system affect savings? The answer: unfavorably. Let us assume that $\tau w_t = \tau w_{t+1}$ and take the derivative of (B.18):

$$\frac{ds_t}{d(\tau w_t)} = \frac{u_1 + \nu u_2''}{u_1 + r u_2''},$$

where u_1 and u_2 are the values of substitution of u at the left- and right-hand sides of (B.18). Savings diminish anyway. Whether the relative reduction, $|ds_t/d(\tau w_t)|$ is less than 1 depends on the validity of $\nu < r$.

The following proposition can be proved similarly:

Theorem B.9. *The introduction of an unfunded system slows down capital accumulation in OLG and reduces the capital stock at the steady state. If $r > \nu$, then the introduction of the unfunded system favors the first generation at the cost of all subsequent generations. If $r < \nu$, then everybody gains, because dynamic inefficiency is eliminated. In the borderline case $r = \nu$, the two systems are equivalent, so the introduction of the unfunded system is neutral in its effect.*

Conclusions

The pioneering article of Samuelson (1958) has already emphasized that, without introducing *social security* or *money*, our OLG economy does not work. Now we have arrived at the end of Appendix B, it would be useful to summarize the conclusions. The family of OLG models successfully explains some phenomena of a dynamic economy which are connected with the interactions of fathers and sons (mothers and daughters). Certain theorems of optimal growth theory (for example, the golden rule) retain their validity, others (like stability) lose it. As a result of the preserved golden rule, the condition of the superiority of the unfunded to the funded system obtains.

On the other hand, in the family of OLG models it is very restrictive that at any given time only two generations overlap (the old and the young). Thus the length of the time-period is very long, say, 30 years, and within this time-period no changes can be considered. We list only two unrealistic consequences. (i) The time spent in labor and in retirement are equal. (ii) Earnings do not increase with age. Unfortunately, the experts of OLG often forget about these (and other) limitations and draw practical conclusions with excessive self-confidence.

Solutions to problems

Problem 1.1. For the perfect smoothing of the consumption path, $c_i \equiv 1/3$. Because of $c_0 > w_0$ and the credit constraint, $c_0^* = 1/4$, that is, $c_1^* = c_2^* = 3/8$.

Problem 2.1. (a) By our assumption, the numerators of (2.4) and (2.5) are common. Breaking down both denominators (according to the stages of work and retirement), the first sum is identical and the second is trivially less in (2.4) than in (2.5).

(b)

$$c_L^I = \frac{1 + 1/2 \cdot 2 \cdot 1/2}{1 + 1/2 \cdot 1/2 + 1/2 \cdot 1/4} = \frac{12}{11} \approx 1.091;$$

$$c_L^N = \frac{1 + 2 \cdot 1/2}{1 + 1/2 + 1/4} = \frac{8}{7} \approx 1.143.$$

Problem 3.1. Let φ be the proportionality coefficient between β_u and τ_w: $\beta_u(1 - \tau_w) = \varphi \tau_w$. The same way $\beta_w = \varphi \tau_w$. In the new system $\beta_u = \beta_w = \varphi \tau_w^*$. Hence $\tau_w^* = \tau_w/(1 - \tau_w)$.

Table S.1. Contribution rate as a function of wage growth and interest rate

Real interest rate $100(r - 1)$	growth rate of real wages $100(\Omega - 1)$	
	0	2
0	20.0	28.7
2	10.8	16.4
5	4.1	6.7

Remark. There is a small discrepancy between these numbers and those of Table 6.1 of the World Bank, probably because of a slightly different formulation and rounding errors.

Problem 3.2. The present value equation is as follows:

$$\sum_{j=0}^{L-1} b_j r^{-j} = \sum_{i=L}^{L+S} x_i r^{-i}.$$

(a) $b_j = b_0$, $x_i = x_L$. Hence

$$x_L = b_0 r^L \frac{I_{L-1}(1/r)}{I_S(1/r)}.$$

(b)

$$\sum_{j=0}^{L-1} b_j r^{-j} = \xi \sum_{i=L}^{L+S} w_i r^{-i}.$$

(c) Numerically: $x_L^a = 160,800$ HUFs, $x_L^b = 72,000$ HUFs, $S^b = 17$ years. The usual bank loan has a rather short repayment period and the first repayment is too high with respect to the student loan. With inflation, the differences between the two schemes are even bigger.

Problem 4.1. Function

$$\frac{T_v \sum_{i=L}^{R} l_i v_i \rho^{-i}}{\sum_{j=R+1}^{D} l_j b_j \rho^{-j}}$$

is obviously increasing with ρ, and for $\rho = 1$ its value is equal to the ratio of expected lifetime contributions to expected lifetime benefits.

Problem 4.2. Inserting identity $v_i \equiv v_R g^{i-R}$ (Example 4.1) into the formula of a point system, yields

$$b_{R+1} = \alpha_2^* \sum_{i=L}^{R} \frac{v_i}{v_i} = \frac{\alpha_2^*}{v_R} \sum_{i=L}^{R} v_i g^{R-i}.$$

Problem 4.3. For a monthly salary $v^{(1)} = \$531$, $b^{(1)} = 0.9 \cdot 531 = \$478$. The actual benefit is equal to $b = b^{(1)} + 0.32 \cdot (2000 - 531) = \$948$.

Problem 5.1. (a) The Netherlands: $b = \min\{b_m, \beta_v v\}$, $b_m = \beta_v v$, that is, $v^\circ = b_m/\beta_v$. (b) Switzerland: $b = b_m^* + \beta_v^* v$. (c) If earning and pension levels are similar in the two countries, then the Swiss minimum is larger than its Dutch counterpart: $b_m^* > b_m$; and the Swiss maximum is lower than in Holland: $b_m^* + \beta_v^* v_M < b_m + \beta_v v_M$. (The minimum earning is ignored.)

Problem 5.2. Let τ_1 and τ_2 be two reals between 0 and 1, the contribution rates of the unfunded and the funded pillars of the mandatory system. Let us assume that the unfunded system relies on the notional defined contribution. The pure unfunded system provides benefit

$$b_{R+1}^1 = \alpha \sum_{i=L}^{R} v_i \left(\tau_1 + \tau_2\right) g_{i+1} \cdots g_R.$$

The benefit provided by the mixed system for a worker having spent $\bar{T}$ years in the pure system is given by Theorem 6.1 with the following modification:

$$b_{R+1}^{12} = \alpha \sum_{i=L}^{R} v_i \tau_1 g_{i+1} \cdots g_R + \alpha \sum_{i=L+\bar{T}}^{R} v_i \tau_2 r_{i+1} \cdots r_R.$$

Hence the gain (loss) formula is easily obtained.

Problem 6.1. (a) Assume that w_i is the total earning in year i, and the worker pays a contribution τw_i. A pensioner receives a gross benefit b_j in year j. After-tax income is equal to $w_i(1 - \tau) - \iota(w_i(1 - \tau))$, or $b_j - \iota(b_j)$.

(b) If we look at the hypothetical situation prevailing before the introduction of the public pension system, then τw_i is the worker's tax-free saving in year i and $\iota(b_j)$ is equal to the personal income tax paid for consumption b_j.

Problem 6.2. Trivial.

Problem 7.1. $E_0 = 73.145$.

Problem 7.2*. (a) With insertion:

$$X(\nu) = \frac{\sum_k k l_k \nu^{-k}}{\sum_k l_k \nu^{-k}}.$$

(b) Take the derivative of the ratio of two functions etc..

(c*) We shall use the idea of the proof rather than the Chebyshev-inequality itself. Assume that $\nu_1 > \nu_2$. We shall show that $X(\nu_1) < X(\nu_2)$. In fact, to prove this inequality, we remove the denominators:

$$\sum_k k l_k \nu_1^{-k} \sum_j l_j \nu_2^{-j} < \sum_k k l_k \nu_2^{-k} \sum_j l_j \nu_1^{-j}.$$

Grouping the terms (k,j) and (j,k), and dropping the factors $l_j l_k$ we can prove the inequality for these two terms: $(k-j)(\nu_1^{-k}\nu_2^{-j} - \nu_1^{-j}\nu_2^{-k}) < 0$ for $j < k$.

Problem 7.3. (a)

$$\pi^*(\nu) = \frac{\sum_{j=R+1}^{D} l_j \nu^{-j}}{\sum_{i=L}^{R} l_i \nu^{-i}}.$$

(b) Let $a(\nu)$ and $b(\nu)$ be the numerator and the denominator of $\pi^*(\nu)$, respectively. Then $\pi^{*\prime}(\nu)$ is given by

$$\left[\frac{a(\nu)}{b(\nu)}\right]' = \frac{a(\nu)}{b(\nu)}\left[\frac{a'(\nu)}{a(\nu)} - \frac{b'(\nu)}{b(\nu)}\right].$$

In view of Problem 7.2, $X_P = \nu a'(\nu)/a(\nu)$ and $X_W = \nu b'(\nu)/b(\nu)$.

(c) $\pi^*(1) = 20/40 = 0.5$ and $X_W = 39.5$, $X_P = 69.5$, hence $\pi^{*\prime}(1) = -15$. For $\nu = 0.99$, $\pi^*(0.99) \approx \pi^*(1) + \pi^{*\prime}(1)(0.99 - 1) = 0.5 + 0.15 = 0.65$. The exact value is given by

$$\pi^*(\nu) = \frac{\sum_{j=R+1}^{D} \nu^{-j}}{\sum_{i=L}^{R} \nu^{-i}} = \frac{\nu^{-(D+1)} - \nu^{-(R+1)}}{\nu^{-(R+1)} - \nu^{-L}} = 0.6725.$$

(d) For $L = 1 = R$, $D = 2$, $l_k \equiv 1$, $\Pi^*(\nu) = (1 + \nu^{-2})/\nu^{-1} = \nu^{-1} + \nu$.

Problem 8.1. Consider the appropriately modified equation (4.3):

$$\tau_v \sum_{i=R-t}^{R} v_i l_i \rho_t^{-i} = \sum_{j=R+1}^{D} b_j l_j \rho_t^{-j}, \tag{4.3*}$$

where

$$\tau_v \sum_{i=0}^{R} v_i l_i (vg)^{-i} = \sum_{j=R+1}^{D} b_j l_j (vg)^{-j}, \tag{4.3**}$$

Problem 8.2. The lifetime budget constraint of a funded system (apart from children) is

$$\sum_{i=L}^{R} w_i r^{-i} = \sum_{j=L}^{D} c_j r^{-j}. \qquad (1.1^*)$$

The lifetime budget constraint of a PAYG1 system (apart from children) is

$$\sum_{i=L}^{R} w_i (\nu g)^{-i} = \sum_{j=L}^{D} c_j (\nu g)^{-j}. \qquad (1.1^{**})$$

Because of monotonicity, for $\nu g < r$ (1.1^{**}) is tighter than (1.1^*), and so the funded system allows a better consumption path than does PAYG1.

Problem 8.3. Different budget constraints imply different optimal consumption paths (compare Chapter 11).

Problem 9.1. Imagine the following triangle: the horizontal base has a length $T + S$, the height at T is equal to b. Then E is the area of the triangle. $E = S^2 b/2$, $Y = 4wT/3$, $b = \beta w$. With substitution: $E = S^2 \beta w/2$, $E/Y = 3S^2 \beta w/(8wT) = 15/8$.

Problem 9.2. (a) About 10% of the aggregate contribution, that is, about 0.8% of GDP, flows to the second pillar. This is close to the upper limit of the pension deficit accepted by the government of 1994–1998. (b) About $0.6 \cdot 0.25 \cdot 0.08 \cdot 100 = 1.2\%$ of GDP will flow to the second pillar.

Problem 10.1. (a) Consider the poor: $1 - \tau = \tau$, hence $\tau = 1/2$. (b) If everybody pays according to contribution rate τ, then the poor, the middle class, and the rich together pay contributions 4τ, $2 \cdot 2\tau$ and $1 \cdot 4\tau$ respectively, totaling 12τ. Since everybody receives a flat benefit, $b = 12\tau/7$. Returning to the poor: $b = 1 - \tau$, that is, $12\tau/7 = 1 - \tau$, that is, $\tau = 7/19 \approx 36.8\%$ in contrast with 50%.

Problem 10.2. Pension. Poor: $b^{(1)} = b_1 + b_2$, middle class: $b^{(2)} = b_1 + 2b_2$, rich: $b^{(3)} = b_1 + 4b_2$, together $B = 7b_1 + 12b_2$. Individual contribution: τ, 2τ and 4τ, total: 12τ. Equality between aggregate benefits and aggregate contributions: $7b_1 + 12b_2 = 12\tau$. For the middle class, the two benefits are equal to each other: $b_1 = 2b_2$. The poor's replacement rate is unity: $b_1 + b_2 = 1 - \tau$. Step-by-step elimination yields $\tau = 13/31$, $b_1 = 12/31$ and $b_2 = 6/31$. Hence $b^{(1)} = 18/31 \approx 0.581$, $b^{(2)} = 24/31 \approx 0.774$ and $b^{(3)} = 36/31 \approx 1.161$.

Problem 11.1.

$$U(c_0, \ldots, c_D) = \sigma^{-1} \sum_{k=0}^{D} \delta^k u \left(\frac{c_k}{g^k} \right). \tag{11.4*}$$

Problem 11.2. (a) For the Leontief utility function, without credit constraint: $U = 1/3$, with credit constraint: $U = 1/4$.

(b) Cobb–Douglas utility function without credit constraint: $U = 3\log(1/3) = -3\log 3$, with credit constraint: $U = \log(1/4) + 2\log(3/8)$.

Problem 11.3. Insert (11.3) into (11.8″).

Problem 11.4. (a) X_c becomes $(L + R)/2$. (b) Then a flat PAYG path is creditor if and only if the retirement period is longer than the childhood period: $D - R > L$.

Problem 11.5. The Lagrange-function of the constrained maximum is

$$\mathcal{L}(c_0, \ldots, c_D) = U(c_0, \ldots, c_D) + \mu \sum_{i=0}^{D} (w_i - c_i) r^{-i}.$$

According to the generalized envelope theorem,

$$V'(r) = -\sum_{i=0}^{D} \mu i \cdot (w_i - c_i) r^{-i-1},$$

etc. In fact, we have proved this theorem in the concrete setting of Theorem 11.2*.

Problem 12.1. Substitute the CRRA-functions into (12.5):

$$\varepsilon \lambda^{(1-\varepsilon)\sigma} a^{\varepsilon\sigma-1} = \varepsilon b^{\varepsilon\sigma-1}$$

and simplify.

Substitute the CRRA-functions into (12.4) and use $b = \beta a$ with (12.5′), yields

$$\sigma^{-1}\beta^{\varepsilon\sigma-1}a^{\varepsilon\sigma} - \sigma^{-1}\beta^{\varepsilon\sigma}a^{\varepsilon\sigma} + \varepsilon\beta^{\varepsilon\sigma-1}a^{\varepsilon\sigma}[1 - a + \beta a] = 0$$

and express a.

Problem 12.2. (a) In the incorrectly differentiated system:

$$\tilde{\beta}_1 = \tau\frac{R_1}{D^* - R_1} \quad \text{and} \quad \tilde{\beta}_2 = \tau\frac{R_2}{D^* - R_2}.$$

In the correctly differentiated system:

$$\beta_1 = \tau\frac{R_1}{D_1 - R_1} \quad \text{and} \quad \beta_2 = \tau\frac{R_2}{D_2 - R_2}.$$

Because of the properties of the average, $D_1 < D^* < D_2$, hence $\tilde{\beta}_1 > \beta_1$ and $\tilde{\beta}_2 < \beta_2$.

(b) Numerically, $\tilde{\beta}_1 = 0.631$, $\tilde{\beta}_2 = 1$; $\beta_1 = 0.68$; $\beta_2 = 0.75$. The average replacement rate in the incorrect system is equal to $\tilde{\beta} = 0.723$; while in the correct one it is equal to $\beta = 0.7$.

Problem 12.3. Fixing j, Theorem 12.3 applies for the subsums.

Problem 12.4. Take the logarithmic derivative.

Problem 13.1. For details, see Appendix B.

(a) Rational expectations:

Individual life-path:

$$s_{0,t}r_{t+1} + s_{1,t+1} = 0. \tag{13.2*}$$

Gale's simplification:

$$s_{0,t} = s(r_{t+1}).$$

Basic equation:

$$S_R(r_t, r_{t+1}) = s(r_{t+1}) - r_t s(r_t) = 0, \tag{13.3*}$$

where r_{-1} given.

(b) Naive expectations:

$$S_N(r_{t-1}, r_t) = s(r_t) - r_t s(r_{t-1}) = 0. \tag{13.4*}$$

For both expectations, there are the same two steady states, and the condition for local stability is $-1 < f'(r_F) < 1$ for the explicit difference equation $r_{t+1} = f(r_t)$. According to the implicit function theorem,

$$\frac{dr_{t+1}}{dr_t} = \frac{-\partial S/\partial r_t}{\partial S/\partial r_{t+1}}.$$

Problem 14.1. $B_t = \sum_{k=R+1}^{D} l_k b_{k,t}$, $W_t = \mathbf{w}_t \sum_{i=L}^{R} l_i$, etc.

Problem 15.1.

$$2\tau_U = b, \tag{15.1*}$$
$$\tau_F r(1 + r) = b. \tag{15.2*}$$

In the mature unfunded system,

$$e_0 = 0, \qquad e_1 = \frac{b}{2}, \qquad e_2 = b, \qquad E_0 = \frac{3b}{2}.$$

In the mature funded system,

$$a_0 = 0, \qquad a_1 = \tau_F r, \qquad a_2 = \tau_F r(1 + r), \qquad A_2 = \tau_F r(2 + r).$$

The transition lasts for only two periods. At the beginning of period $t = 1$, $G_1 = r(b - 2\tau_U + 2\tau_F) = 2\tau_F r$, $a_{1,1} = a_{2,1} = \tau_F r$, $A_1 = 2\tau_F r$, the partial private benefit $b_1 = b/(1+r)$. At the beginning of period $t = 2$, $G_2 = r(b - b_1 - 2\tau_U + 2\tau_F) = b(2+r)/(1+r)$, and the other variables are already known. The reader is advised to go through the very special case $r = 1$, where the formulas become extremely simple.

Problem 17.1. (a) $\bar{k}$: $\sum_{k=0}^{\bar{k}} n_k < 0.5 \leq \sum_{k=0}^{\bar{k}+1} n_k$. (b) If ν increases, then $\bar{k}$ decreases.

Problem 17.2. For $U(c_0, c_1) = \min[u(c_0), u(c_1)]$ and no sawings, $w(1 - \tau) = \nu\tau[\alpha w + (1 - \phi\tau)(1 - \alpha)\mathbf{w}]$, etc.

Problem B1. Inserting the formulas $c_{0,t} = c_{1,t+1}$ and $s_{i,t} = w_i - c_{i,t}$ into (B.1), the system of equations obtains.

Problem B2. Apply the relations $r_t = f'(k_t)$ and $w_t = f(k_t) - k_t f'(k_t)$.

Notations
(in alphabetical order)

$a =$ worker's consumption (Chapter 12 and Appendix A)

$a_i =$ individual assets at age i (Chapters 3, 11, 13, 15)

$A =$ aggregate assets (Chapters 13 and 15)

$A =$ output coefficient (Appendix B)

$b_j =$ benefit at age j

$b^k =$ lower point of pension class k

$\mathbf{b} =$ average benefit

$\tilde{b}_t =$ nominal benefit (Chapter 6)

$\tilde{b} =$ fair (naive) benefit (Chapter 12)

$B =$ subscript of balanced steady state

$B =$ aggregate benefit

$c_j =$ consumption at age j

$\bar{c} =$ iso-utility consumption

$D =$ (maximal) age at death

$\tilde{D} =$ random age at death

$e =$ individual decision

$e_i =$ pension expectancy at age i

$E_i =$ remaining life expectancy at age i (in general)

$E_t =$ aggregate pension expectancy at year t (Chapter 15)

$f =$ production function

$f_i =$ fertility rate at age i

$F =$ subscript of feasible steady state (Chapter 13 and Appendix B)

$F =$ subscript of funded system (Chapters 15 and 17)

$F =$ primary budget deficit (Chapter 15)

$F =$ distribution function of wages (Chapter 17) and of characteristics (Appendix A)

$g =$ growth factor of average national real earnings or productivity (in general)

$g =$ balance function (Appendix A)

$G =$ subscript of golden rule steady state (Chapters 11, 13 and Appendix B)

$G =$ government debt (Chapters 8 and 15)

$G^* =$ government debt plus the present value of undivided future government expenditures

$G =$ general distribution function (Chapter 17)

$h =$ entry pension function

$H =$ subscript of health

$H =$ continued pension function

$i =$ age (of worker), index

$I =$ superscript of insured

$I_n =$ sum of the $(n + 1)$-term geometrical progression

$j =$ age (of pensioner), index

$J =$ number of elasticity brackets (Chapter 12)

$J_k =$ present value of future net contributions of a k-aged (Chapter 8)

$k =$ age, index (in general)

$k =$ per capita capital (Appendix B)

$K =$ number of earning brackets

$K_1, K_2 =$ minimal and maximal ages of fertility

$l_k =$ probability of survival until age k (Chapters 2, 3, 7, 8 and 14)

$l_k =$ leisure at age k (Chapter 15)

$l =$ leisure (Chapter 12)

$L =$ Left

$L =$ age at starting to work

$L^* =$ age (date) of start of attribution

$\mathcal{L} =$ Lagrange-function

$m_G =$ dimension of government parameter vector

$m_P =$ dimension of individual parameter vector

$m =$ minimal

$M =$ maximal

$M =$ number of workers

$M^* =$ number of people at working age

$\mathbf{M} =$ transition matrix

$n =$ dimension of individual decision vector

$n_{k,t} =$ number of people aged k at date t

$N =$ superscript of non-insured (Chapter 2)

$N =$ naive expectations (Chapter 13)

$N_k =$ net contribution of a person of age k in year 0

$p =$ individual parameter vector (Appendix A)

$p =$ polynomial (Chapter 12)

$p_k =$ probability of living D_k years

$P =$ subscript of pensioner (in general)

$P =$ individual index (Appendix A)

PAYG $=$ unfunded system

$P =$ number of pensioners

$P^* =$ number of people above the normal retirement age

$\mathbf{P} =$ probability

$\mathcal{P}_t =$ price level

$q = g^{\theta-1}$ (Chapter 14)

$q_i =$ mortality rate at age i (Chapters 2 and 7)

$q =$ government parameter vector (Appendix A)

$q_j =$ probability of having consumption elasticity ε_j (Chapter 12)

$r =$ interest factor

$\hat{r} =$ relative interest factor

$\tilde{r} =$ net interest factor

$r_{k,j} =$ probability of being in class (k, j)

$R =$ (effective) retirement age

$R^* =$ normal retirement age

R $=$ Rational expectations (Chapter 13)

R $=$ Right (Chapter 17)

$s_k =$ saving of k-aged

$S =$ aggregate saving (Chapters 13, Appendix B)

$S =$ length of retirement or repayment period (Chapters 3 and 14)

$t =$ date, calendar time (year in general)

$t =$ personal income tax (Problem 6.2)

$T =$ actual (number of) years of service (Chapters 1–4)

$T^* =$ normal (number of) years of service (Chapter 4)

$T =$ transition tax (Chapter 15)

$u =$ (worker's) per-period utility function (Chapters 11, 15, 17 and Appendices A, B)

$\mathbf{u} =$ national average net earning (Chapter 8)

$u_i =$ net earnings at age i

U $=$ subscript of unfunded system (Chapters 15 and 17)

$U =$ lifetime utility function

$U^* =$ indirect lifetime utility function

$v =$ pensioner's per-period utility function (Chapters 15, 17 and Appendices A, B)

$v_i = $ gross earnings at age i

$v^k = $ lower point of gross earnings class k

$\bar{v} = $ (individual) average indexed annual (gross) earning

$v^* = $ estimated average indexed annual (gross) earning or reference wage

$\mathbf{v} = $ national average gross earnings

$V = $ indirect utility function (Chapter 11)

$V = $ social welfare function (Chapter 12 and Appendices A, B)

$w = $ wage costs (total earnings)

$\mathbf{w} = $ average wage costs (total earnings)

$w_o = $ median total earning

$W = $ index of worker

$W = $ aggregate wage costs

$\mathbf{x} = $ state vector

$x_j = $ repayment of student's loan at age j

$X_c = $ mean age of consumption

$X_n = $ mean age of population

$X_P = $ mean age of retired population,

$X_w = $ mean age of earning

$X_W = $ mean age of worker population

$\mathbf{y} = $ per-capita GDP

$Y = $ GDP

$z = $ net-gross earning (Chapter 4)

$z = $ individual net contribution (Chapter 12 and Appendix A)

$Z = $ aggregate net contribution

$\alpha = $ pension coefficient (Chapters 4, 12 and Appendix A)

$\alpha_k = $ compensation for contributions for k periods (Chapter 15)

$\alpha = $ weight of proportional benefit (Chapter 17)

$\beta_{\mathbf{v}} = $ average replacement rate

$\hat{\beta}_{\mathbf{w}} = $ average entry replacement rate

$\hat{\beta} = $ individual closing replacement rate

$\beta = $ individual lifetime replacement rate

$\gamma = $ consumption growth factor (in general)

$\gamma = $ benefit for zero employment (Chapter 12 and Appendix A)

$\Gamma = $ output growth factor

$\delta = $ discount factor

$\Delta = $ relative deviation of consumption

$\varepsilon = $ compensated elasticity (Chapter 6)

$\varepsilon = $ correction factor (Chapters 8 and 18)

$\varepsilon = $ elasticity for consumption (Chapters 12, 15 and Appendix A)

$\varepsilon =$ constant (Chapter 17)
$\zeta =$ eligibility rate (Chapter 8)
$\zeta =$ CARA coefficient (Chapter 12)
$\eta =$ wage efficiency
$\theta =$ constant (Chapter 12)
$\theta =$ share of wage indexation (Section 14)
$\vartheta_a = 1-$relative cost with respect to assets
$\vartheta_b =$ money's worth ratio of annuity
$\vartheta_w = 1-$relative cost with respect to contributions
$\iota =$ personal income tax function
$\kappa =$ relative accrual rate (Chapter 12)
$\kappa =$ constant (Appendix B)
$\lambda =$ ratio of leisure coefficients
$\mu =$ participation rate (Chapter 8)
$\mu =$ Lagrange-multiplier (in general)
$\nu =$ population growth factor
$\xi =$ multiplier of the student loan
$\pi =$ system dependency ratio
$\pi_t =$ inflation factor
$\pi^* =$ old-age (demographic) dependency ratio
$\Pi^* =$ total demographic dependency ratio
$\rho =$ internal factor of return
$\sigma = 1 -$ coefficient of constant relative risk aversion
$\tau_1 =$ employer's contribution rate
$\tau_2 =$ employee's contribution rate
$\tau =$ total contribution rate
$\varphi =$ US attribution function (Chapter 4)
$\varphi =$ logarithmic dampening factor (Chapter 12)
$\varphi =$ notation (Appendix A)
$\phi =$ coefficient of social welfare function (Appendix A)
$\phi =$ return function (Appendix B)
$\chi =$ statutory replacement rate
$\psi =$ Hungarian attribution function (Chapter 4)
$\psi =$ transformation function of individual utility (Appendix A)
$\psi =$ amortization coefficient (Appendix B)
$\omega =$ seniority growth factor of wages (Chapter 1)
$\omega = 1-$intertemporal rate of substitution (Part III)
$\Omega =$ growth factor of individual earning

References

AARON, H. J. (1966): "The Social Insurance Paradox", *Canadian Journal of Economics and Political Science 32* 371–374.

ABEL, A., ed. (1980): *Collected Papers of Franco Modigliani*, Cambridge, MA, MIT Press.

AKERLOF, G. (1970): "The Market for Lemons: Quality Uncertainty and the Market Mechanism", *Quarterly Journal of Economics 89* 488–500.

ALIER, M.–VITTAS, D. (2001): "Personal Pension Plans and Stock-Market Volatility", *Holzmann–Stiglitz, eds.* 391–423.

ÁMON, ZS.–BUDAVÁRI, P.–HAMZA, L.–HARASZTI, K.–MÁRKUS, A. (2002): "The First Four Years of the Pension Reform. Model Computations and Facts" (in Hungarian), *Közgazdasági Szemle 49* 518–527.

ANDERSON, M.–TULJAPURKAR, S.–LI, N. (2001): "How Accurate are Demographic Projections Used in Forecasting Pension Expenditures?", *Boeri et al., eds., (2001b)* 9–28.

ANDO, A.–MODIGLIANI, F. (1963): "The 'Life Cycle' Hypothesis of Saving: Aggregate Implications and Tests", *American Economic Review 53* 55–84.

ANTAL, K.–RÉTI, J.–TOLDI, M. (1995): "Loss of Value and Distortions in the Hungarian Pension System", *Ehrlich–Révész, eds.* 184–192.

ARNOLD, R. D.–GRAETZ, M. J.–MUNNELL, A. H., eds. (1999): *Framing the Social Security Debate*, Washington, D.C. National Academy of Social Insurance.

ARROW, K. J. (1963): "Uncertainty and the Welfare Economics of Medical Care", *American Economic Review 53* 941–969.

ARROW, K. J.–DEBREU, G. (1954): "Existence of Equilibrium for a Competitive Economy", *Econometrica 22* 265–290.

ARROW, K. J.–INTRILLIGATOR, M. D., eds. (1986): *Handbook of Mathematical Economics, Vol. III.*, Amsterdam, North-Holland.

ARTHUR, W. B.–McNICOLL, G. (1978): "Samuelson, Population and Intergenerational Transfers", *International Economic Review 19* 241–246.

ATKINSON, A. B.–BOURGUIGNON, F., eds. (2000): *Handbook of Income Distribution, Vol. I.*, Amsterdam, Elsevier.

ATKINSON, A. B.–STIGLITZ, J. E. (1980): *Lectures on Public Economics*, London, McGraw-Hill.

AUERBACH, A. J.–GOKHALE, J.–KOTLIKOFF, L. (1991): "Generational Accounts: A Meaningful Alternative to Deficit Accounting", *Bradford, ed.* 55–110.

AUERBACH, A. J.–GOKHALE, J.–KOTLIKOFF, L. (1994): "Generational Accounting: A Meaningful Way to Evaluate Fiscal Policy", *Journal of Economic Perspectives 8, Winter* 73–94.

AUERBACH, A. J.–HAGEMANN, R. P.–KOTLIKOFF, L. J.– NICOLETTI, G. (1989): "The Economic Dynamics of an Ageing Population: The Case of Four OECD Countries", *OECD Economic Studies 12* 97–130.

AUERBACH, A. J.–HERRMANN, H., eds. (2002): *Ageing, Financial Markets and Monetary Policy*, Berlin, Springer.

AUERBACH, A. J.–KOTLIKOFF, L. J. (1987): *Dynamic Fiscal Policy*, Cambridge, Cambridge University Press.

AUGUSZTINOVICS, M. (1989): "The Costs of Human Life", *Economic Systems Research 1* 5–26.

AUGUSZTINOVICS, M. (1992): "Towards a Theory of Stationary Populations", *typescript*, Institute of Economics, Budapest (earlier version: Discussion Paper, 1991).

AUGUSZTINOVICS, M. (1993): "The Crisis of the Pension System", *Székely–Newbery, eds.* 296–320.

AUGUSZTINOVICS, M. (1995): "The Long-term Financial Balance of the Pension System: Macrosimulation", *Ehrlich–Révész, eds.* 210–228.

AUGUSZTINOVICS, M. (1997a): "Introduction", *Augusztinovics et al.* 7–23.

AUGUSZTINOVICS, M. (1997b): "Gestation and Retirement Financing Applied to Hungary", *Sustaining Social Security*, United Nations.

AUGUSZTINOVICS, M. (1999a): "Pension Systems and Reforms in the Transition Economies", *Economic Survey of Europe, No. 4*, UN ECE, Geneva.

AUGUSZTINOVICS, M. (1999b): "The Demographic and Economic Foundations of the Pension Reform" (in Hungarian), *Demográfia 42* 120–132.

AUGUSZTINOVICS, M. (1999c): "Pension Systems and Reforms— Britain, Hungary, Italy, Poland, Sweden", *European Journal of Social Security 1* 351–382.

AUGUSZTINOVICS, M., eds., (2000a): *Panorama after the Reform: Studies on Pension Systems* (in Hungarian), Budapest, Közgazdasági Szemle Alapítvány.

AUGUSZTINOVICS, M. (2000b): "The Dynamics of Retirement Savings—Theory and Reality", *Structural Change and Economic Dynamics 11* 111–128.

AUGUSZTINOVICS, M. et al. (1997): *Pension Systems and Reforms— Britain, Hungary, Italy, Poland, Sweden, Phare ACE Program P95-2139-R*, Budapest.

AUGUSZTINOVICS M. (coordinator)–GÁL, R. I.–MATITS, Á.–MÁTÉ, L.–SIMONOVITS, A.–STÁHL, J. (2002): "The Hungarian Pension System Before and After the 1998 Reform", *Fultz, ed. Vol. 1* 25–93.

AUGUSZTINOVICS, M.–MARTOS, B. (1996): "Pension Reform: Calculations and Conclusions", *Acta Oeconomica 48* 119–160.

AZARIADIS, C. (1993): *Intertemporal Macroeconomics*, Oxford, Blackwell.

BARR, N. (1987): *The Economics of the Welfare State*, London, Weidenfeld and Nicholson, Stanford University Press (3rd edition in 1998).

BARR, N. (2001): *The Welfare State as a Piggy Bank: Information, Risk, Uncertainty and the Role of the State*, Oxford, Oxford University Press.

BARRO, R. J. (1974): "Are Government Bonds Net Worth?", *Journal of Political Economy 82* 1095–1117.

BEATTIE, R.–McGILLIWRAY, W. (1995): "A Risky Strategy: Reflections on the World Bank Report 'Averting the Old Age Crisis' ", *International Social Security Review 48* 5–22.

BEETS, G.–MILTÉNYI, K., eds. (2000): *Population Ageing in Hungary and the Netherlands, A European Perspective*, Thela Thesis, Amsterdam.

BERMAN, A.–PLEMONS, R. J. (1979): *Nonnegative Matrices in Mathematical Sciences*, New York, Academic Press.

BLAKE, D. (1997): "Pension Choices and Pension Policy in the United Kingdom", *Valdés-Prieto, ed.* 277–317.

BLAKE, D. (2000): "Does it Matter what Kind of Pension Scheme you have?", *Economic Journal 110*, F46–F81.

BLANCHARD, O. J.–FISCHER, S. (1989): *Lectures on Macroeconomics*, Cambridge, MA, MIT Press.

BLONDAL, S.–SCARPETTA, S. (1999): "The Retirement in OECD Countries", OECD, *Economics Department Working Papers 202*.

BOD, P. (1995): "Formation of the Hungarian Social Insurance Based Pension System", *Ehrlich–Révész, eds.* 173–183.

BOD, P. (2000): "Reflections on the Perspectives on the Functioning of the Private Pension Funds" (in Hungarian), *Király et al., eds.* 85–101.

BOERI, T.–BÖRSCH-SUPAN, A.–BRUGIAVINI, D.–DISNEY, R.–KAPTEYN, A.–PERACCHI, R., eds. (2001a): *Pensions: More Information, Less Ideology*, Boston, Kluwer.

BOERI, T.–BRUGIVIANI, A.–MAIGNAN, C. (2001b): "Early Retirement: Reasons and Consequences", *Boeri et al., eds. (2001a)* 29–53.

BOKROS, L.–DETHIER, J-J., eds. (1998): *Public Finance Reform during the Transition: The Experience of Hungary.* Washington, World Bank.

BOVENBERG, L.–MEIJDAM, L. (2001): "The Dutch Pension System", *Börsch-Supan–Miegel, eds.* 39–67.

BOSWORTH, B. P.–DORNBUSCH, R.–LABÁN, R., eds. (1993): *The Chilean Economy, Policy Lessons and Challenges*, Washington D.C., The Brookings Institution.

BÖRSCH-SUPAN, A. (1998): "Incentive Effects of Social Security on Labor Force Participation: Evidence in Germany and Across Europe", *NBER WP 6780*, Cambridge, MA.

BÖRSCH-SUPAN, A. (2000): "A Model under Siege: A Case Study of the German Retirement Insurance System", *Economic Journal 110*, F24–F45.

BÖRSCH-SUPAN, A. (2001a): "Six Countries—And No Pension System Alike", *Börsch-Supan–Miegel, eds.* 1–12. o.

BÖRSCH-SUPAN, A. (2001b): "The German Retirement Insurance System", *Börsch-Supan–Miegel, eds.* 13–38.

BÖRSCH-SUPAN, A.–LUDWIG, A.–WINTER, J. (2002): "Aging, Pension Reform, and Capital Flows", *Auerbach–Herrmann, eds.* 55–83.

BÖRSCH-SUPAN, A.–MIEGEL, M., eds. (2001): *Pension Reform in Six Countries*, Berlin, Springer.

BRADFORD, D., ed. (1991): *Tax Policy and the Economy 5*, Cambridge, MA, MIT Press.

BREYER, F. (1989): "On the Intergenerational Pareto-efficiency of Pay-as-you-go Pension Systems", *Journal of International and Theoretical Economics 145* 643–658.

BREYER, F.–STOLTE, K. (2001): "Demographic Change, Endogenous Labor Supply and the Political Feasibility of Pension Reform", *Journal of Population Economics 14* 409–424.

BROMBACHER STEINER, M. V. (2001): "The Swiss Three-Pillar System", *Börsch-Supan–Miegel, eds.* 69–85.

BROOKS, R. (2000): "What will Happen to Financial Markets when the Baby Boomers Retire?" *IMF WP /00/18*, Washington D.C.

BROWNING, E. K. (1975): "Why the Social Insurance Budget is Too Large in a Democracy", *Economic Inquiry 13* 373–388.

BROWNING, E. (1987): "On the Marginal Welfare Cost of Taxation", *American Economic Review 77* 11–23.

BUDD, A.–CAMPBELL, N. (1998): "The Roles of the Public and Private Sectors in the U.K. Pension System" with comments by R. Disney and others, *Feldstein, ed.* 99–134.

BRUNNER, J. (1996): "Transition from a Pay-as-You-Go to a Fully Funded Pension System: The Case of Diferring Individuals and Intragenerational Fairness", *Journal of Public Economics 60* 131–146.

BÜTLER, M. (2001): "Neoclassical Life-Cycle Consumption: A Textbook Example", *Economic Theory 17* 209–221.

CALLUND, D. (1999): "Chile: Controversy, Difficulty and Solutions", *The Geneva Papers on Risk and Insurance 24* 528–533.

CARROLL, C. D.–OVERLAND, J.–WEIL, D. N. (2000): "Saving and Growth with Habit Formation", *American Economic Review 90* 341–355.

CASAMATTA, G.–CREMER, H.–PESTIEAU, P. (2000): "The Political Economy of Social Security", *Scandinavian Journal of Economics 102* 503–522.

CENTRAL STATISTICAL OFFICE (1996): *Hungary's Population and Economy: Past and Present*, in Hungarian, Budapest, KSH.

CENTRAL STATISTICAL OFFICE (1998): *Demographic Yearbook: Hungary, 1997*, Budapest, KSH.

CHARLTON, R.–MCKINNON, R. (2001): *Pension in Development,* Aldershot, Ashgate.

COILE, C.–DIAMOND, P.–GRUBER, J.–JOUSTEN, A. (1999): "Delays in Claiming Social Security Benefits", *NBER WP 7318,* Cambridge, MA.

COILE, C.–GRUBER, J. (2000): "Social Security Incentives for Retirement", *NBER WP 7651,* Cambridge, MA.

CRAWFORD, V. P.–LILIEN, D. M. (1981): "Social Security and Retirement Decision", *Quarterly Journal of Economics 100* 479–529.

CREEDY, J. (1992): *Income, Inequality and the Life Cycle,* Aldershot, Elgar.

CSONTOS, L.–KORNAI, J.–TÓTH, I. GY. (1998): "Tax Awareness and the Reform of the Welfare State: Hungarian Survey Results", *Economics of Transition 6* 287–312.

DEARDORF, A. W. (1976): "The Optimum Growth Rate for Population: Comment", *International Economic Review 17* 510–514.

DEATON, A. (1992): *Understanding Consumption,* Oxford, Clarendon Press.

DIAMOND, P. A. (1965): "National Debt in a Neoclassical Growth Model", *American Economic Review 55* 1126–1150.

DIAMOND, P. (1997): "Macroeconomic Aspects of Social Security Reform", *Brookings Papers on Economic Activity: 2* 1–87.

DIAMOND, P. (1998): "The Economics of Social Security Reform", *NBER WP 6719,* Cambridge, MA, also *Arnold et al., eds.* 38–64.

DIAMOND, P. (2002a): *Taxation, Incomplete Markets and Social Security,* Munich Lectures, Cambridge, MA, MIT Press.

DIAMOND, P. (2002b): *Social Security Reform,* The Lindahl Lectures, Oxford, Oxford University Press.

DIAMOND, P.–MIRRLEES, J. (1978): "A Model of Social Insurance with Variable Retirement", *Journal of Public Economics 10* 295–336.

DIAMOND, P.–MIRRLEES, J. (1986): "Payroll-Tax Financed Social Security with Variable Retirement", *Scandinavian Journal of Economics 88* 25–50.

DIAMOND, P.–MIRRLEES, J. (2003): "Social Insurance with Variable Retirement and Private Saving", *Journal of Public Economics...*

DIAMOND, P.–ORSZAG, P. R. (2002): "Assessing the Plans Proposed by the President's Commission to Strengthen Social Security", *Tax Notes 73.*

DIAMOND, P.–VALDÉS-PRIETO, S. (1993): "Social Security Reforms", *Bosworth et al., eds.* 257–320.

DISNEY, R. (2000): "Crises in Public Pension Programmes in OECD: What are the Reform Options", *Economic Journal 110* F1-F23.

DISNEY, R. (2001): "The UK System of Pension Provision", *Börsch-Supan–Miegel, eds.* 87–109.

DRÈZE, J. H. (2000): "Economic and Social Security in the Twenty-first Century, with Attention to Europe", *Scandinavian Journal of Economics 102* 327–348.

THE ECONOMIST (2001): "Gordon Says Saving is Good for You", April 7, 41–42.

THE ECONOMIST (2002): "A Survey of Pensions", February 16, after p. 54.

EDWARDS, S. (1998): "The Chilean Pension Reform: A Pioneering Program" with Comments by S. P. Zeldes and others, *Feldstein, ed.* 33–62.

EHRLICH, É.–RÉVÉSZ, G., eds. (1995): *Human Resources and Social Stability during Transition in Hungary,* San Francisco, International Center for Growth.

ELMENDORF, D. W.–LIEBMAN, J. B. (2000): "Social Security Reform and National Savings in an Era of Budget Surpluses", *Brookings Papers on Economic Activity: 2* 1–71.

ENGEN, E. M.–GALE, W. G.–SCHOLZ, J. (1996): "The Illusory Effects of Savings Incentives on Saving", *Journal of Economic Perspectives 10:4,* 111–138.

ESŐ, P.–SIMONOVITS, A. (2002): "Designing Optimal Benefit Rules for Flexible Retirement", *Discussion Paper CMS-EMS 1353,* Northwestern University, Evanston, IL.

FABEL, O. (1994): *The Economics of Pensions and Variable Retirement Schemes,* New York, Wiley.

FEHR, H. (2000): "Pension Reform during the Demographic Transition", *Scandinavian Journal of Economics 102* 419–443.

FELDSTEIN, M. (1974): "Social Security, Induced Retirement and Aggregate Capital Accumulation", *Journal of Political Economy 82* 905–926.

FELDSTEIN, M. S. (1987): "Should Social Security Means Tested?", *Journal of Political Economy 95* 468–484.

FELDSTEIN, M. (1996): "The Missing Piece in Policy Analysis: Social Security Reform", *American Economic Review 86* 1–14.

FELDSTEIN, M., ed. (1998a): *Privatizing Social Security*, Chicago, University of Chicago Press.

FELDSTEIN, M. (1998b): "Introduction", *Feldstein, ed.* 1–29.

FELDSTEIN, M.–LIEBMAN, J. F. (2001): "Social Security", *NBER WP 8451*, Cambridge, MA.

FELDSTEIN, M.–SAMWICK, A. (1998): "The Transition Path in Privatizing Social Security" with comments by J. B. Shoven and others, *Feldstein, ed.* 215–264.

FELLNER, W. et al. (1967): *Ten Economic Studies in the Tradition of Irving Fisher*, New York, Wiley.

FERGE, ZS. (1999): "The Politics of the Hungarian Pension Reform", *Müller et al., eds.* 231–246.

FISCHER, S. (1973): "A Life Cycle Model of Insurance Purchases", *International Economic Review 14* 132–152.

FREDERICK, S.–LOEWENSTEIN, G.–O'DONOGHUE, T. (2002): "Time Discounting and Time Preferences: A Critical Review", *Journal of Economic Literature 40* 351–401.

FREEMAN, R. B.–KATZ, L. F., eds. (1995): *Differences and Changes in Wage Structure*, Chicago, Chicago University Press.

FRIEDMANN, B. M.–WARSHAWSKI, M. J. (1990): "The Cost of Annuities: Implications for Saving Behavior and Bequests", *Quarterly Journal of Economics 105* 135–154.

FUCHS, V. R. (2000): "Medicare Reform: The Larger Picture", *Journal of Economic Perspectives 14:2* 57–70.

FULTZ, E., ed. (2002): *Pension Reform in Central and Eastern Europe*, Budapest, ILO, Volumes 1–2.

GÁL, R. I. (1999): "Hungarian Old-Age Security Prior to the 1998 Reform", *Müller et al., eds.* 201–210.

GÁL, R. I.–SIMONOVITS, A.–SZABÓ, M.–TARCALI, G. (2000): "Generational Accounts in Hungary", Budapest, TÁRKI, http://www.tarki.hu/research-e/welfare/genaccount.pdf.

GÁL, R. I.–SIMONOVITS, A.–TARCALI, G. (2001): "Pension Reform and Generational Accounts", *Social Protection Discussion Paper Series 0127*. World Bank, Washington D.C.

GALE, D. (1973): "Pure Exchange Equilibrium of Dynamic Economic Models", *Journal of Economic Theory 6* 12–36.

GALE, D. (1974): "The Trade Imbalance Story", *Journal of International Economics 4* 119–137.

GEANAKOPLOS, J.–MITCHELL, O. S.–ZELDES, S. P. (1998): Social Security Money's Worth, *NBER WP 6722*, Cambridge, MA; appeared: *Mitchell–Meyers–Young, eds.* (1999a), 137–157.

GILLION, C.–TURNER, J.–BAILEY, C.–LATULIPPE, D., eds. (2000): *Social Security Pension: Development and Reform*, Geneva, ILO.

GOKHALE, J.–KOTLIKOFF, L. (1999): "Social Security Treatment of Postwar Americans: How Bad Can it Get?", *NBER 7362*, Cambridge, MA.

GOKHALE, J.–KOTLIKOFF, L.–SABELHAUS, J. (1996): "Understanding the Postwar Decline in U.S. Saving: A Cohort Analysis", *Brookings Papers on Economic Activity (1)* 315–407.

GRUBER, J.–ORSZAG, P. (1999): "What to Do About the Social Security Earning Test", Issue in Brief #1. Center for Retirement Research, Boston College.

GRUBER, J.–WISE, D., eds. (1999): *Social Security and Retirement around the World*, Chicago, The Chicago University Press.

GUEGANO, Y. (2000): Cessation d'activitè, dèpart en retrait et dècisions individuelles: vers la neutralitè actuarielles de barèmand de retraites et une plus grande libertè de choix, Paris, Caisse des Dèpots et Consignations.

HABLICSEK, L. (1999): "Aging and Diminishing Population: Demographic Scenarios 1997–2050" (in Hungarian), *Demográfia 42* 390–413.

HABLICSEK, L.–DE BEER, J.–VAN HOORN, W. (2000): "Future Population and Household Trends: Projections and Scenarios", *Beets–Miltényi, eds.* 141–180.

HAVEMAN, R. (1994): "Should Generational Accounts Replace Public Budgets and Deficits", *Journal of Economic Perspectives 8. Winter* 95–111.

HINDE, A. (1998): *Demographic Methods*, London, Arnold.

HOLZMANN, R. (1998): "Financing the Transition to Multipillar [Systems]", World Bank; Social Protection Discussion Series.

HOLZMANN, R.–JAMES, E.–BÖRSCH-SUPAN, A.–DIAMOND, P.–VALDÉS-PRIETO, S. (2001): "Comments on Rethinking Pension Reform: Ten Myths about Social Security Systems", *Holzmann–Stiglitz, eds.* 57–89.

HOLZMANN, R.–PALACIOS, R.–ZVINIENE, A. (2001): "Implicit Pension Debt: Issues, Measurement and Scope in International Perspectives", HDNSP for Social Protection Discussion Series, Washington, D.C., World Bank.

HOLZMANN, R.–STIGLITZ, R., eds. (2001): *New Ideas about Old-Age Security: Toward Sustainable Pension Systems in the 21st Century.* Washington, D.C., World Bank.

HOTELLING, H. (1929): "Stability of Competition", *Economic Journal 39* 41–57.

HUBBARD, R. G.–SKINNER, J.–ZELDES, S. P. (1995): "Precautionary Saving and Social Insurance", *Journal of Political Economy 103* 360–399.

HUJO, K. (1999): "Paradigmatic Change in Old-Age Security—Latin American Cases", *Müller et al., eds.* 121–139.

HUNGARIAN PENSION INSTITUTION (1998): *Statistical Yearbook,* Budapest.

JAMES, E.–BROOKS, S. (2001): "The Political Economy of Structural Pension Reforms", *Holzmann–Stiglitz, eds. 2001* 133–170.

JAMES, E.–SMALHOUT, J.–VITTAS, D. (2001): "Administrative Costs and Organization of Individual Account Systems: A Comparative Perspective", *Holzmann–Stiglitz, eds. 2001* 254–307.

JOHNSON, P.–RAKE, K. (1997): "Great-Britain: A Case Study", *Augusztinovics et al.* 25–50.

KEYFITZ, N.–BEEKMAN, J. A. (1984): *Demography through Problems,* New York, Springer.

KIM, O. (1983): "Balanced Equilibrium in a Consumption Loans Model", *Journal of Economic Theory 29* 339–346.

KIRÁLY, J.–SIMONOVITS, A.– SZÁZ, J., eds. (2000): *Rationality and Equity* (in Hungarian), Budapest, Közgazdasági Szemle Alapítvány.

KIRMAN, A. (1992): "Whom or What Does the Representative Individual Represent?" *Journal of Economic Perspectives 6:1* 117–136.

KORNAI, J. (1992): "The Postsocialist Transition and the State", *American Economic Review 82, Papers and Proceedings* 1–21.

KORNAI, J. (1999): *Welfare after Communism,* London, The Social Market Foundation.

KOTLIKOFF, L. (1997): "Privatization of Social Security: How it Works and Why it Matters", *Poterba, ed.* 1–32.

KOTLIKOFF, L. (1998): "Simulating the Privatization of Social Security in General Equilibrium" with comments by T. J. Sargents and others, *Feldstein, ed.* 265–312.

KOTLIKOFF, L.–SMETTERS, K. A.–WALLISER, J. (1998): "Opting Out of Social Security and Adverse Selection", *NBER WP 6430* Cambridge, MA, to appear in *Journal of Public Economics.*

KOTLIKOFF, L.–SUMMERS, L. (1981): "The Role of Intergenerational Transfers in Aggregate Capital Accumulation", *Journal of Political Economy 89* 706–732.

KRUGMAN, P. R.–OBSTFELD, M. (2000): *International Economics. Theory and Policy*, 5th edition, Addison Wesley Longman.

KURIHARA, K. K., ed. (1954): *Post-Keynesian Economics*, New Brunswick, Rutgers University Press.

LACKÓ, M. (2000): "Do Power Consumption Data Tell the Story? (Electricity Intensity and Hidden Economy in Post-Socialist Countries)", *Maskin–Simonovits, eds.* 345–366.

LAIBSON, D. I. (1997): "Golden Eggs and Hyperbolic Discounting", *Quarterly Journal of Economics 112* 443–477.

LAITNER, J. P. (1984): "Transition Time Paths for Overlapping-Generations Models", *Journal of Economic Dynamics and Control 7* 111–129.

LAZEAR, E. P. (1979): "Why is there Mandatory Retirement?", *Journal of Political Economy 87* 1261–1269.

LEE, R. (1980): "Age Structure, Intergenerational Transfers and Economic Growth", *Revue economique 31* 1129–1156.

LEE, R.–TULJAPURKAR, S. (1998): "Uncertain Demographic Future and Social Security Finances", *American Economic Review 88* 237–241.

LEIMER, D. R. (1995): "A Guide to Social Security Money Worth Issues", *Social Security Bulletin 58, Summer*, 3–20.

LEIMER, D. R.–LESNOY, S. (1982): "Social Security and Private Savings: New Time-Series Evidence", *Journal of Political Economy 90* 606–642.

LIEBMAN, J. B. (2001): "Redistribution in the Current U.S. Social Security System", *NBER WP 8625* Cambridge, MA.

LINDBECK, A.–WEIBULL, J. (1988): "Strategic Interaction with Altruism: The Economics of Fait Accompli", *Journal of Political Economy 96* 1165–1182.

LOTKA, A. J.–SHARPE, F. R. (1911): "A Problem in Age Distribution", *Philosophical Magazine 21* 435–438.

MÁCHA, M. (2002): "The Political Economy of Pension Reform in the Czech Republic", *Fultz, ed. Vol. 2* 75–112.

MANKIW, N. G. (1997): *Macroeconomics*, New York, Worth, 3rd edition.

MARTOS, B. (1995): "Point System of Individual Pensions: Setup and Operation", *Ehrlich–Révész, eds.* 229– 241.

MARTOS, B. (1997): "Pension Formulas", *Augusztinovics et al.* 159–169.

MASKIN, E.–SIMONOVITS, A., eds. (2000): *Planning, Shortage and Transformation, Essays in Honor of J. Kornai*, Cambridge, MA, MIT Press.

MCKINNON, R. I. (2001): "The International Dollar Standard and the Sustainability of the U.S. Current Account Deficit", *Brooking Papers on Economic Activity 1*, 227–239.

MINISTRY OF FINANCE–MINISTRY OF WELFARE (1997): *Background Information of the Pension Reform*, Budapest.

MIRRLEES, J. A. (1971): "An Exploration in the Theory of Optimum Income Taxation", *Review of Economic Studies 38* 175–208.

MIRRLEES, J. A. (1986): "The Theory of Optimal Taxation", *Arrow–Intrilligator, eds.* 1197–1249.

MITCHELL, O. S. (1998): "Administrative Costs in Public and Private Retirement Systems" with comments by S. J. Schieber and others, *Feldstein, ed.* 403–456.

MITCHELL, O. S. (2002): "Developments in Decumulation: The Role of Annuity Products in Financing Retirement", *Auerbach–Herrmann, eds.*, 97–125.

MITCHELL, O. S.–MEYERS, R. J.–YOUNG, H., eds. (1999a): *Prospects for Social Security Reform*, Pension Research Council, University of Pennsylvania Press.

MITCHELL, O. S.–POTERBA, J. M.–WARSHAWSKI, M. J.–BROWN, J. R. (1999b): "New Evidence on Money's Worth of Individual Annuities", *American Economic Review 89* 1299–1318.

MODIGLIANI, F. (1976): "Some Economic Policy Implications of Indexing of Financial Assets with Special Reference to Mortgages", *Monti, eds.* 90–116 and *Abel, ed. Volume 3*, 97–123.

MODIGLIANI, F.–BRUMBERG, R. (1954): "Utility Analysis and the Consumption Function: An Interpretation of Cross-Section Data", *Kurihara, ed.* 388–436.

MOLNÁR, GY.–SIMONOVITS, A. (1998): "Expectations, (In)stability and (In)viability in Realistic Overlapping Cohorts Models", *Journal of Economic Dynamics and Control 23* 303–332.

MONTI, M., ed. (1976): *The New Inflation and Monetary Policy*, London and Basington, Macmillan.

MURTHI, M.–ORSZAG, J. M.–ORSZAG, P. R. (2001): "The Charge Ratio on Individual Accounts: Lessons from the UK Experience", *Holzmann–Stiglitz, eds.* 308–335.

MÜLLER, K. (1999): *The Political Economy of Pension Reform in Central-Eastern Europe*, Cheltenham, UK and Northampton, MA, USA: Elgar.

MÜLLER, K.–RYLL, A.–WAGENER, H-J., eds. (1999): *Transformation of Social Security: Pensions in Central-Eastern Europe*, Heidelberg, Physica.

MYLES, G. D. (1995): *Public Economics*, Cambridge, University Press.

NORDHAUS, W. (1973): "The Effects of Inflation on the Distribution of Economic Welfare", *Journal of Money, Credit and Banking 5* 465–508.

OECD (2000) *Economic Outlook 67*, Paris.

ORENSTEIN, M. A. (2000): "How Politics and Institutions Affect Pension Reform in Three Post Communist Countries", *Policy Research WP 2310*, Washington, World Bank.

ORLOWSKI, L., eds. (2000): *Transition and Growth in Post-Communist Countries: Ten Years Experience*, Celtenham, UK, Elgar.

ORSZAG, P.–STIGLITZ, J. E. (2001): "Rethinking Pension Reform: Ten Myths about Social Security Systems", *Holzmann–Stiglitz, eds.* 17–56.

PALACIOS, R.–ROCHA, R. (1998): "The Hungarian Pension System in Transition", *Bokros–Dethier, eds.* 177–216.

PHILIPSON, T. J.–BECKER, G. S. (1998): "Old-Age Longevity and Mortality Contingent Claims", *Journal of Political Economy 106* 551–573.

POTERBA, J. M., ed. (1997): *Tax Policy and the Economy 10*, Cambridge, MA, MIT Press.

POTERBA, J. M. (2001): "Demographic Structure and Asset Returns", *Review of Economics and Statistics 83* 565–584.

POTERBA, J. M.–VENTI, S. F.–WISE, D. A. (1996): "How Retirement Savings Program Increase Savings", *Journal of Economic Perspectives 10:4*, 91–112.

POTERBA, J. M.–VENTI, S. F.–WISE, D. A. (1999): "Pre-Retirement Cashouts and Forgone Retirement Savings: Implications for 401(k) Asset Accumulation", *NBER WP 7314* Cambridge, MA.

PRESIDENT'S COMMISSION TO STRENGTHEN SOCIAL SECURITY (2002): *Strengthening Social Security and Creating Personal Wealth for All Americans*, Washington, (http:/www.csss.gov/reports/)

RAZIN, A.–SADKA, E.–SWAGEL, P. (2002): "The Aging Population and the Size of the Welfare State", *Journal of Political Economy* *110* 900–918.

RÉTI, J. (1996): The Basic Calculations of the Pension Reform: the Possibilities (in Hungarian), *typescript*, Budapest. Pension Self Government.

RÉTI, J. (1997): "The Development of Pension Expenditures and Changes in the Nineties" (in Hungarian), *typescript*, Budapest. Pension Self Government. (For an earlier English version, see *Ehrlich–Révész, eds.* (1995)).

RÉTI J. (2000): "The Pension Risks at the End of the Nineties: (To the History of the Pension Reform)" (in Hungarian), *Király et al., eds.* 134–156.

RÉTI, J. (2002): "Pay-as-You-Go System with Individual Accounts" (in Hungarian), *Közgazdasági Szemle 49* 528–550.

RUTKOWSKI, M. (2000): "Restoring Hope, Rewarding Work: Pension Reforms in Post-Communist Economies", *Orlowski, eds.*.

SAMUELSON, P. A. (1958): "An Exact Consumption-Loan Model of Interest with or without the Social Contrivance of Money", *Journal of Political Economy 66* 467–482.

SAMUELSON, P. A. (1975a): "The Optimum Growth Rate for Population", *International Economic Review 16* 531–538.

SAMUELSON, P. A. (1975b): "Optimum Social Security in a Life-Cycle Growth Model", *International Economic Review 16* 539–544.

SAMUELSON, P. A. (1976): "The Optimum Growth Rate for Population: Agreement and Evaluations", *International Economic Review 17* 516–525.

SAMWICK, A. (1998): "New Evidence on Pensions, Social Security and the Timing of Retirement", *Journal of Public Economics 70* 207–236.

SCHMÄHL, A. (1999): "Pension Reforms in Germany: Major Topics, Decisions and Developments", *Müller et al., eds.* 91–120.

SCHMIDT-HEBBEL, K. (2001): "Chile's Pension Revolution Coming of Age", *Börsch-Supan–Miegel, eds.* 139–170.

SHAFIR, E.–DIAMOND, P.–TVERSKY, A. (1997): "Money Illusion", *Quarterly Journal of Economics 112* 341–347.

SHESHINSKI, E. (1972): "The Optimal Linear Income Tax", *Review of Economic Studies 39* 297–302.

SHESHINSKI, E. (1978): "A Model of Social Security and Retirement Decisions", *Journal of Public Economics 10* 337–360.

SIMONOVITS, A. (1992): "Indexed Mortgages and Expectations: Mathematical Analysis and Simulation", *Acta Oeconomica 44* 144–160.

SIMONOVITS, A. (1995a): "Three Economic Applications of Chebyshev's Algebraic Inequality", *Mathematical Social Sciences 30* 207–220.

SIMONOVITS, A. (1995b): "On the Number of Balanced Steady States in Overlapping Cohorts Model", *Acta Oeconomica 47* 51–67.

SIMONOVITS, A. (1996): "Pensions and Family Allowances: A Reconsideration of the Social Insurance Paradox", *Acta Oeconomica 47* 337–347.

SIMONOVITS, A. (1999): "The New Hungarian Pension System and its Problems", *Müller et al., eds.* 211–230.

SIMONOVITS, A. (2000a): *Mathematical Methods in Economic Dynamics*, Oxford, Macmillan.

SIMONOVITS, A. (2000b): "Parables and Realism in Overlapping Cohorts Models", *Maskin–Simonovits, eds.* 95–107.

SIMONOVITS, A. (2000c): "Introduction into Pension Modeling", Budapest, CEU Department of Economics, *Working Paper 6.*

SIMONOVITS, A. (2001): "Employment Length, Leisure and Pension: Incentives with Limits", Budapest, CEU Department of Economics, *Working Paper 3.*

SIMONOVITS, A. (2002): "Designing Optimal Linear Rules for Flexible Retirement", Budapest, CEU Department of Economics, *Working Paper 6.*

SIMONOVITS, A. (2003): "Introduction into Pension Modeling", *Bulletin of Social Security.*

SINN, H. W. (2000): "Why a Funded Pension System is Useful and why it is not Useful", *NBER WP 7592*, also *International Tax and Public Finance 7* 389–410.

SKINNER, J. (1989): "Risky Income, Life-Cycle Consumption and Precautionary Savings", *Journal of Monetary Economics 22* 237–255.

SPIEZIA, V. (2002): "The Greying Population: A Wasted Human Capital or Just a Social Liability?", *International Labour Review 141* 71–113.

STIGLITZ, J. E. (1988): *Economics of the Public Sector*, New York–London, Norton, 2nd edition.

SOCIAL SECURITY ADMINISTRATION, OFFICE OF RESEARCH, EVALUATION AND STATISTICS (1998): "Fast Facts and Figures about Social Security", Washington, Government Printing Office.

SPÉDER, ZS. (1999): "Relative Advantages and Increasing Differences: The Pensioners' Welfare between 1987 and 1996 in Hungary" (in Hungarian), Budapest University of Economic Sciences, Household and Family Research Unit.

STOCK, J.–WISE, D. (1990): "Pensions, the Option Value of Work, and Retirement", *Econometrica 58* 1151–1180.

SYDSATER, K.–HAMMOND, P. (1995): *Mathematics for Economic Analysis*, Prentice Hall.

SZÉKELY, I. P.–NEWBERY, D. M. G., eds. (1993): *Hungary: An Economy in Transition*, Cambridge, Cambridge University Press.

TANZI, V., eds. (1983): *The Underground Economy in the United States and Abroad*, Lexington, MA.

THALER, R. H.–SHEFRIN, H. M. (1981): "An Economic Theory of Self-Control", *Journal of Political Economy 89* 392–406.

THOMPSON, L. (1998): *Older and Wiser: The Economics of Public Pension*, Washington D. C., The Urban Institute Press.

TOBIN, J. (1967): "Life Cycle Saving and Balanced Growth", *Fellner et al.* 231–256.

YAARI, M. E. (1965): "Uncertain Lifetime, Life Insurance and the Theory of Consumer", *Review of Economic Studies 32* 137–150.

VALDÉS-PRIETO, S., ed. (1997): *The Economics of Pensions: Principles, Policies and International Experience*, Cambridge, Cambridge University Press.

VALDÉS-PRIETO, S. (2000): "The Financial Stability of Notional Account Pensions", *Scandinavian Journal of Economics 102* 395–417.

VAN GROEZEN, B.–LEERS, T.–MEIJDAM, L. (2003): "Social Security and Endogeneous Fertility: Pension and Child Allowances as Siamese Twins", *Journal of Public Economics 87* 233–251.

VARIAN, H. (1992): *Microeconomic Analysis*, 3rd edition, New York, Norton.

VARIAN, H. (1999): *Intermediate Microeconomics*, New York, Norton.

VERBON, H. (1988): *The Evolution of Public Pension Schemes*, Berlin, Springer Verlag.

VITTAS, D. (1997): "Designing Pension Reform Programs: Lessons from Recent Experience", *Working Paper Series*, University of Ljubljana.

WAGENER, A. (2001): "Pension Risk, Saving and Retirement Decisions", *International Workshop on Ageing, Skills and Labour Markets*, Nantes, September 7–8.

WALDRON, H. (2001): "Links between Early Retirement and Mortality", ORES *Working Paper 93*, Division of Economic Research, SS Administration.

WALLISER, J. (2000): "Adverse Selection in the Annuities Market and the Privatizing of Social Security", *Scandinavian Journal of Economics 102* 373–393.

WALLISER, J. (2001): "Regulation of Withdrawals in Individual Account Systems", *Holzmann–Stiglitz, eds.* 367–390.

WISE, D. A. (2001): "United States: Support in Retirement: Where We are and Where We are Going", *Börsch-Supan–Miegel, eds.* 111–138.

WORLD BANK (1994): *Averting the Old-Age Crisis*, New York, N.Y., Oxford University Press.

Index